I dedicate *Girl Talk* to my grandmother, Mary, and my mother, Anne. They gave me life, hope, strength and courage. I also dedicate it to Sandra and Deborah—my daughters—who have given me love, joy, adventure and comfort. My last dedication is to my granddaughters—Melanie, Cheyenne and Sierra—who fill my life with happiness that knows no bounds. I treasure the fact that we have been women together. This, then, is a book by a woman, about women, for all women.

Girl Talk

Daily Reflections for Women of All Ages

SHARON WEGSCHEIDER-CRUSE

Health Communications, Inc.
Deerfield Beach, Florida

www.hci-online.com

Library of Congress Cataloging-in-Publication Data

Wegscheider-Cruse, Sharon, date.
    Girl Talk: daily reflections for women of all ages / Sharon Wegscheider-Cruse.
       p.   cm.
    Includes index.
    ISBN 1-55874-551-3 (trade pbk.)
      1. Women—Psychology—Miscellanea. 2. Self-esteem in women—Miscellanea.
    3. Self-actualization (Psychology)—Miscellanea.   4. Affirmations.   I. Title.
    HQ1206.W44   1998   97-47009
    646.7'082—dc21   CIP

Publisher: Health Communications, Inc.
                3201 S.W. 15th Street
                Deerfield Beach, Florida 33442-8190

Icon illustrations designed by Larissa Hise
Cover design by Lawna Patterson Oldfield
Artwork from Wood River Gallery, San Rafael, CA

Preface—About This Book

For the last fifteen years I have enjoyed being an author, and I have published several books. Each time a new book came out, there was this nagging feeling inside me that someday I wanted to write a book for and about women. On a hike in the sacred hills of Bear Butte, South Dakota, I made the commitment to the memories of my mother and grandmother, and I promised them and myself that I would write this book. The ideas lay dormant until I attended an authors' meeting that my publisher sponsored. After meeting with other authors and professionals in the publishing industry, several people suggested to me that this was the right time for me to share my life's experiences in a book for women.

After meditating, I sat down at the word processor. Except for eating, sleeping and a little tap dancing, that is where I have been for many months. It is as though the book wrote itself. My thinking, my research and my typing were steady and the ideas flowed. There were days when I woke up early and stayed up late because I could not wait to see the things about which that day's writing were going to be. It has been the most satisfying and joyful book I have ever written.

I am an ordinary woman blessed with an extraordinary life. I have known many women who had unique skills and gifts—they blessed me by sharing those skills and gifts with me. Other women have become my friends through their writings or the books that others wrote about them. These role models helped me find myself and define who I was and who I wanted to become. The lessons they have taught me will come out throughout this entire book, and particularly in the part devoted to role models.

Throughout my lengthy career as a marriage and family therapist, and later as a public speaker and author, I have spoken to thousands of women and listened to their concerns and the areas of life where they were seeking information and guidance. Using their input as my guide, I selected twelve subjects on which to focus: body image and health, making the most of your time, rituals and traditions, managing money, humor and laughter, spirituality, relationships, sacred places, stages and passages, role models, choices, and qualities.

I hope that the words and ideas in this book inspire you with new thoughts, old memories and warm feelings. Writing this book has been one of the most fulfilling joys of my life and has reminded me of how proud and happy I am to be a woman. I have shared this book with my husband and son, who told me that they are also proud and happy to be men. Perhaps what sex we are at birth is not so important as our coming to know ourselves as either men or women. The riches of my life are abundant as I come to know more deeply and appreciate my womanliness. May this book help you know and love yourself.

Acknowledgments

While this book was being written, many of my friends, colleagues and family showed their interest and gave their support. I want to thank all those who asked creative questions, who told me their stories and who believed in the book as much as I did. As I thought about the women who have gone before me and showed me the path that I have followed, I felt an immense gratitude. And, as always, God was the power and the inspiration that kept me full of ideas and memories.

The influence of my friends is present throughout the pages of this book. I want to thank Elaine, Lorrie, Gertie, Harriet, Lana, Lisa, Margie, Beth, Ann, Kathy, Irene, Evie, Mary, Verna, Nancy, Virgilia, Sandy, Deb, Mary Ann, Marty, Bitsie, Joan, Dee, Linda, Sybil, Shirley, Pat, Jackie, Sue, Lois, Lorraine, Ellie, Cheryl, Mary Jo, Sharon, Marian and many more. Each of you knows who you are.

Much love goes to my husband, who takes such good care of me as I write, and who shows endless patience when the spirit moves me to sit at the computer for hours at a time. Special thanks to Ellie Gore, who makes sure the typing gets done and the book takes form. Her support is valuable to me.

In writing several books over the years, I have been most fortunate to work with Peter Vegso and Gary Seidler of Health Communications, Inc., who are always one step ahead. They are both visionaries who make dreams come true for their authors and those who work in their organization. It has been my privilege to work with this creative and talented team.

Special thanks goes to Matthew Diener, Lisa Drucker and L.A. Justice, whose editing skills are invaluable, and to Ronni O'Brien, who puts the book before the public. It may take a village to raise a child, but it takes a team to publish a book.

It's always a joy to be part of this team.

Introduction

I organized the book as a daily meditation book with a different subject highlighted each day. It can be used as a daily reading book, or a reference book on individual topics. You can read the book as organized or you may refer to the topic(s) whenever you choose.

Instead of a table of contents, you will find the twelve sections and the corresponding icons following this introduction. At the back of the book you will also find a cross-reference index, pointing out the number of the reflection. There is one for each day of the year, so they are numbered 1 through 365.

During my years as a therapist, I observed a pattern of issues that kept surfacing in counseling sessions. The topics that continually recurred were:

1. Body Image
   and Health

 2. Making the Most
   of Your Time

 3. Rituals and Traditions

 4. Managing Money

 5. Humor and Laughter

 6. Spirituality

 7. Relationships

 8. Sacred Places

 9. Stages and
   Passages

 10. Role Models

 11. Choices

 12. Qualities

My intent in writing *Girl Talk* is to address these twelve topics in ways that bring new thoughts and ideas to the reader.

As you prepare to take the journey of 365 days of reflections, it will be helpful to meditate on each of the topics. May each reflection give you a thought, an inspiration and an idea for action that will help you take a step forward in your own growth.

Character contributes to beauty . . .
A mode of conduct, a standard of courage,
discipline, fortitude and integrity
can do a great deal to make a woman beautiful.
—JACQUELINE BISSET

Body Image and Health

B ody image and health are linked. How we feel about our bodies can influence our health, and how we care for our health can affect our body image. When speaking of body image, I refer to the picture a person has of her body. It includes how one's body looks to one's self and what we think it looks like to others. It may include a total picture or we may concentrate on one feature. Some see themselves only as short, tall, fat, thin, or centered around a disability, surgery or handicap. Certain times may also impact body feelings—events such as pregnancy, pre- and post-menstruation changes, teenage acne, gray hair, etc. There is an overwhelming interest in cosmetics, diets, fitness, clothes, etc., designed to enhance women's body image.

Many women have a positive body image. It has come about because of positive reinforcing experiences. These women take good care of their bodies and have a history of knowing how to see their bodies as just one part of who they are. Many other women have had histories and experiences that have brought them to a place of poor body image, and this image interferes with every other aspect of their lives. Often, these women have negative body images not because they have unattractive bodies, but because they see themselves inaccurately. Their images are sometimes distorted harshly, and they view themselves as less than adequate when in fact that is not true. Individuals with whom these women were in relationships in the past may have viewed them this way, and the women began to believe it.

Some women are estranged from their bodies. Rather than feeling connected to all of whom she is, early training or values taught have separated her from her body. She may see it as something separate from her identity. When she becomes ill, she may see her body as letting her down. She may not know what pleases her sexually. She may not know what exercise makes her feel better and at what weight she functions best. Because of her lack of knowledge about herself, she looks to outside measurements to tell her how she should be. This can become very confusing because we live in a culture that worships women of very different proportions. There are the Marilyn Monroe-, Sophia Loren-type, with very ample voluptuous shapes. Then there is the very thin, almost boyish shape of Goldie Hawn and many women athletes. Then we have the ultra-thin world of Kate Moss and the models we see in every magazine. If a woman does not know who she is and how her body looks and feels, she could be led in many differing directions, all of which may decrease her positive feelings about her own body image.

At any given time, there are millions of women on some kind of diet. Our newsstands and bookstores have an abundance of articles and books with the latest diet plan. While it's important to have a body that is healthy, the focus on being ultra-thin more often stems from someone's worries about how she looks. There is also a double standard in regard to weight. Luciano Pavarotti, Rush Limbaugh and James Earl Jones are seen as powerful and lovable, while an overweight woman is scorned.

Poor body image can also lead to poor health. When a woman does not love her body, it becomes less important for her to take care of it. She will sometimes postpone dental appointments, forget to get mammograms, avoid exercise, etc. Too often a negative cycle gets set up that includes both poor body image and declining health.

The body image days in this book will be devoted to developing a positive body image and improved health. This is the time to say, "Now is the time for me to devote some special thoughts and behaviors to my body. I will plan to get to know myself better and commit to caring for my body."

Time: the measured or measurable period during which
an action, process, or condition exists or continues.
—Webster's Collegiate Dictionary

Making the Most of Your Time

I am an ordinary woman leading an extraordinary life. My greatest accomplishment has been rearing my three most wonderful and beautiful children. More changes for challenge and pleasure have been given to me in the six very different and very special grandchildren I love. Perhaps the most challenging and wonderful relationship that I treasure is my soul connection —my husband. While nurturing and enjoying these relationships, my professional life has included founding and building three companies, traveling nationally and internationally, designing addiction treatment programs, speaking in hundreds of conferences, authoring fifteen books, and making two films and several videotapes. My hobbies have been to garden, entertain, travel, walk and listen to music. My most recent interest is tap dancing.

One could say, "How hectic." Yet it's been a manageable lifestyle because I learned to SIMPLIFY, over and over again.

Sometimes in my life I've felt overwhelmed by commitment, activities and business. Years ago, I went to see my mentor and complained of a lack of time in my life to enjoy what I had. My mentor listened very intently to my complaints and when I finished said: " Simplify." I began my list of reasons why I could not simplify and my mentor continued, "You must always be simplifying. In our lives when we are faced with good things and bad things, it's easy to simplify. We eliminate the bad things over time and choose to keep the good. Then our lives are filled with good things. It becomes more difficult to simplify when we must eliminate good things, activities and people from our lives in order to gain manageability and time. However, when we do continue to simplify, we are left with very little that is good, and we have more of the better things. Now our lives are filled with better and better things. Yet we need time to enjoy what we have, so in time we need to simplify again. That means that we eliminate some of our better activities, things and people. This process gets increasingly difficult, but if we remember to keep simplifying, we are left with all our choices being between the best and the best—and having the time to enjoy what we have. It's part of the journey of life, and when we have continued to eliminate, gain and simplify, we become increasingly fulfilled."

The challenge is to be able to let go and give up portions of my life when something new and better presents itself. It may not always be better qualitatively, but better for me in a particular time of my life. If we kept every piece of clothing and furniture we ever owned, if we kept every automobile, book, gift or photo we have ever enjoyed, if we nurtured every acquaintance, friend and coworker we have shared with, we would be exhausted and our energy would be spent. Our challenge is in recognizing the seasons of our life and keeping the appropriate belongings for that stage, and letting go of the rest.

This section will help you explore ways to evaluate, let go and simplify your life. There will always be a certain book, piece of jewelry, photo, friend and family member that we will want in our life forever. That is how we honor those special people and possessions. Yet in order to enjoy them, we have to let go of others so that we have the time and energy for the choices we value.

Corporations coined the word *downsizing.* It's a wonderful word and applies to the message of this section of the book. As we eliminate clutter and excess obligation in our lives, we are left with a purer and clearer vision of who we are and what we want as women. In another book I wrote, called *Dancing with Destiny*, I speak of grace as "spiritual energy" that helps us on our journey of discovery of our own lives. This search, and willingness to live life to its fullest and as authentically as we can, is our spiritual mission. Fulfilling our own individual and unique mission is the basis of contentment and inner peace.

As you walk through the days devoted to time, enjoy the lift and energy you feel as you unclutter your surroundings, your work, your closet, your decisions and your social life.

One faces the future with one's past.

—PEARL S. BUCK

Rituals and Traditions

L ife has always had rituals to mark important events and traditions to bond people together. In my childhood, there
were many. On May 1, we would bring our friends May baskets
filled with candy and cookies. We'd set them on the front porch
and run, leaving them to guess who left the baskets. My father,
who owned a chicken hatchery, would dip little chicks in food
coloring each April. The cute little pink, yellow and blue chicks
would then run around under a light in the front window of his
business, and he would give them away to children for Easter.

Today, however, many people feel they are too busy for these
little acts of ritual and tradition. Such gestures might even seem
a bit corny. Yet when you are ill and someone shows up at your
doorstep with hot chicken noodle soup, you are grateful for the
soup and touched by the gesture. There are countless ways to
bring a little sunshine into your life and the lives of others. They
aren't expensive or time-consuming. They are just thoughtful
touches that let people know you care.

While we sometimes remember to exchange thoughtful gestures with friends and coworkers, all too often we forget family
members, especially those living right in our own house. With
all the pressures and interruptions in daily life, the outside world
can crowd our time with each other. Little rituals and traditions,
however, can form protective walls around our relationships,

creating a bit of intimacy. An individual or family with rich traditions brings information and celebration from the past into the future. The more we can bring strength and courage from the past, the easier and more full will be the present and the future. Our responses today reflect our experiences yesterday, and those roots lie in the past. Those experiences are not coincidental. They will be given to us consistent with our talents and lessons we need to learn in order to play out our role in life.

When we are involved in a ritual or tradition, we connect first of all to ourselves, and our energy and spirit become active. This spirit we feel is connected to our ancestors, to the people in our lives right now and maybe even in the community or world we live in. The act or event becomes like a magical thread connecting many people. It's as though each person connected is a dot, and when the ritual takes place it connects the dots and there is a bigger picture of life.

A very important lesson was given to me by my grandmother. I had recently been through a divorce, and my three children and I were looking toward the holidays with a bit of sadness. As that time approached, I decided to take a big step and plan a trip to Disney World for us. Flying out of the snow and winter to a Florida vacation was a thought that lifted all our spirits.

About a month before the departure date, my mother called with the message that she and my grandmother decided to visit us for the holidays. When I told her that we had already made plans to take a two-week vacation to Florida, she said, "But Sharon, we don't know how long Grandma will be with us, and perhaps you should change your plans." Just try and tell children that you are not going to Disney World! I didn't know what to do. Before I could make a decision, my grandmother called and said, "I heard you were thinking of going to Disney World. That's great! Go! Every mom is responsible for following some traditions. That's important when we all get together. However, every mom is also responsible for starting a few new traditions. Perhaps a holiday at Disney World will be part of a new tradition.

We'll get together later." We did go to Disney World that year, and Disney trips have become a tradition. Just this year, we took all the grandchildren. Grandma was a prophet and shared her adventuresome spirit with us all. (We did have some additional wonderful visits with her.)

One night after seeing a movie together, my son said, "Let's go for a pizza; we always go for a pizza after a movie." I started to laugh because we had done that twice before, and now it was perceived as a tradition. The same son said to me this last holiday, "I'm sure you're bringing that meat spread for our crackers, aren't you?" He's in his thirties and yet he remembers the special traditions with family and friends. Traditions and rituals celebrate our shared experiences in life and become the source of happy memories for a lifetime.

As we read through the many ideas of the tradition meditations, may we think about what traditions we would like to pass on, and what rituals and traditions we would like to start.

We become what we do.

Managing Money

As a successful businesswoman in my forties, I was surprised when a wealthy mentor asked me what I was doing to develop *passive income*. My ability to save a bit, buy some CDs and invest in an IRA comprised my idea of planning for the future. He quickly advised me that my goals were too small and financial security would be out of my reach until I learned the value of passive income.

His words took me on a journey of exploration and discovery. I'm grateful for that nudge that my friend gave me when I was in my forties, because today I have found financial security. Learning how to use credit rather than allow credit to use me is one of the lessons I learned. Learning how to spend wisely, save wisely and invest wisely were all new lessons for me.

Both opportunities and handicaps arise for those born to wealthy parents. My birth was into a family of poverty, yet my career took me into the intimate lives of many wealthy people. Interestingly, the problems that both groups face have been quite similar. The challenge is how to deal with those issues.

Regardless of how much money one has, it is important to address:

investments
credit

financial blocks
financial tips to get ahead
employment
self-worth
wants
needs

As you read each of the meditations on money, you will be able to evaluate your personal situation and your attitudes toward money. Money can work for or against us.

There is probably no other subject that is as volatile and emotionally charged. In addition to facing all her own money issues, every individual must also face the money issues of her partner and/or mate. The addition of children and grandchildren further complicates these issues. Perhaps the most conflict and pain come with divorce, remarriage and stepchildren. Lucky is the family that is able to work through all these issues.

I have chosen the meditations on money management to stimulate you to think about many different approaches to your relationship with money.

Take time to laugh. It's the music of the soul.
—A<small>NONYMOUS</small>

Humor and Laughter

There was a time in my life when I thought I would die of terminal seriousness. My perception was that the concerns of my life were somehow different from those of the rest of the world and required my somber dedication. Granted, there was plenty to be somber about in my life. (I'll spare you the details.) But I couldn't help noticing that there were many who had as much to worry about as I did, yet they did it with a sense of humor and a lightness of heart. I wondered, *How did they do that?* Then fortunately, I met my husband, who has the best-developed sense of humor of anyone I know. Little by little, he taught me to laugh, to sometimes be silly, and to see the lighter side of life. Many of the somber issues continued to touch my life and new ones have surfaced, but I've learned I do not need to live in the sadness and difficulty. Facing the realities of life is easier with a sense of humor.

It's hard to pick up a magazine without reading an article about the benefits of laughter. Health benefits alone would justify a few laughs every day. Wonderful physicians, who are great leaders in this new understanding of humor and laughter (Norman Cousins, Andrew Weil, Bernie Siegel, etc.), are teaching us of humor's benefits. Laughter decreases blood pressure and heart rate. It stimulates alertness and increases endorphins. Stress is reduced as laughter and humor improve coping skills and decrease anxiety and tension. The majority of people who come to a family physician's office come because of some form of stress and the rest have chronic problems like arthritis or diabetes. Since stress makes all the symptoms worse, wouldn't it be a good idea to use humor to relieve that stress? Laughter has been referred to as "internal jogging." Socially, laughter creates bonding, encourages trust, heals relationships and enhances creativity. Laughter has been referred to as a "social lubricant."

Steve Allen Jr., M.D., prescribes laughter and juggling "as needed" to reduce stress. In his own words, Dr. Allen has said that he inherited a funny bone from his famous dad and he uses it, both in his medical practice and as a consultant who teaches juggling for stress management. Bernie Siegel, M.D., recommends that his exceptional cancer patients take a survival kit to the hospital with them. The kit includes a whistle for calling nurses and a water gun if necessary. These physicians do not avoid how complicated and serious medicine is, but they try to give us all the tools we can handle to best cope with our crisis of illness. Even though there have been scientific articles written for a long time, it was the book *Anatomy of an Illness,* published by Norman Cousins, M.D., in 1979, that brought the idea of humor and laughter as healing to the attention of the general public. In this book, Dr. Cousins describes how he improved his healing by reading humorous books and watching comedies. He found that laughter gave him pain relief and allowed him to sleep.

Laughter prevents "hardening of the attitudes." The ability to laugh at yourself or your circumstances will relieve tension. Choosing to find humor in your predicament and admitting your humanity will help you and endear you to others. Laughing with someone allows you to connect with them for a moment, to have a shared experience and feel closer to each other. This is an important antidote to loneliness, isolation and depression.

In addition to the health benefits, laughter is fun for its own sake. When you think of your favorite friends, you'll find that those with a sense of humor top the list. Humor covers many situations. I can remember when my girlfriends and I were starting to date boys. We would frequently say, "I really like him— he doesn't have a car and is not too cute, but he is so funny and so much fun to be with."

Enjoy the meditations on laughter and humor. May they bring a smile or a giggle to you.

We wait for life to keep unfolding.
We try to understand its meaning year by year,
experience by experience. We may control our actions,
speed up our movement, resist schedules, but in
truth life will unfold at its own pace.

—Dancing with Destiny[1]

Spirituality

Spirituality is a powerful word and means so many different things to so many. For purposes of meditation on this topic, I will try to do my best to come up with a definition we can all use. To me, spirituality is whatever leads us or reminds us to transform ourselves and the area we live in to wider channels of possibility and fulfillment. It's a sort of lens that, when we look through it, can give clarity and meaning to the stress and the chaos of our minute-to-minute experiences. It helps us make sense of the struggles of the past and conceive of a future full of possibility, it also gives us the energy and courage to live in the present.

I will use the terms *spiritual resources* and *spirituality.* It will be my words for the many spiritual frames of reference people use. You may substitute Higher Self, Mother Nature, God, Holy Spirit, Jesus, Buddha, Truth, Force, Higher Power, etc. It's important that I state that I am not using *spirituality* and *religion* as synonyms. They do not mean the same thing. What we will be doing in this topic's meditations is taking a journey within to explore what

1. Sharon Wegscheider-Cruse, *Dancing with Destiny* (Deerfield Beach, Florida: Health Communications, 1997), p. xxii.

spirituality means to each of us, and how it is recognized and demonstrated in our personal lives.

Signs of spiritual revolution are everywhere as people in all walks of life, in every economic bracket, search for added meaning in their lives. They seek contentment, serenity, understanding and inner peace. The fixations on material goods, physical beauty, failed relationships, broken families and financial striving have not nourished people's souls.

There are very different ways to begin to experience a power outside of ourselves. Sometimes it is a sense of awe—the majesty of a snow-capped mountain, the sound of pine crackling in the fireplace at holiday times or the delicate fragrance of a freshly bathed infant. When we see a spectacular sunset, or hear a powerful piece of music, we are lifted out of the ordinary. The unfolding of our spiritual self comes in stages.

As we watch children grow—from infancy to the first day of school, then through the rites of passage (first communion, bar mitzvah) to the first date, graduation, wedding, and then the birth of a child—we are touched by a powerful sense of life's steady yet irrepressible flow. We begin to see where and how we fit into the grand scheme of things.

When we lose a parent or someone dearly loved and are forced to become the head of a family, the awareness becomes more acute. We realize that we are merely drops in a stream, circles in the trunk of a tree—part of something much bigger than we can ever be individually. I love the words of Helen Keller: "I put my hand in yours and together we can do what each of us cannot do alone."

Many people find their spiritual resource in the laws of nature. Nature provides us with numerous ways to experience a feeling of grandeur and mysteries. In the timeless cycle of spring blossoms and falling leaves, in the crashing surf of the seashore, we can embrace the certainty that life will go on, with or without us. While we are here, we can be part of nature, sense its strength and beauty and feel reassured by its ever-changing ways.

My own spiritual journey started many years ago as a small child and has gone through countless transitions that have given me understanding, security and inner peace. In my early life, I was very fortunate to have many spiritual and loving female role models. They were my mother and grandmother and several very special aunts. From them, I learned about the spirituality of raising a family, cooking a meal, creating a home and then sharing that home with others. Nature was also a part of those early years. In the woods, I had an outdoor (fantasy) cathedral that was a safe place for me.

From my earliest memories, I felt close to God. As a child, I had a brass bed with a headboard filled with decorative holes. I tied pencils on the bedposts, and after being tucked in at night, plugged the pencils into the holes like the old-time telephone operators did. With the divine "headboard," I pretended to connect myself with God and the angels so we could talk. As a child, the connection was as real as a regular telephone conversation. Later in my life, those conversations became prayers. For me, prayer and meditations have been a lifelong practice.

As I grew older, experiences and circumstances challenged my sense of a power outside my self. My faith needed to mature and grow with me. The traumas and losses in my life seemed out of character with a loving God. In time, I came to realize that these very traumas and losses were part of the maturing of my faith. The message of love, loss, faith and courage is not only for me. It is for all souls. The great figures in history have also had experiences that have given glimpses of light, clarity and a tangible inner peace. I invite you to explore the journey of your spirituality in many of the meditations.

Love doesn't just sit there, like a stone, it has to be made,
like bread, remade all the time.

—URSULA K. LE GUIN

Relationships

The art of being related to another is a special gift. Relationships offer support and warmth, fun and pleasure, pain and problems, hurt and fear—and often all of those with the same person. Relationships are a challenge and perhaps one of the most important and valued connections a person can have. We will reflect on the relationships in our life.

Relationships can be rewarding experiences that we value a great deal. In those connections, it's important to learn more and more ways to nurture and strengthen those people in our lives who bring so much richness just by being themselves—knowing them enriches us. It is important to invest emotion, time and resources to sustain valuable relationships.

Some relationships are strained. This can happen for any number of reasons. It may be disappointment, unresolved hurt or anger, fear, or misunderstandings. If the relationship has enough history of feeling involved and both parties want to bridge the gap, then efforts can be made to heal the pain between people, and the relationship has a chance to grow in a positive way.

Sometimes a relationship needs to end. There are too few rituals or traditions that help people successfully end relationships. It would never be possible to keep every connection we have made in a lifetime. Reality demands that we will end some relationships. When we do so in a direct and clear way, with gratitude and intention, everyone benefits. Without that, people drift apart—with issues left unresolved and sometimes with hurt feelings.

In our early years, many of our relationships are chosen for us. Parents, children, grandchildren, siblings, etc. do not get a great deal of choice as to whom they are related. These are all relationships that are connected to roles in our life. While there will always be some role definition, it is as people mature that they make a decision as to whether to develop a close relationship with someone they were originally connected to by a role. We'll explore this further in the meditations on relationships.

Friends are a very important value in life. Chosen friends can sometimes be the person you connect to most closely and chosen friendships certainly bring much joy to the people involved. Some friendships are important to a specific time in life and then end. Geographic changes, changing lifestyles and changing interests all can impact a friendship. If entered and left with honor and respect, these treasured (although temporary) friendships are a very important part of a person's life. Other friendships (usually much fewer in number) may last a lifetime and even outlive certain family relationships.

Years ago, someone gave me this reading. It was on a plain piece of paper and I have no idea whom to credit. If it belongs to someone, may he or she come forth to claim it. I would be happy to give credit.

People are gifts that God has sent—wrapped.
Some are wrapped very beautifully and are very attractive.
Some come in ordinary wrapping paper.
Some have been mishandled in the mail.
Once in a while there is a Special Delivery.
Some persons are gifts which come loosely wrapped, others very tightly.
But the wrapping is not the gift. It's so easy to make that mistake.

Sometimes the gift is easy to open up. Sometimes it's difficult.
Sometimes the gift has been opened up before and thrown away.
I, too, am a gift. A gift to myself and then to others.
Have I ever really looked at the gift that I am?

Do I give myself to others as a gift
or do I only let others look at the wrappings?
Every meeting of persons is an exchange of gifts.
Relationships are the connections between people and are an exchange of gifts.

May the meditations devoted to relationships help you to discover the gift that you are to others. May they help you evaluate all your relationships—those you want to nurture, those you may want to heal and those that perhaps you should end.

The doors we open and close each day
decide the lives we live.

—FLORA WHITTLEMORE

Sacred Places

My journey in life has taken me many places. Early years were in small Midwestern towns in farming areas. There is a whole lifestyle that goes with small-town living. My father was a town merchant and dependent on the farmers as his customers. When weather or disaster affected the crops of the farmer, it also affected the lives of the townspeople. I learned much by being a small-town girl, and I will be forever grateful to have grown up in this kind of community. It's been easy for me to feel a sense of belonging and importance because in this small community, everyone did belong and we were important to the life in that community.

During those young and formative years, my family traveled a great deal, perhaps quite a bit more than the usual Midwestern family. My mother and I traveled during World War II to try to stay close to my father. As a child, my world became quite large through these travels and also through train trips with my grandmother, who managed a depot for the Great Northern Railroad. There were times when I felt very special when traveling with my mother and/or my grandmother.

In my young adulthood, I left for the big city. At seventeen, the city and its ways were new to me. Yet as I learned my way around, I felt powerful and safe as the city became increasingly familiar to me. It was as though my Higher Power (God) was showing me the way to the rest of my future. The city became a friendly place to me.

My early married life took me into another lifestyle and new places. This was the prime time of the suburbs. We bought a couple of acres in a beautiful suburb and became suburbanites. Our time and our resources were spent on lawns, gardens and neighborly pursuits. Once again, the space we lived in shaped and influenced our lives. By now it was clear to me that there were spaces that influenced how we lived, what we felt and how we behaved.

My living experiences, which were varied and quite different, were teaching me that space and place were important factors in personal development. Some of the places I lived in and visited were spaces that were painful to me, and I learned to avoid being in that kind of space. Other spaces were nurturing and gave me gifts of strength and clarity. In time, I began to be very conscious of the time I spent in certain spaces. It became important to me to choose spaces where I could feel the power of my God. Those were spaces I would return to again and again and let the awareness and learning surround me. I would like to share with you some of the "sacred places" that have brought me closer to my God. In telling you about those places, the lessons learned from them will be my gift to you.

I have made my world and it is a much better
world than I ever saw outside.

—Louise Nevelson

Stages and Passages

All of us are on a journey that begins with our birth and ends with our death. In between, we move from stage to stage. Each part of the journey has special pains, challenges and joys. Our trip will be so much easier if we do not get stuck in any one of the stages and know that everything changes and nothing is forever.

As a child, it seemed that life would be a time of freedom. Much of life seemed controlled by both the calendar and the clock. So much of the time was spent in school. I can remember watching the big classroom clock during the afternoon and thinking that my choices in life would begin at 4:00, when the school bell rang. Then during high school, I didn't want the school day to end because my whole life was wrapped up in friends and activities.

My young adult years were spent in a very early marriage and soon followed by the births of three children. It seemed in many ways that everything went on hold while I took care of the responsibilities that were right in front of me all the time. It seemed that there would never be another time in life that wasn't filled with little children, diapers, baby food, baby-sitters and laundry. Those years took a long time—and then one day, the last child went out of diapers. It felt like I had been given three or four extra hours per day.

Eventually, I came to mark passages by the events in my children's lives. There came a time when there was no need for baby-sitters. The next stage was drivers' licenses. Then came dating. Then came the bittersweet time of the children going to college. It was exciting as they embarked on their own journeys, and yet it was such a signal that the family was coming to an end. It was hard for me to go through this passage; I wanted us to be a family forever. The next big passage was the choosing of partners and adding more people to our basic core family. Nothing would ever be the same again.

Then for me, once the family was raised, it was time for me to pursue my education. Many of you readers also took the same journey I did. It was my choice to parent first and educate myself afterwards. Others of you went to college right out of high school and postponed marriage and/or parenting until later. It really doesn't matter which choices we made. What matters is that both types of journeys were full of stages and passages.

It was interesting and yet strange to be back in school at thirty-three. After years of believing there would never be anything other than child care, it felt scary to be responsible for my mind, my choices and my activities. It had been a long time since I had thought of myself in this way. It was also very satisfying and fulfilling. Nine years of college and training was a major shift for me.

By now, my children had lives of their own. It was still difficult for me to let them go and become who they needed to become. I thank God every day that I love each of their partners because it made the letting to a little easier.

Following college as an older student, it became time for me to start my career. Little did I know that it was going to be a career that would take me all over the world, change my way of living, lead me to my soul mate and introduce me to the world of being an author. It has been a whirlwind from day one, and the journey has been an unpredictable lifestyle beyond my wildest dreams. My career days were an incredible gift and a spiritual experience.

The next big passage for me was the coming of grandchildren in my life. I had always wanted grandchildren. After my girls married, it seemed like forever before they announced their pregnancies (a few years, in fact.) Finally, I bought a rocking chair and put it in my bedroom, and rocked and prayed. When they became pregnant it happened at the same time, and my first two grandchildren were born just days apart. I was unprepared for the impact their births would have on me. No longer did I want to work, no longer did I want to travel. I wanted to be as much a part of their lives as my girls would welcome. Fortunately, they welcomed both my husband and me into the lives of the grandchildren with open arms and hearts, and this passage has become one of great importance.

The birth of my grandchildren forced my decision to want to retire and free myself to be able to share in their lives. For someone who had such a full and complicated career, retiring was not an easy task. It meant selling a company, teaching others to take over my work and changing the nature of relationships with hundreds of people who had been part of my professional career. It actually took years to be able to retire and feel good about all my choices.

Life was settling into the kind of style for which I had hoped. It looked like there would be many wonderful years of enjoying my partner, children, grandchildren and friends. This bubble burst shortly after retirement with the surprise diagnosis of two serious illnesses. At first it seemed like a cruel joke, but as time went on and the adjustments were made, it was clear that it was only another passage for me to face, understand and go through successfully. Today, many things have happened and much physical healing has taken place, and the journey goes on.

The people in my life remain primary in my life, health has an important place in my daily living and I'm ready for new adventures. God has blessed my life with supportive and joyful relatives, interesting and valued friendships and a strong sense of the meaning in my life. I've come to know that every day we have choices in the way we choose to live and connect in our relationships. We cannot change the inevitable. The only thing we can do is give our best to every day. Someone once said, "I am not afraid of tomorrow . . . for I have seen yesterday and I love today."

My story of passages and stages is my story, and you have a story and set of passages that are yours. As you read about stages, you will explore some of those stages and take from them the learning, courage and strength to keep going on this journey we call life.

The timeless wisdom that is passed from woman to woman is one of life's greatest gifts.

—ANONYMOUS

Role Models

If you could pick any woman as your model, whom would you choose? There are the well-known—Eleanor Roosevelt, Meryl Streep, Coretta Scott King, Gail Sheehy, Oprah Winfrey, etc.— and there are the unknown—all are women who have fulfilled their dreams, inspired us, taught us lessons, and lived their lives with grace. We need female role models. For so long, men were in positions of visibility and power and women were in the background.

Yet women have been the strength and power behind many a man, working with and beside him at the same time, being the primary manager of home and children. Women's ability to have many roles at once often has been undernoticed and the visibility of her role often neglected. In more recent times, women have taken their place in history, boardrooms, the workforce, the entertainment industry, medicine, education and politics. Role models are currently available and women are networking to help each other.

There are two different kinds of role models. One type lives her life in such a way that she teaches us how to be. There are women who can show each other how to learn, how to manage money, how to earn that money, how to play, how to make choices, how to walk a spiritual path, how to successfully raise children, etc. The second kind of role model is not the teacher, but the inspiration that goes inside each of us and finds the treasures buried there. These women bring qualities to the surface that had always been inside, but that needed an outside trigger to release them.

There are women who have touched our hearts and minds and given us a look at what we might become and what we might achieve. They come in all shapes and sizes. They can be of any color or background. What they share is a self-knowledge and the courage and strength to live their lives authentically. They are who they are and do not tend to be part of a crowd. They are individualists and they are real.

We learn from them by listening, by reading and by watching. Often the women who become role models are not aware of how deeply they impact the lives of those who are touched so deeply by them. By living their own lives with power and grace, they are able to teach lessons that challenge others into becoming the best they can be.

My role models are varied. Some are young, some are old. Some I know personally and others have touched me through words they have written or that have been written about them. What they share is that I respect each of them profoundly, and they have touched my life with their qualities and warmth.

*I am not afraid of storms, for I am
learning how to sail my ship.*

—Louisa May Alcott

Choices

Perhaps one of the most important skills we can develop is the skill to make choices. Our entire life is bombarded with information, requests, obligations, people and possibilities. If we do not learn how to make positive choices on our own behalf, we will feel overwhelmed, stuck, burned out and lonely. *Choice* simply means "to choose between alternatives." Some choices are relatively easy. If we are to choose between doing the laundry or going to a movie and out to dinner, no problem—the choice is easy. However, some choices get more difficult. To choose between going to dinner and going dancing might be more difficult. Choosing between cleaning house and going for a walk on a spring day is not a difficult choice. Choosing between taking a vacation in the mountains or taking a vacation on the beach might be more difficult. Every choice means there is a loss. The loss is whatever we do not choose. When that loss is the loss of a relationship, or loss of a job, loss of safety, etc., we sometimes will avoid making a decision because we are not willing to lose anything. However, we won't have room or energy in our lives if we never let go of anything. This is how we become overwhelmed or burned out. Therefore, learning to make choices is really learning how to let go and become comfortable with loss. Learning and accepting the grieving process is a part of learning to make choices.

Our lives are filled with decisions and selections. There are classes to take, careers to plan, hobbies to choose, sports to play, friendships to cultivate, budgets to make, vacations to take and clothes to wear. We need to choose houses or apartments to live in, whether to get married and whether to have children. When we get in our car, we have to choose what to listen to and where to go. The list goes on and on. The talents we each have been blessed with can only be developed fully if we do not squander our energy on too many things in our lives. Sometimes important choices have to be made just to protect ourselves and the time and energy we have. The more talents and opportunities we have, the more difficult it becomes to make choices and simplify. As Anne Morrow Lindbergh said, "One cannot collect all the beautiful shells on the beach, one can collect only a *few*."

There have been times in history when women felt they did not have many choices in their lives. They felt that it wasn't possible to mold and shape their lives. Even our grandmothers and mothers lived in circumstances where much of their lives consisted of fulfilling predestined roles. A woman at that time could choose to become a teacher, nurse or secretary, if she desired a career, or she could become a wife and/or a mother. Those are still wonderful roles for women to choose for themselves, but there are many more occupations available to women today, and a variety of options on how to be a wife and mother and still have an abundance of choices. Our identity as women is strengthened each time we thoughtfully make a choice.

Being alive is our invitation to become a choice maker. We are free to make decisions in new, fresh and creative ways. To have this ability requires that we concentrate on an inner vision of what we want in life and then bring it forth to combine with our external reality. When our vision and our reality meet, the decisions we need to make for ourselves become much clearer.

In my life, I learned early on to make decisions between bad things and good things. It was a little harder to choose between the good and the better in my life. So often, because I struggled to make these decisions, my life would get very full and complicated before I would be willing to let go of something. By the time my life was full of all the best, I was too tired to enjoy any of it. I remember a time when I said to myself, "I'm taking three months and taking a break from training, consulting, writing and lecturing." About three weeks later, a publisher called and offered me a very attractive advance to write a particular book. The only problem was that they needed it quite soon. My excitement was high and I told them I'd make a decision in a week. Sometime during that week, I asked my husband what he thought of my attractive offer. He simply asked, "What about the gift of time you were going to give to yourself?" Once again, the temptation to grab the brass ring was right in front of me. After doing some serious thinking, I made the decision that the brass ring would come again, and my three months of time off were more important than writing a book. It was a very important turning point for me as I realized the gift of time.

When we understand that most situations are resolvable and that opportunities will always be there, it will become easier to make wise decisions. Our purpose in life is to make the selections that enhance our whole being, and we can learn to develop the gift of discernment (knowing which decisions to make).

*To live is so startling it leaves little
time for anything else.*

—EMILY DICKINSON

Qualities

My life has been graced by wonderful family and friends. Family came with the territory but friends have been chosen. Some family members have become close friends and some remain connected by blood only. All of us meet many people in a lifetime and we can't keep everyone we've met in our lives— therefore we have to make choices. Some people we meet and in time they pass through our lives. Others we meet and they will be part of our lives forever. In thinking about all the people in my life that are special, it seems that they have certain similar qualities. The more I explored this idea, it seemed that while these special people were varied—from different backgrounds and with different interests—they all did share qualities I respected and led lives that inspired me.

Webster defines *qualities* as "attributes, characteristics, traits or kinds." It's so interesting how each of my friends can be so different, and yet share many of the same traits, values and attributes. My friends all have a sense of adventure and the courage to live fully in the world and make it a better place because they have been here.

We share our lives with each other. We share both the valleys and the peaks. When a friend loses a child to suicide, my heart breaks for her and her husband. When a friend becomes a new grandparent, we celebrate the joy together. We go to air shows and we visit Las Vegas showrooms. We take walks together in the sacred hills and we go shopping. Woven into our relationships are the qualities of courage, risk, joy, love, effort, creation, laughter, tears, silence, speaking up, compassion, fidelity, kindness, adventure and many more. We enrich each other's lives by sharing ourselves fully.

It's as though each of the friends I have in my life is a different color, and when we put them all together, with different shapes and shades, we end up with a patchwork quilt that is a place in which to curl up in comfort. Each of the people adds something and creates something more than any one person can do alone.

I treasure these friendships and am willing to invest myself to nurture and cherish them. That takes letters, phone calls and visits. It demands an authentic interest in the life of each person. It also means that we give each other space to lead a private life at the same time we share these special bonds.

I used to believe that if we didn't get together frequently, the friendship would suffer and maybe even fall apart. Today I know that with the type of friends I have, we are bonded—heart and soul—and nothing cuts that bond. There are so many ways to connect even if we can't get together. The glue that holds us together is the nature of the qualities of people who can bond and give space at the same time.

In the meditations devoted to qualities, I want to explore some of the qualities that make a person a wonderful individual, partner, friend, coworker and neighbor. Family members can be friends as well. Parents, adult children and siblings as well as extended family members all have great friend potential. After all, there is a shared history. May we all be blessed with as many high-quality friends as possible. May we also do what we can to develop and nurture these qualities in ourselves.

I hope you will use this book for daily meditation. Or you can use it as a reference book, for those times when you need a helping hand or a sympathetic ear.

Hopefully the words and ideas contained within these pages will inspire new thoughts for each of you, as well as bring back old memories and warm fuzzy feelings. As for me, writing it has been one of the most fulfilling and enriching experiences of my life. Each day reminds me how proud and happy I am to be a woman. May this book help you to know and love yourself.

Girl Talk

GIRL TALK #1: Today I will think about how I want to spend New Year's Day and what traditions would bring pleasure and meaning to me. Then I'll set out to make my dreams come true.

New Year's Day is one of my favorite holidays—a day to sleep in and linger over coffee. It's a good time to reflect on what has happened during the past year. Then I bring out the new calendars and mark all the special days I want to remember: birthdays, anniversaries, meaningful memory days. There's a feeling of getting organized that brings a sense of harmony and enthusiasm for this day and the 364 that lie ahead.

Our football appetizer party is the first of many rituals and traditions that come throughout the year. While my husband sets up the football betting pools and the televisions, I plan a light and easy dinner. When the guests arrive, each with his or her unique appetizer, the party begins. With wagers won and lost, eating, drinking, sharing plans and listening to our friends' resolutions, the day passes quickly. When everyone is "footballed out," we say goodnight to our guests.

This is the one day of the year when everything seems possible. When the future lies ahead fresh and unsullied.

It is important to take some time to dream and plan—for only dreams give birth to change. Take a leap of faith this year and believe in yourself. Choose your dreams wisely and believe that the energy and the people around you will help realize your goals.

Happiness is like manna, it is to be
gathered and enjoyed every day.

—TRYON EDWARDS

GIRL TALK #2: Life goes by so quickly. Today I will meditate on the need to embrace all the holy moments and weave them into the fabric of my life.

My first two grandchildren were born only a few days apart and I realized that I wanted regular visits at our home for our growing family. During our first "Grandparents' Week" there were three little ones to romp and play in the yard, to take on picnics and to share our joy. Since the children were young, they needed constant supervision—a challenge indeed. Yet I was determined to make the get-togethers a tradition.

After a full day of activity, complete with laughter and a few tears, we settled in the yard for iced tea and a few moments of rest. As my daughters and their husbands settled in lawn chairs, Grandpa went to fetch some old kites from the garage. Soon all three youngsters were racing through the field behind the house, pulling their kites behind them. Without warning I started to cry. This was one of those magic moments—an idyllic setting with my most cherished family members—and I was totally overcome with sentimentality.

Taking a deep breath, I said a private prayer of gratitude that I recognized my connection to my family and a Higher Power. It became one of the special memories in my mental treasure chest. These moments of holiness are nourishment for the human spirit. Those who recognize them will know they have a unique connection to their spiritual resources.

*If one advances confidently in the direction of his
dreams and endeavors to live the life which he has imagined,
he will meet with a success unimagined in common hours.*
—HENRY DAVID THOREAU

GIRL TALK #3: Today I will think about the role of food and how I can use the sharing of food to connect with others.

Aside from providing nourishment, there are many foods that comfort us. Homecooked meals are the best—rather than store-bought. Mashed potatoes, casseroles, breads and pies are some of my favorites.

Growing up was a wonder of delight when I spent time in the kitchens of my aunts or grandmother. They grew fruits, vegetables and herbs in their back yards. At the summer's end, everything had to be canned or preserved until needed. Nothing was wasted.

Food was synonymous with caring. It also provided special consolation during funerals and extra added joy for baptisms, graduations and family reunions. Gathering around the table for holidays, gazing at the bowls of delicious things to eat, made me realize how blessed we are when food is part of our daily lives.

I think something has been lost with the fast-food and restaurant meals on which many busy people rely. Is there caring in the preparation? Where is the kindness shared? I truly believe that food is more than just nourishment. It is love.

A good cook is like a sorceress who dispenses happiness.
—ELSA SCHIAPARELLI

GIRL TALK #4: Today is the day I will examine the people and activities in my life to see how I can get closer to my goals.

Many years ago I had a wonderful mentor. He helped me make some very difficult decisions. At that time of my life, things were exciting. My tendency was to take on too many projects and obligations at one time and become overwhelmed. When that happened, I went to my mentor.

"Simplify," he'd say. "Simply, simplify your life and you will regain your energy and well-being."

The hardest part, of course, was giving up something that was precious. I had to choose between the good, better and best parts of my life. It all boiled down to choices. However, there is just so much time and each of us has a limited amount of energy. We must choose the better part of the best of our life. Only by letting the rest drop away—the toxic people, the ones who drain our spirit and energy, the mundane chores that we can delegate to others—will we arrive at a place where each and every moment is fulfilling.

> *Discernment: to be able to discriminate*
> *and understand the difference.*
>
> —WEBSTER'S DICTIONARY

GIRL TALK #5: Helpful hints can save time. Today I'll choose one or two.

I find that the following ideas help me keep my home organized and prevent the accumulation of out-of-date clothing, magazines and catalogs.

- A phone call to your favorite charity will bring a truck to your door. They will gladly take away your clutter and give you a tax deduction, too. Your closets will be neater, your house cleaner and you will have done a good deed for others.
- When you buy furniture, keep in mind extra storage space. I always look for tables and wall cabinets with drawers and ottomans that open. When you have a place for everything, your life (and your home) will be less jumbled.
- A large, attractive wicker basket in your living room, den, office or bedroom makes a great way to keep magazines and newspapers organized. Once a week throw out what you don't need, or those you've read. You can even spray-paint the baskets to match your decor.
- Using a plastic bucket with a handle is a terrific way of keeping gardening tools, gloves and knee pads together. When I'm ready to trim plants or set in some new ones, I simply grab my bucket and head outside.

Each day provides its own gifts.

—RUTH P. FREEDOM

GIRL TALK #6: Today I will pay attention to my body and take good care of myself. Should an illness befall me, I will use my best resources to stay positive so I can heal.

A few summers ago, during a routine health checkup, I had the shock of my life. I thought I was in great shape. In fact, the month before my exam I had been to a health spa and worked out for a week. Imagine my surprise when the doctor told me I was facing not one but TWO life-threatening illnesses. One was heart disease, the other was breast cancer.

Right from the beginning I knew I had to make some choices. I could panic—which would complicate my heart condition—or I could live in paralyzing fear—which would complicate my breast cancer—or I could make other choices.

So I made these choices:

1. To do whatever was necessary to get better
2. To pray
3. To ask for emotional support from my loved ones
4. To get on with my life

I felt it was important to accept myself, even with my physical limitations. And I had to trust that the doctors would help me work toward my own healing.

Now, years later, I am a grateful survivor. And I know that one need not wait for illness to strike before developing confidence in one's ability to rise to a serious challenge.

We are all stronger than we think.

Change your thoughts and you will change your world.

—ANONYMOUS

GIRL TALK #7: Today's the day for a good belly laugh. There's no better way to wash away the blues.

There was a time in my life when I thought I'd die of terminal seriousness. I'll spare you the grim details but there was plenty to be somber about. Yet I couldn't help but notice that there were many people around me, with even worse problems, who still had a sense of humor and a lightness of heart. I wondered how they did it. Since that time I've learned that facing the realities of life is easier with a sense of humor.

The health benefits of laughter alone would justify a few daily chuckles. Some of the best doctors in the world are teaching us about the healing properties of a good giggle. It decreases the heart rate and lowers blood pressure. It stimulates alertness and increases endorphins. Humor improves coping skills, decreases anxiety and tension, and reduces stress. Laughter has been called "internal jogging."

Social laughter promotes bonding, encourages trust, heals relationships and enhances creativity. It's also been referred to as a "social lubricant."

Laughter prevents hardening of the attitudes. And having the ability to laugh at yourself or your circumstances certainly relieves tension and helps endear you to others.

But best of all, laughter is fun for its own sake. So laugh a little every day. It's good for what ails you.

> *You grow up the day you have your*
> *first real laugh—at yourself.*
>
> —ETHEL BARRYMORE

9

GIRL TALK #8: Today I will explore my relationship to children and make a promise to connect with a child every week—either my own, one who lives nearby or a stranger that I meet.

Throughout my life I have always connected with kids. I had two younger siblings. I had nine cousins living nearby. And when I was a young adult and had no youngsters around me, I joined the Big Sister organization, which gave me a chance to reconnect.

Children are a promise, a new chance and a miracle. Their qualities are varied and remarkable: curiosity, trust, joy, affection and so many more. They force us to slow down, to smell the flowers, watch the ants and walk in rain puddles. With them we revisit the movies that were so much a part of our childhood, like *Bambi, Snow White, Dumbo*—and who could ever forget *The Wizard of Oz*?

With a hug or a kiss, they take away pain. Kids bring out the best in us—and also the worst. They can be trying at times, of that there can be no doubt. But becoming a mother three times over changed my life profoundly and permanently. I learned lessons in patience, acceptance, respect, courage and love—both given and received. Those lessons doubled when I became a grandmother.

If you have a child or children in your life, enjoy them to the fullest. If you don't, explore all the ways you can to reach out and touch one or two. The gift will be shared both ways, I assure you. The give-and-take is miraculous. It will be a special, gifted relationship.

> **Genius is childhood revisited.**
>
> —René Dubos

GIRL TALK #9: Today I will meditate on the experiences and spaces in my life when I know my Higher Power touched me.

The very first time I was hospitalized was at the Methodist Hospital in Minnesota. It was only a minor illness, and I was only there for a few days, but I learned that good things can happen in a medical facility.

My next two visits were times of joy: the births of my daughters. The maternity ward was a happy place, decorated in pink and blue, where visitors brought gifts and congratulations. And we new mothers cuddled with our precious infants for the first time.

Then came the nightmare visits when my eleven-year-old daughter needed major surgery and I sat in the chapel and prayed she would be all right. Someone up there must have been listening, for the doctors finally found me and said, "Our prayers were answered; your little girl will make a full recovery."

Just a few years ago one more miracle took place. The daughter who had been so gravely ill gave birth to her first child, making me a grandmother at last. Once again tears of gratitude trickled down my face as I thanked the doctors for being so gifted and caring.

*The only thing that makes life
possible is permanent, intolerable uncertainty,
not knowing what comes next.*
—Ursula K. Le Guin

GIRL TALK #10: Today is the day I ask myself a few questions about money. My goal is to see if I can neutralize its power.

Money is a powerful commodity. Some people think it will solve their problems. Others believe it will bring happiness and wash away all their troubles. Others rob, steal or kill for it. First Timothy 6:10 New King James Version says, "For the love of money is a root of all kinds of evil." But, in reality, it is merely a medium of exchange. It is only when we give it too much power that it causes such difficulty.

For me, money has three primary values: It can help provide food, shelter, transportation, clothing and medical care. It can offer the opportunity for education, travel, entertainment and hobbies. And lastly, it can give me freedom—when I no longer have to work to earn it.

Here are the questions I am asking myself today. I am also asking you.

1. Do you think you have enough money?
2. Does your job or lifestyle reflect your values?
3. Do you have enough saved to get you through a six-month crisis?
4. Do you feel comfortable financially around others?
5. Do you feel overwhelmed by money problems?
6. Do you overspend, then feel guilty?
7. Do you deprive yourself, then feel sad?
8. Do you want more financial security in your life?

> *Money: any form or denomination of coin or paper lawfully current as money.*
> —WEBSTER'S DICTIONARY

GIRL TALK #11: Today I will think about myself as an infant. If I missed out on early nurturing from my parents, I will find ways to give it to myself.

It is a mistake to think that our lives start when we are born. Each of us was born into a situation that developed long before we arrived. For some their birth was a burden, for others a long-awaited joy. Some were born to single parents, others into large, extended families. Some were born rich, others poor.

Every soul that arrives on earth has the chance to accomplish things left undone, to right wrongs and bring new hope to others. We all arrive naked and helpless. As we grow, we strive to become the center of our own personal universe. We learn to have our many needs met by primary caregivers. We learn to respond to love and to anger.

Parents who are in a position of filling their own needs are in a position to give unconditional love, without any expectation of receiving something in return. This gives the child a chance to develop naturally, at his or her own pace. But when parents are needy, the return they expect becomes more than the child can give. This, then, leads to undue pressure on the infant, and the baby is pushed too fast or too harshly. Nothing comes naturally, and problems down the road are bound to develop.

For prospective parents, the most important factor is whether or not their own needs are met so that they can offer unconditional love in meeting the needs of their precious offspring.

There's a time when you have to explain to your children why they're born, and it's a marvelous thing if you know the reason by then.

—HAZEL SCOTT

GIRL TALK #12: Today I will examine my sense of humor to see if I can see the ridiculous side of life. If I need practice, I will commit to reading at least one of Erma Bombeck's books.

The world lost a great role model for all women with the death of Erma Bombeck. She had the uncanny ability to put into words what every homemaker experiences on a day-to-day basis. Her columns were taped to refrigerator doors across America, copied for friends, and mailed interstate and worldwide.

She approached living with courage and humor. Early on she learned that happiness is not something you seek but something you find by living life to the fullest. She shared her wisdom with the rest of us: If you live with goodness and kindness and let life happen, happiness will find YOU.

Through the years we laughed with her as we read about her pregnancy, cooking, cleaning, entertaining and becoming a new mother—just trying to cope in a crazy world. She had no time for the rush to stay young and wrinkle-free. Instead, she truly believed that what we need most in our lives is a well-developed sense of humor.

I've been on a constant diet for the past two decades.
I've lost a total of 789 pounds. By all accounts,
I should be hanging from a charm bracelet.

—ERMA BOMBECK

GIRL TALK #13: Today I will think about faith and what it means to me. I will take comfort knowing that faith is there for me if I choose to nurture it.

When I was a young girl, my father was in the army, stationed in Germany during World War II. My mother, like other women her age, rolled bandages for hours as a volunteer with the Red Cross. On Sunday mornings all the children would gather together, our arms filled with flowers from our gardens or picked by the roadside. Then we'd march in a procession, singing as we walked toward a creek that flowed on the outskirts of town. When we reached the water's edge, we'd throw the flowers in and say a prayer that our daddies would come home safe and sound.

It never occurred to me at that tender age to doubt that our flowers, songs and prayers were indeed keeping our fathers from harm. Yet when I became an adult—a pragmatic, thinking person—it was harder for me to understand some of the miracles in which I once believed.

Today, however, it's clear to me that faith is a choice. And it's given me great comfort through the years. Now it never occurs to me to doubt that belief. Indeed, it brings me closer to my Higher Power, not only in times of turmoil, but on a daily basis.

> *Faith is the bird that sings when the dawn is still dark.*
>
> —RABINDRANATH TAGORE

GIRL TALK #14: Today I will think about who I am apart from my work.

I t's easy to over-identify with our work. We feel as though we ARE our job or profession. There was a time when earning a living was the means to an end. The earning was the job and we did it to support our living.

For too many, the earning has become the living and there is precious little time left for enjoying the quality of life we desire. Work can be so demanding and draining that dinner becomes fast food, take-out, ordered-in or microwaved, eaten in front of the television while we unwind. We fall into bed in a daze, ready to do it again, and again, with no relief in sight.

When work becomes our primary focus, we lose our own sense of self. Instead of saying, "I do nursing," we say, "I am a nurse." We don't say, "I program computers," we say, "I am a computer programmer." There is a difference, not only in the words themselves, but in the way we view them.

That brings me to a final thought: Do you see your work as something you do, or are you completely identified as a person through your work? Think about it.

I believe that true identity is found in creative activity springing from within. It is found, paradoxically, when one loses oneself. Woman can best refind herself by losing herself in some kind of creative activity of her own.

—Anne Morrow Lindbergh

GIRL TALK #15: Today I'll think of ways I have needed to believe in myself, even when circumstances are difficult. I believe that truth will conquer our fears.

Everyone must take risks at some time during his or her life. It's part of the human experience; only the level of intensity changes.

Martin Luther King Jr. took huge risks when he committed himself—and millions of African-Americans—to equality through non-violent resistance. He risked the wrath of the establishment for breaking the strict rules that governed the color barrier. His success is a shining example of how risk can work to everyone's advantage.

Of course, my story of risk pales by comparison. Nevertheless, it was a monumental turning point in my life.

I had written my first book dealing with addiction. The president of the agency I was working for asked to see it. But he found it objectionable and threatened to fire me if I went ahead and had it published.

Eventually, I risked my job and reputation to rewrite and publish it. It was a huge gamble for me at the time. But in the end, it has paid off many times over. Testimonial letters from those who have read my books and learned from them let me know that sometimes we have to put ourselves out on that limb. Whether it breaks or not, we've got to take the chance.

> *If you're never scared or embarrassed or hurt,*
> *it means you never take any chances.*
>
> —JULIA SOUL

GIRL TALK #16: Today I will begin my plan to commit to "timeless time" for myself and set a date to start the process. If I'm in a relationship, I'll discuss the possibilities with my partner.

In the frantic pace of today's hectic world, it's often impossible to schedule what I've called "timeless time." That's time to spend with you and you alone. It can be half an hour each day, a half-day each week, a weekend a month or a week a year. However you want to break it down, it gives you a chance to destress and unwind.

Of course, it means setting priorities. If you are busy from morning to night, something's got to give. To follow through with your plan to make timeless time, at least one activity will have to be set aside.

Since I'm married, I find that my husband's schedule and mine often prevent us from spending quality time with each other. To bring balance into our relationship, we tried scheduling specific time together and alone. When we are together we can discuss topics of interest to both of us, climb into the hot tub, listen to music or take a walk. What's important is that nothing is planned. We allow ourselves to be spontaneous.

The best part of this notion of timeless time is that it forces us to make a commitment to ourselves as individuals, and to the relationship as well.

I wake each morning with the thrill of
expectation and the joy of being truly alive.
And I'm thankful for this day.

—ANGELA L. WOZNIAK

GIRL TALK #17: Today I will boost my confidence in one very specific way. Then I will try another way. With each accomplishment I will appreciate my own efforts.

Confidence is the art of believing in yourself. Sometimes we feel proud of our accomplishments, sometimes we are anxious and afraid. During those times, acting assured may actually bring about a real sense of security in yourself.

Confidence gives us energy, increases our willingness to try new things and allows us to explore new places. Here are a few tips for boosting your feelings of self-worth:

- Walk tall.
- Look people in the eye.
- Smile.
- Dress in clothes that make you feel good about yourself.
- Take an interest in others and stop worrying about you.
- Set goals for yourself, then make a plan to reach them.
- Seek out others whose confidence you admire. Learn from them.

Go forth into the busy world and love it.
Interest yourself in its life, mingle kindly
with its joys and sorrows.

—RALPH WALDO EMERSON

GIRL TALK #18: Today I'll remember that it is the little remembrances that are every bit as important as the big things.

There's a small gift shop in the town where I live, a recovery bookstore that is crammed with cards and gifts for about a dollar each. Periodically, I visit this inspirational store, where I stock up on cards with special sayings, angels with comforting messages, bookmarks with proverbs, and so on.

My stash of goodies never lasts long. The occasions to use these small items are many and varied. Illness is all too frequent. And just the other day a waitress in my favorite restaurant was verbally abused by a rude customer. When I got home I pulled out one of my gifts and dropped it off, just to let her know she was appreciated.

I'm coming to believe that it's not the big things in life that matter as much as the small ones, if they come when they are needed.

The way we treat others mirrors the way we feel about ourselves. When we feel at peace and we want to share it with others, it's easy and natural. A conscious effort to convey our good intentions may take some effort, but it will always come back a thousand times.

I am now treated like royalty whenever I stop into that restaurant. It was only a small item I gave the waitress, but she greatly appreciated it.

Love is a force. It is not a result, it is a course.
It is not a product, it produces. It is a power, like money
or steam or electricity. It is valueless unless you can
give something else by means of it.
—ANNE MORROW LINDBERGH

GIRL TALK #19: Today I'll remember what's important and what's not. Some things just aren't worth making a fuss over and some are small potatoes in the big picture.

Snoopy was a sheltie with coal-black fur and a lovable personality. She loved to cuddle across my feet at the end of the bed. But she was as lazy as dogs get. So we took her to obedience training, held in the school gymnasium.

As much as my son tried to follow the instructions of the trainer, it was obvious Snoopy had a mind of her own. One night the teacher asked all masters to have their dogs stand up at attention. Of course, Snoopy was leaning against my son's leg. No matter what he tried, Snoopy would not follow instructions.

"Get that dog off the floor," shouted the trainer over the loudspeaker. "She's too lazy to be in this class."

Coming quickly to his pet's defense, my son shouted back, "She's not lazy, she's just independent."

As my son turned to leave, Snoopy—who was still using his leg as a leaning post—fell flat on the floor. Sheepishly my son looked up at the trainer and said, "Maybe you're right."

He scooped her up, carried her to the car and that was that. She never was trained, but it didn't matter. We enjoyed many years of loyalty and love from that lazy pooch.

> *But Grandma, it doesn't matter if my shoes*
> *are on the wrong feet. They still work.*
>
> —CHRISTOPHER, AGE 4

GIRL TALK #20: Today I will recognize that when I'm feeling depressed, maybe I just need to talk to someone who will listen and support me.

During my twenties I was bombarded by grief, loss and stress. My father committed suicide on Christmas Eve at the age of 46. Two weeks later one of my girlfriends died from cancer. Two weeks after that my mother nearly died and was hospitalized with a very serious illness.

All this trauma occurred just after I had given birth to my second child. It was simply too much for me to bear emotionally. I awoke one morning and could not get out of bed. The paramedics transported me to the hospital to determine whether I was paralyzed. The doctors diagnosed it as an "emotional freeze." There was nothing physically wrong, but my body had shut down.

After sleeping for forty-eight hours straight, I was sent for a psychiatric consultation. He suggested medication.

"No," I said, "I just want to talk."

He insisted on medicating me but I decided to wait and see what happened. Later that night three patients on my ward came to my room looking for a fourth hand for a game of bridge. I figured, *Why not?* During the game a visitor brought a pizza.

This is crazy, I thought. *I have a home of my own, I can order my own pizza and I don't want to take pills. What am I doing here?*

When I returned to my room, I flushed the pills down the toilet. Then I checked myself out. I knew the only way to face my demons was to conquer my fears and struggle with my losses. I did not want to be stuck in a hospital where the doctors prescribed drugs instead of talking to their patients.

The lesson was a valuable one. I learned that often all we need is a sympathetic ear when the going gets tough. And, likewise, whenever someone has a problem and wants to talk, I'm ready to listen.

> *The truth shall set you free, but first it will make you miserable.*
>
> —GARFIELD

GIRL TALK #21: Today I will meditate on the times in my life when divine protection took care of me.

As we venture forward in our spiritual quest, one way to increase trust and faith is to go back over our lives and look at the times it seemed like someone or something was guiding and protecting us from harm. This is what I call "divine protection."

When I moved from Minnesota to Texas during the winter of 1983, I found out just what divine protection really was and how it worked.

I left on a cold December day, driving a small Honda. Looking back it might not have been the best idea, but I was hell-bent on heading south. I drove a gray car, dressed in a gray jacket, down-lined boots and a red knit cap. Only a few hours into the trip, a blizzard turned the world white. After three days of treacherous driving, I was a tense bundle of nerves. I was alone, isolated from friends and colleagues. I drove and cried, praying, "Dear God, please give me a sign that I'm doing the right thing."

A little while later I spotted a diner and stopped for a break. As I settled in a booth and took off my cap, the waitress said, "You must be Red Rose."

Puzzled, I asked her to explain.

"The truck drivers coming down from up north are all talking about Red Rose," she said. "Seems some gal left Minnesota in a snowstorm and they've been watching to make sure she was safe on the roads. I'll let them know you're here."

Suddenly, I began to cry. Perfect strangers cared about me. They didn't even know my name, yet they were watching over me, nicknaming me Red Rose. It was really touching and comforting.

It's an amazing world we live in. Whether we acknowledge it or not, there's a divine providence watching over us. So keep the faith, even when you're ready to give up. The Red Rose knows!

Believing is not seeing. I walk in the shadows of faith.
Each step makes me more certain, toward horizons
that are ever more shrouded in mist.

—Pierre Teilhard de Chardin

GIRL TALK #22: Today is a good day to think about my siblings. I think I might just send a card or give a call.

Siblings are people who have shared your history and your past. In large measure, they are responsible for the way you have grown into adulthood. One of my children said to me, "If you died I would be sad and I'd miss you. But if my sister or brother died, I'd be devastated. They are the people who know me best."

At first I was saddened. Then I realized that the bond between siblings is truly amazing.

Birth positions affect family dynamics. Oldest children change the nature of the parents. First there were two, now there are three. They often bond closely with one parent or both. They become leaders and often dominate younger siblings. When the next one comes along, they are expected to grow up fast.

Middle children can be rebellious, wanting attention, too. Others are placid and become withdrawn and quiet. They feel inferior to the older one but more dominant than the youngest.

Last-born children have a unique position that never changes. They are the babies and often feel they've got to catch up. They are also protected by parents and older siblings alike.

What's most important is that everyone understands his or her position and each knows the benefits and drawbacks. That way siblings can provide a support system and share close and loving relationships, instead of constantly competing for their parents' attention and love.

A joy shared is a joy made double.

—ENGLISH PROVERB

25

GIRL TALK #23: Today I will think about where I came from and where I'm going.

When I was eight I received my first camera. It was an old Brownie that took black-and-white photos. Before long I had started a scrapbook. It was a way of recapturing special moments in my life.

The first lesson I learned was to not let the pictures accumulate. I tried to paste them in a scrapbook right away. The second lesson was not to worry about them being perfect or I wouldn't do it at all. Then they'd accumulate in an old shoebox and it would take three times as long to sort them and put them in some semblance of order.

These days I have one shelf set aside strictly for scrapbooks. I have them in every size and shape. Some are full, others empty. I work on a few at a time. When developing film I have duplicates made. That way I can make a small album and give it as a gift.

Knowing my hobby has prompted family members to send me old photos. Over the years I have accumulated six generations' worth of pictures. What a legacy I can pass on to my children and their children—and so on down the line.

You are a child of the universe . . .
You have a right to be here.

—DESIDERATA

GIRL TALK #24: Today I'll consider what success really means. It may be time to define it for me.

Too often when we think of success we think of money, power, possessions or fame. Yet each of these measurements alone has nothing to do with success *per se*. The person who lives life according to his or her own value system is a success. The person who makes a positive contribution to society is a success.

People who are kind, and those who watch over the safety of children, are successful. Whenever we make a commitment and keep it, that spells success. So does brightening someone's day.

Success is taking action or finding a solution to a nagging problem. Success is the ability to handle an encounter so everyone wins.

As long as we fully embrace life and make decisions according to our own truth, we are assured of success.

I am not bound to win, but I am bound
to be true. I am not bound to succeed, but I am
bound to live up to what light I have.

—ABRAHAM LINCOLN

GIRL TALK #25: Today I'll look at ways to protect myself and when I should do so. It's always better to be embarrassed than sorry.

Before my first trip to Washington, D.C., during the 1970s, when I started traveling professionally, I had read several articles about how women should protect themselves. Not only was I a natural worrier, but I had spent a sheltered life in Minnesota and knew virtually nothing about Eastern big-city life.

I arrived at 11 P.M. and took a cab to the hotel, checking in at midnight. I was given a key and a room number. Since it was only an overnight trip, I had only a cosmetic case, garment bag, purse and briefcase. As I stepped into the elevator, a large man wedged in near me. I could feel him breathing down my neck and I was terrified. Certainly he was going to rape or rob me—or both.

When we reached my floor, I stepped off. He was right behind me so I screamed at the top of my lungs, "Get away from me!"

"I would, if you'd take the hanger of your garment bag out of my pocket," he said to the crowd that had gathered.

Mortified, I spent the next few minutes apologizing. But I learned a valuable lesson: Some fears are based on reality and some are based on our wild and out-of-control imaginations. If it's hard to tell which is which, err on the side of being embarrassed.

I can stand what I know.
It's what I don't know that frightens me.

—FRANCES NEWTON

GIRL TALK #26: Today I will evaluate and balance my life in a realistic way. My goal is to include everything I need to be guided on my own unique spiritual path.

The search for enlightenment can be overwhelming. Often I have exhausted myself seeking inner peace and serenity. The two most difficult emotions for me to control are patience and intensity, which are connected. The minute I get an idea I want to act on it. I become stressed and my world turns chaotic.

Balance is the answer.

In addition to meditation and regular exercise, I have learned these pearls of wisdom from spiritual teachers, mystics and sages I have encountered.

1. Make sure the physical needs of the body are met.
2. Use your innermost feelings to guide your decision.
3. Analyze your experiences based on feelings as well as facts.
4. Learn to accept and forgive others—as well as yourself.
5. Make room for spontaneity and humor in your life.
6. Follow your passion, whatever it is. We are most alive when filled with excitement and energy.
7. Let go of resentment; avoid conflict.
8. Connect with your Higher Power. Ask for guidance, wisdom and discernment to find balance and peace.

God respects me when I work, but
he loves me when I sing.

—Rabindranath Tagore

GIRL TALK #27: Today I will start a project that is often too easy to postpone.

One of my favorite hobbies is collecting recipes and planning special parties and get-togethers. I regularly buy magazines and clip articles, recipes, and decorating ideas. Until recently, I would throw all my clippings in a basket and in spite of good intensions, never get back to them. It was too overwhelming to be useful.

Then I had an idea. My favorite parties feature an Italian, French, Southwestern or Hawaiian theme and food. The occasions I like to celebrate are birthdays, anniversaries and congratulations. I now have a folder labeled for each of the above seven categories. I do not clip ideas that do not fit into one of my seven categories. This way I don't have things I don't want and my seven categories are always ready and sorted for my use. It works and is manageable.

The road to hell is paved with good intentions.

—OLD PROVERB

GIRL TALK #28: Today I will make sure I do not become a victim or a doormat. My choices are my own and I will make them on my behalf.

Having a doormat as a role model instills anger in the child. We grow up seeing our shining role model become dependent, depressed and used. We become disillusioned.

"I'll only count on myself," was a lesson I learned early in life. I could not trust my elders to be there for me. Consequently, throughout my adult life, I have had trouble trusting others, especially in relationships.

Sadly, a person in this position cannot voice her anger toward her fragile, pitiful family. So she bottles it up inside where it simmers and stews.

Others become the martyrs, controlling the family with depression. In finding a release for anger, it is easy to suffer an emotional breakdown or a serious physical illness. This increases the victim status and makes everyone feel guilty.

A person with a martyr family must not fall into the trap of becoming the savior. It simply cannot be done. Family members must save themselves by altering beliefs and behavior, and dealing with anger. Children can be victims, but adults VOLUNTEER to be victims. The best thing one can do for oneself is refuse to follow in historical footsteps. They can be deadly.

I cannot give you the formula for success, but
I can give you the formula for failure:
try to please everybody.

—HERBERT BAYARD SWOPE

GIRL TALK #29: Today I will remember some of the comfort items that made me feel safe and secure.

Grade school is the time we start branching out, leaving home for short stretches of time to connect with the larger world. Whenever I was asked to stay overnight at a girlfriend's home, I'd pack my bag and head over in high spirits.

We'd have dinner, play games and listen to the radio. I felt so grown up being away from home. Then we'd bathe, brush our teeth, crawl into bed and tell scary stories or giggle for hours. But when the time came to go to sleep, I wanted to go home. A quick call and my parents would soon be at the door to pick me up.

I'm grateful my folks always said, "We'll be right over," and my friend always said, "It's okay, see you tomorrow." The wisdom from both parties allowed me to mature at the rate I needed so I could eventually feel safe and secure away from home.

As children, it helps if we are able to anchor ourselves with bits of the familiar (security blankets, toys, special music or certain favorite pieces of clothing). Later, as we grow older, we find the anchor within ourselves. Yet I still have my security blanket—a white crocheted afghan that brings me comfort. When I'm having a bad day I simply wrap that old, familiar afghan around me, and suddenly everything seems okay again.

> *Everyone is a child of his past.*
> —EDNA G. ROSTOW

GIRL TALK #30: Today I will think about my pain and make a commitment to deal with it and not run from it. In doing so, I trust that I will heal.

Mary Jo and I were good friends. We were both therapists and our husbands were physicians. We had a lot in common and shared many good times. We all took up hiking in the beautiful hills of South Dakota, and we two women would often share our thoughts and feelings.

I had been away on a trip and returned exhausted. As I lay in bed catching up on my mail and the local news, I happened to glance at the obituaries. It seemed unreal to see Mary Jo's husband there, dead at the age of forty-two.

He had been playing basketball when down he went. His heart had simply stopped.

Over the next few weeks I saw Mary Jo a great deal. She faced her grief with courage, anger, sadness, fear and humor. Her feelings were totally unpredictable. Yet she never covered them up or pretended to be what she was not.

Within a year her emotions had leveled out and by the second anniversary of his death, Mary Jo was making a new life for herself.

Mary Jo taught me about pain. She dealt with it, felt it, faced it and lived with it. She inspired me to have the courage and strength to face loss when it happened to me.

> *You must do the thing you think*
> *you cannot do.*
>
> —ELEANOR ROOSEVELT

GIRL TALK #31: Today I will make a decision. If it's the right one, I'll celebrate. If it's the wrong one, I'll learn from my mistake.

I t's not uncommon to be immobilized with the fear of making a wrong decision. As a therapist, I'd tell my clients who were stuck to "do something, get off dead center."

Any decision, whether right or wrong, will get you unstuck. It will awaken your senses. If it is a good decision, you'll celebrate your good fortune. If not, you'll learn a lesson for next time. Above all, decisions and choices are opportunities for growth.

When I was thinking of semi-retirement, I was unsure of where I'd like to have a second home. So I kept working and signing contracts that obligated me to keep going. Of course, under it all was my fear of retirement, period!

At last I picked Florida. After three years I knew I had made a mistake. The lifestyle was not what I wanted. So I sold the property and moved to Nevada. That was the right choice.

The attitudes we develop and the decisions we make influence the outcome for better or worse. But there's nothing less productive than doing nothing at all.

Those who are mentally and emotionally
healthy are those who have learned when to say yes,
when to say no, and when to say whoopee!

—WILARD S. KRABILL

GIRL TALK #32: Today I will see if there is something I want to pursue. The choice of how I want to spend my time is completely up to me.

I never could understand why people liked the game of golf. It seems strange since I live on a golf course. Come rain or shine, wind or calm, hot or cold, the golfers are out there swinging away at those little white dimpled balls. On a lazy weekend morning, I'll take my coffee and the newspaper back to bed. From the window I can see that they've been on the course since dawn.

Once, out of sheer curiosity, I visited the pro shop. There, on display, were garments only a peacock would wear, in pink, lilac, baby blue, and plaids in garish shades of red, yellow and green. On a board outside the shop was a list of rankings and winners of recent tournaments.

It was a whole culture I knew nothing about. We recently had a celebrity golf tournament in our back yard and I admit I was there, right along with the rest, following the sport's latest sensation, Tiger Woods.

I may not have time in my life right now for golf as a full-time hobby. But I do have enough interest to take a few lessons. So if you're looking for me, try the first hole, where I'll be teeing off.

They believed they could, and they could . . .
I believe I can, too.

—ANONYMOUS

GIRL TALK #33: Today I will think about how to increase my passive income.

By the time I was thirty-three, I had completed college, given birth to three children, finished an internship at a social service agency and received my graduate degree. Then I was hired for a dream job that allowed me to learn while traveling around the country and to other lands. I was earning a respectable income and was quite content—until I had breakfast with one of the company's executives.

"Now that you are secure with your job, what are you doing for passive income?" he asked. When I didn't reply, he continued. "You've got to learn the difference between what you need and what you want."

Simply put, he meant that in order to enjoy life with the best financial advantage, I had to make money that could be used solely to EARN money. In other words, something other than my salary that could be invested.

The most amazing thing happened after that chat. I began brown-bagging lunch instead of eating out. I was less quick to make spontaneous purchases at the mall. The amounts were small at first but they helped me start working toward my goal of financial independence.

What corners can you cut so you can reward yourself with assets that will bring monetary security in the future?

Man does not simply exist, but always decides what his existence will be and what he will become in the next moment.

—VIKTOR FRANKL

GIRL TALK #34: Today I will pay attention to the important aspects of my life and do my best to achieve a balance.

Setting goals and steadily moving toward them ultimately accomplish more than do procrastinating and trying to cram. There was a time in my life that I can now call "management by crisis." Whatever or whoever demanded my attention had the most influence over what I did. My own goals and needs were ignored. I'd simply have to set them aside, then scramble at the last minute to get caught up. It often meant I went without sleep or cancelled events that were important to me.

I often thought of my uncle's farm. He had found a balance with his daily chores and his seasonal tasks. How could he not feed the cows while he planted the corn? He couldn't! He managed to do it all. And that is the lesson I had to learn.

Nature and life have a balance. It's our task to find this stability in our own lives.

To be really great in little things,
to be truly noble and heroic in the insipid details of
everyday life, is a virtue so rare as to be
worthy of canonization.

—Harriet Beecher Stowe

GIRL TALK #35: Today I will have faith that all is well and my life will become manageable again.

Some days are overwhelming. Even our usual methods of solace—like chocolate, wine, a movie, a hot bath or a delicious dinner—are not enough to soothe our frazzled spirit or calm our frayed nerves. The disappointment may be too great, the loss too large, the problems too many.

When life seems unmanageable, we need help—someone to throw us a life preserver.

When this happens to me, I find a quiet place and repeat this poem. It's saved me from many a terrible day.

> God created me to do him
> Some definite service
> He has committed some work to me
> Which he has not committed to another.
> I have my mission
> I am a link in a chain,
> A bond of connection between persons.
> He has not created me for naught
> I shall do good. I shall do his work
> I shall be an angel of peace
> A healer of truth in my own way.
> Therefore, I will trust him
> Whatever, wherever I am
> I can never be thrown away.
> If I am in sickness, my illness will serve
> If I am perplexed, my confusion may serve
> If I am in sorrow, my grief may serve
> God does nothing in vain
> He knows what he and I are about.
>
> —ANONYMOUS

Concern should drive us into action and not into depression.
—KAREN HORNEY

GIRL TALK #36: Today I will set up two private drawers. One will be at home for treats on days when I need to be treated. The other will be at work with treats for my coworkers.

Growing up at home I had my own private treasure drawer. It had tickets from favorite movies, photos, a package of sunflower seeds. Among my siblings, it was understood that nobody went into anyone else's private drawers.

Now that I'm grown, I still have my drawer at home, but I also have one at work. It is stocked with stamps, birthday cards, aspirin, Band-Aids, unopened packages of pantyhose, sample boxes of chocolate, a disposable camera (for those special occasions), and an assortment of inspirational things. Being able to fill an immediate need for others goes a long way toward creating an endless supply of goodwill. And the best part is, the drawer can easily be restocked with goodies.

I also keep a supply of angel pins in my purse for that special moment. Like the time I was in a restaurant where the short-order cook was clearly overwhelmed by rude and abusive customers. One man ran out of patience completely and hurled his food at her. She calmly cleaned up and continued serving up meals for the rest of us.

When the din quieted down, I went over to her and gave her a hug and an angel pin to remind her that she was appreciated. She later told me that the small gesture kept her from quitting a job she liked and could not afford to lose.

We must be true inside, true to ourselves, before we can know a truth that is outside us.

—THOMAS MERTON

GIRL TALK #37: Today I'll do something for fun. Then I'll promise to do that every day. My well-being depends on it.

A life without play is incomplete. And there are so many ways to play: the movies, theater, sports, cards, games, walking, swimming.

If you don't know how to play, watch children. They may climb the ladder and go down the slide dozens of times and get a thrill on each ride. They may stop and watch ants carry crumbs across a sidewalk, or throw a ball for hours on end.

Fly a kite, watch a ball game, walk on crunchy leaves or splash through a puddle barefoot. Build a snowman or an ice fort in winter. Play a musical instrument for fun or listen to music. Gaze at the stars on a summer night, make a wish, or just be.

Take an energizing walk to start the day or throw a potluck dinner for your friends. There's no preparation and everyone brings a dish to share. Eat, relax and unwind with your family, friends or neighbors.

Play is a quality that we all need in our daily lives. It may require some thought or planning—or it may be spontaneous and fancy-free. It's not expensive, risky or fattening. How do you beat that combination? So, enjoy.

> *Work is not always required—there is*
> *such a thing as sacred idleness, the cultivation*
> *of which is now fearfully neglected.*
>
> —George MacDonald

GIRL TALK #38: Today I will make it easier for myself and everyone around me to look for the humor in life and to enjoy a good laugh.

Every afternoon my father would lie on the sofa after lunch and take a nap before going back to work for the afternoon. While he was sleeping, I'd play beauty shop. I'd comb his curly black hair and put bobby pins in to create new hair styles. I loved the bonding time we had when he woke up.

Once, during the year my dad volunteered as a driver for the local fire department, I tried an experiment while he napped on the couch. I took out my little pink sponge curlers and rolled them in his thick hair. I thought it would be fun to see the look on his face when he saw them.

But suddenly the fire alarm sounded, and before I could say anything, he jumped up and dashed out the front door. He raced to his car and sped down Main Street to the firehouse.

There's no need to explain what happened. Use your imagination. Fortunately, he had a great sense of humor and was able to laugh right along with everyone else.

*A complete revaluation takes place
in your physical and mental being when
you've laughed and had some fun.*

—CATHERINE PONDER

GIRL TALK #39: Today I will meditate on the different ways I can link up with someone in my life that I love. Then I will put my spiritual energy into keeping that connection alive.

My grandson was living in Alaska—about 2,000 miles from the desert of Nevada, though it seemed more like 10,000. So whenever he came to visit, we had long talks and walks. We'd stay in touch by phone, and by the time he was five, we were great friends.

When my daughter became ill, I had to fly to the frozen North to see her. It was a depressing journey. The only solace was that I'd see my grandchildren. One afternoon I took them to the mall where a vendor had set up a table of bottles, sand, buttons, fringe and other decorations to make a sand man. We bought one, and worked mighty hard.

Parting was extraordinarily difficult. My daughter still was not feeling well. A family member had died while we were gone and we'd missed the funeral. The planes were grounded because of a snowstorm. It was dismal all around.

Then my little grandson came running toward me with a box. "Grandma, you and me both love the sand man," he said. "Take it home and he'll make you feel better." I did, and he did.

Now, whenever we meet, we share the sand man. Sometimes he has it, sometimes I do. It travels back and forth between snow and desert, connecting that special link of love between us.

If you would be loved, love and be lovable.
—BENJAMIN FRANKLIN

GIRL TALK #40: Today I will let go of resentment and trouble, which steal my inner peace, and let serenity come into my life.

As the end of each day comes, we should close our eyes and minds to the stress and turmoil. We must let our minds meander down a path of beauty and let our Higher Power give us the courage and strength to face a new day. When we do this, we can feel the tension and pressure draining away. Serenity falls over us and we feel a sense of inner peace.

Peace of mind is of utmost importance. But it's not something we can buy in a store. It isn't for sale. Serenity is something we earn when we reach a stage of life when we feel satisfied with the way things are going. When we have found the spiritual practices that bring meaning to our lives, there is no longer the need to add more turmoil and unrest to our cluttered existence. Instead, we let stressful situations, toxic environments or depressing people fall away from us. We replace them with healthy, peaceful choices.

The world is full of people looking for spectacular happiness while they snub contentment.

—DOUG LARSON

GIRL TALK #41: Today I will be grateful for a pet. If I don't have one, I'll explore the possibility of getting one.

A nimals are the most loyal friends we can have. They act as natural therapists, offering unconditional love. They can pick up on moods and know just what to do. They make us feel needed and important. It's not surprising that we relax, lower our voice, and become loving and caring as we talk to our pet.

Playing with, touching and interacting with a pet is beneficial to the body. It reduces blood pressure and lowers tension. It relieves stress. The constant and unpredictable antics of pets bring smiles and laughter—two other healing properties.

Companionship, security and joy are some of the benefits. In my practice, I had a young client, a very shy girl. Her parents divorced and she felt abandoned by her dad. For her thirteenth birthday her mom bought her a puppy. She named him Sunshine. Every time he learned something new, she felt a sense of accomplishment and pride.

As the months went by, the girl became less shy and more outgoing. The relationship with the pup allowed her to develop self-confidence. And by the time she graduated from high school, her days of loneliness and shyness were long past.

Her dog Sunshine had truly become the sunshine of her life. Through her pet she learned to love and be loved.

Animals are such agreeable friends; they ask no questions, they pass no criticisms.

—George Eliot

Body image and health are linked hand-in-hand. When I say body image, I mean how a woman relates to her own body and how she thinks others perceive it. Too often we see it only as short, fat, thin or misshapen. We center our feelings around a disability or scar. We obsess over diets, fitness and food to make our body fit an unreal ideal.

Quite a few women have a good sense of self when it comes to their bodies. They've learned to accept the way they look. But too many women have a very poor image of themselves. Their negative outlook comes not from their bodies, but because they see themselves inaccurately. The image is distorted to reflect a less-than-adequate figure.

Some women are estranged from their bodies altogether. When they become ill, they blame their bodies for letting them down. They don't know what pleases them sexually or that exercise will make them feel better. So they look to others for feedback—a risky proposition at best. We live in a society that flaunts the thin, waif-like bodies of models like Kate Moss. We worship the bodies of Cindy Crawford or Elle MacPherson. And men fantasize about shapely, curvy Marilyn Monroes or Sophia Lorens.

So it's easy to see that if a woman doesn't have confidence that comes from accepting her own body, she could make herself miserable and crazy.

And women do.

At any given time there are tens of millions of women on some kind of diet. They shell out hundreds of millions of dollars to diet centers and special low-fat frozen foods guaranteed to melt the pounds away. You cannot walk into a bookstore without being swamped by low-fat cookbooks.

Poor body image, therefore, leads to poor health. It is most obvious with college-age girls. On campuses across the country, eating disorders like anorexia and bulimia are so prevalent that many schools have set up free counseling to stop this death-inducing behavior.

When a woman does not love her body, it becomes less important for her to take care of it. She'll avoid mammograms, exercise, annual PAP exams and dental appointments. It's a negative cycle that needs to be broken. We must learn to accept ourselves, fat, skinny, short or tall. We are what we are, and we are all beautiful.

A miracle has happened! The light of understanding has shone upon my little pupil's mind, and behold, all things are changed!

—ANNE SULLIVAN

GIRL TALK # 43: Today I'll think about how hard it is to stay true to oneself when life makes so many demands on me.

We celebrate Abraham Lincoln's birthday each year (these days he shares Presidents' Day with George Washington) without giving a thought to his loyal wife, Mary Todd Lincoln.

She was the daughter of Kentucky pioneers. She lost her mother when she was only seven. When her father remarried, she described her life as "desolate." Mary was diminutive, only five-foot-two, with clear blue eyes and long lashes. She was quite the opposite of the tall, gangly, shy Abe, whom she described as a "poor nobody." Although opposites, the attraction was mutual.

Their first years together were difficult. She bore sons and worked—a chore to which she was unaccustomed. But she had high social ambitions and she triumphed when she was installed in the White House in 1860 as first lady. Misery soon followed. Her spending habits were criticized; she was accused of unpatriotic extravagance. Then, when her son tragically died, she was accused of shirking her social duties. During the Civil War she was scorned by Southerners as a traitor to the land of her birth.

Yet Abe stood by her. "My wife is as handsome as when I fell in love with her, and what's more, I have never fallen out," he said.

Mary was shattered by his sudden death and never recovered. For seventeen years afterward she traveled with her son, Tad, searching to heal herself. When Tad died, she lived her remaining years with her sister, slipping into a world of delusion and paranoia—a misunderstood and tragic figure in the end.

She died in the same house from which she had walked as a bride, forty years before.

Although she survived great losses, and life did not take the path she planned, Mary Todd Lincoln never gave up hope. For me, she is a true hero and an inspiration.

Expecting life to treat you well because you
are a good person is like expecting an angry bull
not to charge because you are a vegetarian.

—SHARI R. BARR

GIRL TALK #44: Today I will examine the relationships in my life and make sure I'm giving people the freedom they need to find their own way. Whenever I need to, I will let go.

Some years ago I saw a banner that read, "Sometimes the pain of hanging on is greater than the pain of letting go." Whenever we hang onto another person—or a part of life—we impede the natural flow. It's natural to want to hold on to what we value and find precious. But life's true reward is going with the ebb and flow.

Too often we hold on to fear, thus missing the good times. Or we embrace the good times and do everything possible to avoid the bad times. In doing so, we hold back life's forward motion.

Letting go of the need to be right is another major hurdle. It's only when we give up the struggle to win every argument that we truly win.

We must learn to admit when we are wrong or when we've made a mistake and let go of the fear that others will reject us.

Feeling responsible for the well-being of children, siblings, mates and friends is another area where we must loosen our grip and let go. We want to spare them pain, so we hang on. But nobody learns from somebody else's mistakes. We must all make our own, and learn through the process.

In the end, we must let our faith guide us. We must trust that the same God who cares for us also cares for them.

I think I must let go. Must fear not, must be quiet so
that my children can hear the sound of creation
and dance the dance that is in them.

—Russell Hoban

GIRL TALK #45: Today I'll remember that loving myself is the cake, loving others is the frosting.

Valentine's Day is one of my favorite holidays. After all, it's a celebration of love. The best part of this day is that it doesn't have to focus on a husband or a lover. Everyone can be included.

Decorating adds to the joy with red hearts, fresh flowers, red candles and a box of chocolates. If you have little ones in your life—even if they're not living with you—get a box of kiddie valentines and send them to loved ones far away.

Even more important, Valentine's Day is a day to love and appreciate YOU. I like to give myself a pat on the back and say, "Job well done, Sharon." Every woman should do that. After all, each and every one of us does far more than expected, with household chores, work, children, spouses and responsibilities outside the home. So feed your soul on this day. Love yourself, and everything else in your life will fall into place.

If you're a party gal, how about giving a Valentine party? Have a few friends bring potluck dinner dishes and decorate the house with homemade valentines. Make a special dessert and add a few bottles of blush wine to the festivities. For singles, it's a great way to celebrate the day instead of sitting home and wishing "if only . . ."

Be happy and love yourself. If you do, others will, too.

People need joy as much as clothing.
Some of them need it far more.

—MARGARET COLLIER GRAHAM

GIRL TALK #46: Today I will strengthen my assets by believing in myself and limiting my use of credit.

When I became a divorced woman with three young children, one of my tasks was to obtain a credit card in my own name. In the 1970s, banks did not easily approve applications for single female parents. Four companies turned me down, which amazed me since my former husband had no problem obtaining one. To make matters worse, my salary was higher than his!

I was outraged at this unfair practice, and it was of utmost importance to me to receive equal treatment. So I hired an attorney.

It didn't take long for him to arrange a credit card for me with a $1,000 limit. By paying off the bill each month in a timely manner, that limit was quickly raised to $10,000. Now I enjoy unlimited spending. But I still pay off my bills in thirty days. If I can't afford it, I don't buy it.

The value of credit cards cannot be denied. However, just as important is learning how to use—not abuse—them.

I think self-awareness is probably the
most important thing toward being a champion.
—BILLIE JEAN KING

GIRL TALK #47: Today I will meditate on the soul connection. If there's a soul mate in my life, I'll be thankful. If not, I'll try to understand why.

A soul mate is someone to whom you feel profoundly connected. Although we've all had relationships, and some were quite deep, a soul mate stands out as someone special. There is probably nothing as precious.

To share your soul with another person takes courage and demands vulnerability. Yet, to have another person know you completely—assets and liabilities alike—and still love and respect you deeply, is the greatest gift.

With a soul mate there is no fear of rejection or ridicule. Feelings of safety, trust and loyalty pervade the relationship. In fact, soul mates do not have to be physically together to know the other's presence is nearby.

It matters not if the external habits and traits match. They might hold different political views or have dissimilar tastes in music, food or hobbies. But in matters of the heart and soul they are fused.

Unfortunately, there's no formula or recipe for creating a soul mate. It's something that happens spontaneously when two people meet and connect on important levels.

Some people believe there is only one soul mate for each of us during our lifetime; others say you can have more than one.

I say if you've had one, you're a lucky lady.

> *Love does not consist of gazing at each other but*
> *in looking together in the same direction.*
> —ANTOINE DE SAINT-EXUPÉRY

GIRL TALK #48: Today I'll remember that we underestimate the influence we have over other people and make sure I keep other people's best interests at heart.

I was in Hawaii conducting a workshop, and was staying at a beautiful high-rise hotel. It had an outside glass elevator that was quite spectacular.

One evening I overheard a couple arguing about it. The woman was afraid to get in and the man was angry at her. As he publicly berated her, she became more embarrassed. I sympathized but was unsure whether or not to interfere in their private altercation.

Finally I walked over to them, introduced myself and said that as a professional hypnotist, I thought I could be of some service. Truthfully, I know nothing about hypnotizing a subject, but they both seemed eager for my assistance.

I took the woman outside, held her hands and looked deep into her eyes. "You'll be safe, you'll enjoy the ride," I said over and over. "Now close your eyes and feel my message."

She followed my instructions and said she was ready to try. Before I could turn around, she had returned to her husband, stepped into the elevator and been whisked away.

The following morning at breakfast, the couple came over to my table and thanked me. I smiled to myself. The power of suggestion is remarkable.

What I said never changed anybody,
what they understood did.

—Paul P.

GIRL TALK #49: Today I'll think about what it takes to hold a family together. I will recognize that from time to time, connecting with family teaches us more about ourselves.

Nestled in the Black Hills in Custer, South Dakota, is a tourist town with a great deal of history. On the edge of town is the Mountain Music Show, headed by Pee Wee Dennis, who looks like a mountain hillbilly with his tall, pointed black hat, polka dot tie and overalls.

When the music starts, you quickly notice the blend of young and old performers. The mountain music fills the room, as musicians perform on guitars, banjos, fiddles, drums and horns with equal dexterity. An amazed audience finds out at the end of the show that the guitarist is a lumberjack, the drummer is a schoolteacher and Pee Wee is an accountant. I later found out that whole families participate—sons, daughters, mothers and fathers—pooling their talents for an extraordinary evening of fun.

If you're ever in the area, treat yourself to a different kind of entertainment. It's family fun that's sure to touch your soul!

If only we'd stop trying to be happy,
we could have a pretty good time.

—EDITH WHARTON

GIRL TALK #50: Today I'll think about myself as a child. Perhaps I'll find a photo and keep it where I can remember to love myself. It's never too late to have a happy childhood.

In going through my photo album, I came across pictures of a little girl with brown, baggy stockings and a pony tail. She looked very much like my granddaughter. Actually, the picture was of me. But I couldn't remember my life at the tender age of three, so I asked my aunt what was going on in my parents' lives at the time.

I learned that my father was drinking quite a bit. However, my aunt assured me that he adored me. Money was tight and he worked long, hard hours to support his growing family. My mother, who was not yet twenty, was the primary caretaker for her grandmother. Times were hard as she divided her energy between her husband, her child, her mother and her grandmother.

Looking more carefully at the picture, I saw innocence, trust and also fear—fear that has been a handicap throughout my life. I felt love and compassion for this sad little girl and I was sorry there wasn't more security in her life to make her carefree.

Today that photo sits in a frame on my dresser. Whenever I glance at it, I feel a special tugging at my heart. I am determined to give her the security she needed when she was three. Now I can see to it that she feels safe and cared for.

> *Children require guidance and sympathy*
> *far more than instruction.*

—ANNE SULLIVAN

GIRL TALK #51: Today I'll look at the stress in my life and figure out ways to reduce it.

In this crazy, stress-filled world we all live in, it's too easy to be overwhelmed by the anxieties and worries that build up. Since medical experts say it can make us physically ill, it's up to each of us to try to reduce the chaos in our lives.

- Exercise. Start now, even if you just walk around the block after dinner or in the morning. Stick with it and add to that basic regimen, making it a part of your daily routine.
- Share. Nothing beats "getting it off your chest." Bottled up emotions turn to depression and eating disorders. So talk to a friend, relative or even a stranger. Unload those bad vibes.
- Set priorities. To avoid utter confusion, decide what needs to be done first, second and third. If some things have to go, let them go. Nobody says you have to do it ALL.
- Create a support system. Networking with your peers can help relieve the pressure at work. It's a give-and-take that works both ways.
- Let go of control. Nobody can be in charge every minute of the day. Delegate responsibility to others. It makes them feel part of the team and relieves you of the burden.
- Be flexible. You can change your mind any time you want, even at the last moment. Don't feel obligated to do what you absolutely don't want to do.

Have the courage to act instead of react.

—DARLENE LARSON JENKS

GIRL TALK #52: Today I will plan some ways to share with the people in my life who could use a little boost.

Palanca (pronounced pa-LON-ka) is not a rice or pasta dish. It's a wonderful Spanish word that means "tangible spiritual energy."

Years ago I was part of a network of people who regularly met to help themselves and others define what our spirituality meant. We explored ways of incorporating our beliefs and actions into our daily lives. We did this on periodic, four-day retreats that were designed to help us probe into our commitments and beliefs.

Palanca was the support given to us by family and friends during this special time, through letters, books, tapes, articles or photographs. It's not hard to imagine the love we felt when the mailman would arrive with his goodies. Palanca was food for the soul.

But palanca is important all the time, not only during retreats. There isn't a day that goes by that someone I know couldn't use a little palanca. So I keep a full supply of cards and uplifting articles to stay connected with my friends and colleagues. It's the gift of spiritual energy that keeps on giving.

Love is when each person is more concerned for the other than for one's self.

—DAVID FROST

GIRL TALK #53: Today I will commit to setting aside time every day to evaluate the demands on me. I will see what changes can be made to help me focus my time.

For many people, interruptions and demands are the number one problem. George Washington, the first president of the United States, was no exception. As a military officer during the war for independence, and as a husband and provider, he had tremendous pressure. Yet he managed. How? By setting priorities.

Urgent demands must be met immediately. But constant interruptions also take their toll in terms of depleting our energy. By using a voice mail service or answering machine, we can eliminate the phone as a distraction. Posting a *Do Not Disturb* sign on an office door will help cut down unnecessary visits. Keep a note pad nearby at all times to jot down important ideas without losing a train of thought.

Above all, FOCUS. Do one thing at a time. Do it well and finish it. Washington's war was over before he became president. Take life in order; don't make a jumble of it or nothing is accomplished, and you'll feel scattered and unfulfilled.

Save the best of yourself for the most important and urgent tasks. Let everything else sort itself into priorities so you can manage your time without becoming a ball of stress.

It works for me. It can work for you, too.

It's always something.

—GILDA RADNER

GIRL TALK #54: Today I will internalize the fact that I know how to generate income. I have done it before and can do it again.

W
omen often overlook the importance of being able to earn a living. Too often we rely on our partners to generate the money that keeps the household going. Are you one of these women? Even if you're not, sit down and estimate how much money you've earned in your lifetime. Start adding up those baby-sitting jobs, paper delivery routes and other odd jobs over the years. Look at old tax returns. You may be disappointed to see how little has been saved or how little you have to show for it.

You can get exact figures from the Social Security office. They will send you a print-out showing how much you've paid into the system and how much you can expect to receive upon retirement.

But more important than the facts and figures is the knowledge that you have the ability to earn money. We all do, although most people—women especially—underestimate the amount that they have earned, or will earn. They use lack of education or lack of experience as a crutch for "I can't" or "I'm not worth it."

So quit fretting. If you've got someone to support you, go back to school full-time right now and further your education. If you don't, do it a little bit at a time. Learn a skill or a trade; become proficient in something—anything. You never know what life will bring. So be prepared.

I came, I saw, I conquered.

—JULIUS CAESAR

GIRL TALK #55: Today I'll think back on how I learned about sex and say thanks to anyone who helped me discover what the mystery was all about.

My family didn't talk about sex. The little I did learn about it came from my girlfriends. When I asked my mom where babies came from, she showed me a book that she kept hidden in a drawer.

One night when I was in seventh grade, I went to a slumber party. Joyce started telling us about her older sister, and what she did with her boyfriend. Our ears perked up as we listened to her shocking and exciting stories. Needless to say, we all learned far more from Joyce than from our parents.

At one of the parties, Joyce invited us to sleep over at her house. "You can look through the keyhole when my parents go to bed," she offered. "I've done it. You can really learn a lot."

Although we were flabbergasted at her offer, we said yes.

On the appointed night, we waited impatiently for the moment of enlightenment. After her folks had retired, one by one we each took a turn at the keyhole, then reported to the others what we had seen. By the end of the night we had a pretty good idea of what sex was all about!

Spying on your friend's parents may not be the ideal way of learning. However, we did learn that sex between two people who love each other can be a beautiful thing. So Joyce, wherever you are, thanks. And to her parents, although they still don't know what a service they provided, a double thanks.

It's the good girls who keep the diaries,
the bad girls never have the time.

—Tallulah Bankhead

GIRL TALK #56: Today I'll think about the lessons I've learned from hard times. And also the choices I've made when faced with adversity.

I grew up in a family with a long history of drinking. It was seen as a problem, a weakness of will, instead of a disease.

Both grandfathers were alcoholics. Both grandmothers took care of the home and children, and on occasion held jobs. By the time my parents married, the die was cast and they easily joined in the tradition of booze and pills.

As an adult there were two questions that nagged at me:

1. What made someone dependent on alcohol or pills?
2. What was the effect on the rest of the family?

The answers to both queries came during my schooling and during my training as a therapist. Personally as well as professionally, I learned how to deal with dysfunctional families and how not to pass on those traits to the next generation.

In my case, addiction turned out to be the catalyst for learning and a way of stopping a destructive family tradition. I only wish there was a way in which new and different choices could set free everyone caught in the terrible cycle of addiction.

> **Growth is the only evidence of life.**
>
> —CARDINAL NEWMAN

GIRL TALK #57: Today I'll give myself permission to have a ten-minute daydream.

"Stop daydreaming and get busy!"

How many times have we heard that refrain? But daydreaming is a good thing; it's a way of letting creativity play in your head. Just before falling asleep at night is when our most imaginative ideas happen.

In fact, whenever I have a nagging problem, I focus on it just before bedtime. Usually I'll wake up the next morning with the answer.

If you can find a few minutes in your busy day to indulge in daydreaming, you will be rewarded with ideas and clarity. But first, get rid of that old notion that it's a waste of time. Nothing could be further from the truth. It's our mind's play time and it's as important as eating and breathing.

Even the dictionary describes it as "a reverie filled with pleasing, often illusory, visions or anticipations."

So give yourself a treat. At work or at home, just close your eyes and catnap into a refreshing pause. Enjoy your special time to daydream.

A man who wants to lead the orchestra
must turn his back on the crowd.

—James Crook

GIRL TALK #58: Today I will look at my life and see if I'm running away from anything. If so, I'll address that issue right now.

As a youngster, my home was filled with stress. I was too young to know what the dynamics were, but I was filled with fear. When this feeling was too powerful, I'd run away.

We lived in a small town and nearby was a ditch with concrete culverts under the road. I'd hide in the deep grass until darkness came. Then I'd slip into the culverts and stay until somebody found me. From my hiding place I could see neighbors and police searching for me.

Sometimes, just to be different, I'd go to the cemetery and hide behind the headstones. Other times, I'd convince some of the train engineers that I needed to visit my grandmother, who owned a restaurant that served the Great Northern Railway. I'd crawl up in the engine and travel in the locomotive—always to be caught. I did this kind of running away from the ages of five to eight.

Later in my life, my career included a great deal of travel. As a therapist, I came to realize that my way of coping with stress was to either stay busy with projects or go on the road.

Today I choose to stay put. I've learned to face the problems in my life head-on, instead of running. Whatever I was running from has been found. Now I don't want to leave.

When all is said and done, willingness is everything.

—FRANK D.

GIRL TALK #59: Today I'll think about having some people over for dinner. Whether formal or informal, the most important thing is that we are all together.

When I was a young bride, having company for dinner meant cleaning the entire house, looking for outstanding recipes, and a week of stress and anticipation. Over the years, I've learned to take it all in stride.

Sometimes I sit down with my recipe books and plan a special meal, complete with candles, flowers and the best china. Or it might be a last-minute, throw-together meal served in the kitchen with paper napkins. Sometimes I like to fuss, at other times I simply want company. Both are great ways of getting together with the people I most care about.

Sharing a meal, a drink and good conversation is a terrific way of strengthening bonds and relaxing. If you tend to fuss, break the habit by using paper plates and disposable utensils so there's no cleanup. Enjoy the sharing and don't think of the preparation and planning as a chore. For most of us, it's the getting together that counts. The food is secondary.

So plan a get-together as soon as possible. Kick off your shoes and let your hair down. Unwind with company. Don't waste any opportunities to enjoy each other.

We can do no great things—
only small things with great love.

—KATHERINE MANSFIELD

GIRL TALK #60: Today I will feel worthy of all the good things in my life.

In my office I kept a bowl of graham cracker crumbs. Why? To remind my clients that it's too easy to settle for the crumbs when we deserve the whole cookie!

Most of us have more ability, creativity, energy and desire than we use. So why don't we make use of our talents?

The answer is self-denial. It's a negative and limiting behavior that makes us settle for less than the whole. Thinking poor is a useless exercise that gets us nowhere. Thinking prosperously will move us toward the idea that wealth is within our grasp—if only we put forth the effort.

It's important to dream your dream; to visualize it and take the necessary action to make it come true. It may require an attitude adjustment, but it's worth the struggle. Self-acceptance, self-confidence and a loving, caring sense of self are all connected.

How do you feel about deserving prosperity?

Can you articulate your dreams?

Are you directing your behavior toward getting what you want and what you deserve?

> *Within our dreams and aspirations*
> *we find our opportunities.*
>
> —SUE ATCHLEY EBLAUGH

GIRL TALK #61: Today I will think about my values and commit myself to making choices that fit MY value system, instead of just going along with the crowd.

During the late 1960s, the Esalen training center was the "in" place for budding and established therapists to share ideas and make connections. So this young Midwesterner took off for sunny California to see for myself.

I held my own in the professional workshops, but when it came to socializing, I was out of my league. Quite a few people were indulging in smoking pot (which I didn't) and hanging out in the hot tub (which I thought would be fun—until I learned they were nude).

The tub area was enchanting and mystical. The baths were three-sided, surrounded by candles. Along the open side, white leather massage tables were set up. I put on my black bathing suit and went to join the others.

I stood there feeling conspicuous and completely overdressed. The next night I figured that going naked would be a growing experience. I wrapped a blanket around me and when I got there, I hung up the blanket, stepped in the tub, and that was the last thing I remembered until I awoke on a massage table.

Apparently the hot water, coupled with stress and fear, caused me to faint. Ironically, while trying not to attract attention, I made quite a spectacle of myself. But I learned a valuable lesson.

As the week passed, I tried the hot tub many times, sometimes naked, sometimes in my bathing suit. I did whatever I felt comfortable doing. It was a learning experience about choice.

You have got to know what it is you want,
or someone is going to sell you a bill of goods somewhere
along the line that can do irreparable damage
to your self-esteem, your sense of worth, and your
stewardship of the talents God gave you.

—RICHARD NELSON BOLLES

GIRL TALK #62: Today I will think of times I've had the opportunity to share. There is no audience too small or subject too unimportant to ignore the possibility of influencing others.

I had returned from a road trip late at night, exhausted and in need of sleep. But the next morning the phone rang at six o'clock and whoever was on the other end would not give up. When I begrudgingly picked it up, I was told that the producer of the Oprah Winfrey show was on the line.

"We want you to come to Chicago and appear on her show," said the producer.

At the time I didn't know who Oprah was (she was just getting started with her own show).

"She's interested in having a show on children of alcoholic parents and she would like you as a guest on her show," the producer explained. That did it. I was hooked.

Not only did I appear on the show, I was asked back a second time. For my return engagement I brought a family who had recovered from the devastating effects of alcoholism.

Oprah has used her widely-watched show to highlight many of today's problems. She is a remarkable role model for whites, blacks, men, women and children. From Oprah I learned that if you have the opportunity to educate others, you have an obligation to do so.

To affect the quality of the day,
that is the highest of arts.

—HENRY DAVID THOREAU

GIRL TALK #63: Today I will respect my imagination, giving myself time to explore my hopes and dreams.

My grandchildren have trunks of play clothes so they can pretend to be firemen, teachers, pilots and scary monsters. They have blocks and toy logs and a myriad of things to stimulate their imaginations.

As a writer, I also try to keep my imagination well oiled. Inventiveness is stimulated by doing things in a different way. When I have a party, I give it a theme and decorate my home to match the occasion. When I work in the garden, I'll buy a cactus instead of flowers.

It may be that our Higher Power speaks to us through our imagination. I do know that our creativity helps us find the special gifts we have to offer the world. And as we develop those gifts, we become prepared for whatever path our Higher Power intends for us to take. Picturing our goals will help us take steps in the right direction. And envisioning ourselves courageous and strong will allow us to get there.

Make time to sit quietly, taking slow, deep breaths. Watch the images that form in your mind. There you will find the clues to help you discover the dreams and hopes of YOUR life. Then all you have to do is follow the Yellow Brick Road to get wherever it is you want to go.

> *Imagination has always*
> *had power of resurrection that no*
> *science can match.*

—INGRID BENJIS

GIRL TALK #64: Today I will tell myself there are no learning limitations. I will commit to starting a new project that will fulfill my need to learn and grow.

Growing up in a town of 600 meant that the variety of classes offered at the high school was quite limited. Since learning was important, I took every opportunity to study whatever was available, including typing and speech. It turned out to be a great decision, since I've become a writer and public speaker!

To this day, whenever I have an opportunity to learn something new, I'll give it a try. Since those early days, I've become proficient as an author and a cook. I can dance, plant an attractive garden and speak before a large audience. I have helped set up three companies and a non-profit philanthropic foundation, where I have been able to teach and train others.

When choosing to learn, there are no limits to the way we can improve our lives and the lives of those we touch.

Our greatest happiness does not depend
on the condition of life in which chance has placed us,
but is always the result of a good conscience,
good health, occupation and freedom
in all just pursuits.

—THOMAS JEFFERSON

GIRL TALK #65: Today I will think of the close calls in my life and the divine protection that pulled me through unharmed, and perhaps a bit wiser.

The only thing that could have brought me to Juneau, Alaska, was the birth of my granddaughter. And so I went.

It's an interesting place to visit, especially in winter, when there are only six hours of daylight and it snows, snows, snows. From the window at the bed-and-breakfast where I stayed, I gazed at majestic mountains, feeling isolated. Television coverage was limited and newspapers carried no world news, only local. Visitors were virtually cut off from society.

On the day of my departure there was an ice storm. Although I made it to the airport okay, I was sure the plane would be delayed. After deicing the wings twice, the pilot announced, "Buckle up tightly. You're going to experience a takeoff like never before."

Terrorized as the plane took off into a blinding snow, we banked and rose higher. I knew we were heading right into the mountains; I prayed we'd miss them. Later I learned that the airport at Juneau is the most dangerous place for takeoffs in the world. Sometimes ignorance is bliss.

And, by the way, my daughter was fine and my granddaughter was a delicious bundle of joy. Now I know that divine providence is truly with us at all times.

> *The beauty of the world, which is so soon*
> *to perish, has two edges: one of laughter, one of*
> *anguish, cutting the heart asunder.*
>
> —Virginia Woolf

GIRL TALK #66: Today I will reflect on my high school years and try to remember what I felt like at that time.

High school was a major life shift. At that time we wanted to be treated like adults, we wanted to rupture the parent/child bond to allow us some freedom. Yet the adolescent transition was filled with conflict; at least it was for me. Although I wanted my folks to leave me alone and trust me, I was relieved when my mother would come fetch me when I broke curfew. While I pushed against the limits she set, I was grateful they were there.

Those years were filled with idealism. Perhaps we teens became carried away at times and unrealistic at others, but the intention was to make the world a better place. The greatest change came from those who respected the past but who had a vision of the future and the courage to change the present. Finding that delicate balance was what high school was all about.

Most people remember those years with clarity, since they formed the basis for our adult lives. We developed values and those values helped us find our direction. We learned about the strength of commitment and the bonds of enduring friendships. Lucky was the adolescent who found the strength and ability to cope and forge ahead during those turbulent times.

Never show a child what cannot be seen.
While you are thinking about what will be useful
when older, talk of what can be used now.

—JEAN JACQUES ROUSSEAU

GIRL TALK #67: Today I'll think about my own death. Even though I don't like the thought of leaving this world, I want to think about how I'll be remembered.

I find cemeteries to be sacred places. There is something spiritual about connecting with the past. It makes the present more precious and it reminds me that the future is precarious, at best.

In a cemetery in New Orleans, I learned that the white masters were buried in front of the black slaves. In Hawaii, I saw a young man's grave marked with half-full beer bottles to remind visitors not to drink and drive. And I saw a young bride's veil hung in a Plexiglas container near her marker, a testament to her short time as a married woman. Perhaps the most touching was the grave of an infant with the baby bottle and pacifier cemented into the headstone.

I find that the presence of those buried in these cemeteries seems to be nearby. And as I browse through the headstones reading inscriptions, I realize how important it is to make the passage of one's life known to others. Markers like these become a shrine where others can come and meditate on the wonders of life and death. Or in my case, when I visit my parents' graves, to feel close to them once again.

We are apt to call barbarous whatever departs
widely from our taste and apprehension.
But soon find the epithet of reproach retorted on us.

—DAVID HUME

GIRL TALK #68: Today I will explore a new way to challenge myself and take the steps to add this new behavior to my life.

To best use our mind-body healing abilities, go outside your daily habits and create new ways of tapping into your strength and potential. These are a few of the ways I have found to increase my capacity for growth:

1. Become a family historian. Collect stories, photographs and mementos. Learn about your roots and pass that information down to your children and grandchildren.
2. Take up an instrument. It's never too late to learn to play music. Do it for fun, not for a new career.
3. Make tapes. Record your favorite music on a tape, then pop it in your Walkman and go out for a long stroll. If you put on fast music, your pace will automatically pick up and you'll burn calories without even feeling it.
4. Take a class. Most high schools and colleges offer adult education studies—from past-life regression to financial planning. The range is wide and varied. Try tap dancing, like I did, or a computer workshop so you can cyber-chat with your grandkids.

There's nothing as exciting as a new challenge. It will promote confidence, dispel boredom and even boost your immune system. Why wait? Don't be a slacker, get with the program! Start today.

If only I may grow firmer, simpler, quieter, warmer.
—DAG HAMMARSKJÖLD

GIRL TALK #69: If my grandmother were alive today, I would call her or write a letter. As a grandmother myself, I will meditate on the ways I can offer my grandchildren security and love.

As a young girl I adored my maternal grandma, and she adored me. She was my supporter who always had an extra hug, an extra quarter and an extra doughnut. She taught me what unconditional love is all about. Even today, if I close my eyes I can smell her perfume, feel her warmth, hear her laugh.

Now that I have grandkids of my own, I can relate to how she related to me. I love them the way she loved me—unconditionally and with no limits. I can spoil them as much as I want and give them all the hugs, toys and cotton candy I choose.

Grandparents can offer their child's offspring social security—a financial and emotional cushion to protect them from the harsh bumps encountered on the road of life. They can provide a safe haven when times at home are too stressful. Being consistent is the key to offering stability for grandchildren. They know where they can turn in times of turmoil and trouble—a place where they are loved and appreciated just for themselves, with no demands.

> *Nothing is so strong as gentleness, and*
> *nothing is so gentle as real strength.*
>
> —RALPH W. SOCKMAN

GIRL TALK #70: Today I'll think about having fun. I'll add one new activity to my growing list.

It may seem strange, but many of us need permission to have fun. This is especially true for people who were raised in a serious home atmosphere, where money was short, parents were neglectful or abusive, and where depression ruled and laughter was not shared.

How does one learn to be carefree and spontaneous in a home like that?

It's difficult to let the little child in you come out and play. So I hereby give you permission to have a good time!

The first step is to allow yourself some physical and mental time off. Then you'll need fun activities to stimulate and invigorate. You may start passively by visiting parks, museums, movies or the theater. Graduate to dancing, painting or playing a sport. Read, make model airplanes or visit a craft supply store and stock up.

Fun is an attitude as much as a behavior. It's a way of looking at life with zest, enthusiasm and a sense of humor. It's energizing and provides an escape from the seriousness that surrounds us. Fun makes reality more tolerable and builds positive memories to bond us to those with whom we share our fun times.

> *I, God, am your playmate!*
> *I will lead the child in you in wonderful*
> *ways for I have chosen you.*
> —MECHTILD OF MAGDEBURG

GIRL TALK #71: Today I'll think of the miracle of birth. I'll remember my mother with love and gratitude for giving me life.

I had just returned to South Dakota bone-tired but overjoyed. My daughter Deb in Minnesota had given birth a few days before to my first grandchild, and I could still hear that first tentative cry. Tears filled my eyes as I walked through the airport.

My husband met me, gave me a big welcoming hug, then said, "Sandra's in labor, she's waiting for you!"

How was it possible that two sisters could give birth within such a short time span? But it was happening. So I turned around, booked a flight back to Minnesota and arrived in her hospital room as she was fighting her way through a monumental contraction.

"You'll be just fine," I said, taking her hands in mine. Naturally, she wasn't buying such platitudes. So I went to work; I knew the drill. Ice chips to suck on, cold compresses for her head, soft encouraging words. From having three children of my own, I knew a comforting presence in the room was essential.

I was lucky to be able to watch the whole birthing process as my first granddaughter was born. It is one of God's most awesome gifts, and being blessed with two grandchildren in one week was simply joyous, miraculous and marvelous.

> *A baby is God's opinion that the*
> *world should go on.*
>
> —CARL SANDBURG

GIRL TALK #72: Today I'll meditate on whether I can change my attitude.

When I was a teenager my social life was severely hampered by my kid sister, for whom I often had to babysit. It was humiliating to tell my dates that I was bringing my seven-year-old sibling along. Some canceled, others said, "Bring her." But I knew they weren't thrilled at the prospect.

Then I met Gary, one of the high school softball players. To my amazement, he was excited when I said I had to bring my sister on our third date, a game in which he was playing.

"Why don't we dress her as the school mascot?" he suggested. Incredibly, she agreed. So we dolled her up as a teddy bear and the team dubbed her their good-luck charm. We both felt special and wanted.

From Gary I learned how to turn a problem into something that can be solved in a positive way. That lesson has stuck with me. Often circumstances arise that I wish I could change. And now I know that a simple attitude alteration has the power to turn a predicament around full circle into something delightful.

Every outlook, desirable or undesirable,
remains possible for anyone, no matter
what his present outlook is.
—Dr. George Weinberg

GIRL TALK #73: Today I will give up the myths about money and define my own personal beliefs.

To feel guilty about spending money on yourself reflects a lack of self-esteem. The message you send to your brain is that you aren't worth it. While it's not a good idea to blow your budget to prove you are, spending money on yourself is an affirming act of self-love.

There are many myths about money. Some consider it security, so they hoard it, spending it only on essentials. For these people, financial security means emotional security.

Others see money as power. Giving or withholding puts them in control; they can make you dance for a dime.

If you have stumbling blocks about spending money on yourself, ask why. Was it frowned upon in your house when you were growing up? Was money scarce or hoarded for a rainy day? Do you feel you are worth it?

Today's a good day to start exploring your feelings and attitudes about money. See how spending it affects your mood, whether you use it as a crutch to feel better, to reward yourself or give yourself a pat on the back. Or do you deny your needs and tell yourself you're not worthy?

Think about it. There's more on money yet to come.

If I am not for myself, who will be?

—THE TALMUD

GIRL TALK #74: Today I will look at my clutter and decide what I want to keep and what I can get rid of.

Most people have at least a hobby or two. This, naturally, involves a certain amount of clutter, with supplies and ongoing projects. For me it's scrapbooks. To date I have amassed at least thirty of them. Inside are photographs going back seven generations. Some of my favorite pictures grace the walls of my home. Part of my nesting is to be surrounded by the faces I love and who love me. A sign near my work area declares, "This is not clutter, it's my hobby!"

While most men can squirrel their hobbies in a garage, women tend to keep their clutter in full view. Knitting or crocheting is usually done on a couch or chair while watching television. Embroidery is also done in the living room. Sewing, painting or stained glass usually requires a separate area.

It's important to keep that space as your own. It defines your presence and makes you feel at home in your nest. While it's fine to put things away when company comes, it's also okay to leave your projects out where they can be seen and admired. Chances are they'll be a conversation starter and a way to show off your talents in a subtle way. A few pats on the back will no doubt be the result. And there's nothing wrong with that.

> *To be happy at home is the ultimate*
> *result of all ambition.*
>
> —SAMUEL JOHNSON

GIRL TALK #75: Today I will look at the places in my home that could be improved by a little candlelight—especially from candles with a special fragrance.

The mood and drama of candlelight is intoxicating. Dinners become more intimate, bath times more relaxing, homes more inviting. The strategic use of candles sets an ambience that is very inviting.

Candles bring back a flood of memories for me. They are used in a first communion. In my faith they are made of beeswax, and the aroma stays with me after all these years. The power of a wedding candle is similar, when the bride and groom light each other's candles and then a joint candle to symbolize their union.

I keep several votive candles on a tray in my bedroom. When I need to calm down and relax, I watch the flames dancing off the walls. When I write in the evening, a flickering candle keeps me company and gives me comfort. And any meal, even if it's from the deli, is special when I sit down at the table and light a candle to dine by.

Try this simple, inexpensive way of making yourself feel good. Candles are a guaranteed way of relaxing and becoming mellow.

When we are authentic, when we keep our spaces
simple, simply bountiful living takes place.

—ALEXANDRA STODDARD

GIRL TALK #76: Today I'll look in my garden and plan for spring planting.

S ince I don't have a message for St. Patrick's Day, I thought that talking about having a green thumb would be appropriate. As spring approaches, the thought of planning my garden for summer thrills me. Watching my seedlings grow and bloom makes me realize how miraculous nature can be.

In the desert where I live, having a green thumb is a challenge. The same goes if you live in the city. But balconies, window sills and patios present a special opportunity.

There is a satisfaction I experience when my hands are covered with soil and my muscles ache from bending over. Although sweat drips down my brow, I feel like an artist painting a masterpiece. The most wonderful part of the process is that the plants will become stronger and more beautiful as they mature, just like a woman!

A home filled with green, growing plants is a delight. They don't fare so well in a tension-filled house. They require a gentle touch, nurturing, soft voices and people who care. You can tell a great deal about a home and the inhabitants by the green things found within.

Check out your home and see where you could add a plant or two. If you have a garden, now is a good time to pick out the flowers and plan the arrangement. Remember, flowers and plants feed our souls.

This could be such a beautiful world.

—ROSALIND WELCHER

GIRL TALK #77: Today I'll see how I can cultivate happiness in my life. If I need to work at it, I'll put in the effort.

Happiness is the joy and comfort that permeates your being when you're completely at peace. It bubbles up as an all-is-well feeling. People who are chronically happy tend to be sick less often, and live longer. Look at Bob Hope and comedian George Burns, who lived to the ripe age of 100, laughing all the way.

Likewise, to be angry or to harbor hostility weakens the immune system. Countless books and articles have documented the mind-body emotional link. Doctors who believe in natural healing are now prescribing not pills, but alternative ways of finding happiness, like:

1. Take a walk and drink in the beauty of nature.
2. Take a news break and steer clear of violence and sadness.
3. Keep an inspirational book nearby and pick it up often.
4. Stay away from angry, depressed people.
5. Count your blessings each night.

Happiness is a choice. Some have to work harder at it than others. Goldie Hawn is almost apologetic when she says, "I'm happy all the time, I can't help it." How wonderful if we could all be that way.

Happiness is the result of positive self-worth, personal attitudes and the way we relate to each other. Too many people pursue success only to find themselves alone and unhappy. They find out too late that money can't buy happiness.

So wake up, walk, smell the roses, drink from the cup of joy. Stay away from toxic people and stressful situations as much as possible. Don't let the little things get you down.

Don't worry. Be happy!

Happiness comes of the capacity to feel deeply, to enjoy simply, to think freely, to risk life, to be needed.

—STORM JAMESON

GIRL TALK #78: Today I'll think about my high school years and celebrate the decisions I made. Then I'll see if there are any more decisions that need making.

High school graduation is a major crossroad. The direction we take is filled with possibilities. Yet the overwhelming majority of students find that it's time to move away from home.

Some choose marriage, thus going from one nest to another. Others go to college or technical school, making education a high priority. Still others go straight to work, assuming the responsibilities of an adult.

Relationships also offer options. Some students go it alone. They see the world as full of excitement and opportunity. Others are less secure and want to go away with a friend or become engaged to their high school sweetheart to avoid loneliness.

The selections made at this juncture will shape the course of one's life. How much to commit, how much responsibility to take on and whom to spend time with are all factors.

I went to work and postponed my education. It was my only choice at the time. Later, however, I had a chance to make other choices, which led to college and graduate school. Luckily, most of us have that opportunity. We can also go home again, and many do, at least for a short time. So if you were not happy with your decision, reassess it now and fix it the way you want.

I do not believe in a child world. I believe the child should be taught from the very first that the whole world is his world, that adult and child share one world, that all generations are needed.

—PEARL S. BUCK

GIRL TALK #79: Today I'll think about my relationship to credit cards.

Back in the 1950s, my high school social studies teacher taught me about positive and negative credit. His rather simplistic philosophy, which makes more sense than ever in today's world, was: If you can't pay for it, don't buy it.

I use my credit card for specific items and purposes.

- For renting a car
- For establishing good credit
- For accumulating bonus points or frequent flyer miles
- For spontaneous purchases when I don't have money on me
- For emergency repairs when I'm caught short

I am always aware of the negatives:

- That there's a tendency to overspend
- That overspending can lead to debt
- That service costs and interest accumulate

If you've found yourself over the credit limit or close to it, make a concrete plan to end your credit card blues. Cut them all up, except for one. Then make steady payments on each, always paying more than the minimum and making sure you mail it before the due date (so you don't get additional late charges). Start paying with cash and make a solemn promise to use the card for emergencies ONLY!

> *I had plastic surgery last week.*
> *I cut up my credit card.*
>
> —Henny Youngman

GIRL TALK #80: Today I will determine whether or not I act like a doormat for anybody. If so, I will take back my own personal power.

One of the families who came to my office was a classic for illustrating this point. As a family therapist I often dealt with situations where one or both parents were alcoholics.

In this particular situation, the alcoholic father had been in a recovery program for two years. Although the dad was sober, the family was still dysfunctional. During the sessions, the father or eldest son did all the talking. The mother and younger siblings stayed silent. To shake things up I asked the mother to lie in front of my office door, since she seemed to be acting like a doormat in the dynamics of the family. She promptly did so and stayed there throughout the hour. The following session she didn't even sit in a chair to start. She went straight for the floor and lay down.

Halfway through the hour, the oldest boy jumped up and said, "I've had it. Mom is the parent. I want to be a kid but I'm doing all the talking and she's lying on the floor. I'm leaving!"

The mother stood slowly, put her arms around her son and apologized. "I'm sorry. I thought I had nothing to offer," she said. "But you're right. I am the mother and I'll try to act more like one from now on."

Do you act like a doormat? Think about it. If you do, the time has come for you to stand up and be counted. You've got a role to play. Play it.

You can't be walked on unless
you're lying on the floor.

—Sylvia L.

GIRL TALK #81: Today I will count my blessings.

One of the most interesting workshops I ever attended was focused on appreciating what we had. The workshop facilitator asked the participants to sit and meditate on their jobs, their families and their lifestyles. The facilitator then told us that there had been an accident and we each had lost someone important to us.

Next, the facilitator told us to process our feelings about this personal tragedy. After an hour of soul-searching through this unbearable grief, the facilitator told us that it was all a mistake. The accident happened to someone else, not to us.

The relief and joy were overwhelming. I felt whole again.

The point was that we all have that relief and joy within our lives at this very moment. But we overshadow it with doom and gloom, obscuring the blessings that we already have.

It was a valuable lesson in appreciating life as it is.

*If the only prayer you ever
say in your entire life is thank you,
it will be enough.*

—Meister Eckhart

GIRL TALK #82: Today I will simplify my bathroom routine in at least one way.

On the edge of my bathtub I keep a plastic basket with all my personal items: pumice stone, bath salts, oils, clippers, nail brush. I also have fragrant candles, attractive bottles of scents and bath gels, and a waterproof pillow for my head. When I need to relax and unwind, the tub is my favorite place.

An open basket on the vanity is a good holder for rolled-up washcloths or hand towels. A pretty wicker basket on the sink holds cosmetic items neatly. A few special photos, a small radio and I've got a room in which to retire.

Whenever my husband can't find me, he knows where to look. With a book, a glass of wine and no telephone, I'm in heaven. I don't even need a *Do Not Disturb* sign on the door. Everyone knows my bathroom time is MY time. It took many years to train them, and now, finally, I can reap the rewards.

If your life is filled with stress, or if you simply need pampering, try meditating in the tub. Then watch your cares swirl down the drain and step out refreshed and rejuvenated.

> *Noble deeds and hot baths are*
> *the best cures for depression.*
>
> —DODIE SMITH

GIRL TALK #83: Today I'll think back on some decisions I've made and see how they have affected my life. If there are new decisions to be made, I'll make them and move on with my business.

We make good choices and bad choices. At other times we don't know whether or not we've made a choice at all.

When I graduated from high school, I went to work. For me it wasn't even a choice. It was simply something I had to do. My father had lost his business in a catastrophic fire and my mother was struggling to keep the family together. There was no extra money and our small town had no guidance for obtaining scholarship money or financial aid. At the time I thought college was simply out of my reach.

My excellent typing skills allowed me to obtain a good position as a secretary in a large corporation. It paid well and before long, I had bought a used car and some nice clothes. I even had money to send back home and some extra for singing and tennis lessons.

At seventeen I was self-supporting. And while I feel I might have missed out on the fun kids have during college, I was grateful to be able to earn a living. So was it a good choice or a bad choice? Who's to say?

Someone once said, "Once you make a decision, then make it the right decision." In other words, learn to make lemonade from sour lemons.

> *When you have to make a choice and*
> *don't make it, that is a choice.*
>
> —WILLIAM JAMES

GIRL TALK #84: Today I'll reflect on listening: when I've listened and when I've been heard.

Mary was a spunky Irish lass who worked hard, yet learned to sing and dance. At the age of sixteen, she was smitten with a thirty-three-year-old stonemason from Scotland. Sparks flew between them and they quickly married, scandalizing our small town of 600 folks.

After raising her children and losing her farm to the Depression, she went to work in the local bowling alley. There, she came up with an original doughnut recipe that made her famous in town and in the nearby villages. She became a legend when she opened her own shop.

Growing up, I had many opportunities to watch Mary at work, dispensing sage advice along with her decorated doughnuts and steaming hot coffee. People came to Mary not only for her sweet treats but simply to talk and listen. And from her I learned that listening, comforting and showing support for someone else's troubles will bring a sense of relief and good will.

She was a terrific role model for me. And over the years, I've tried to incorporate Mary's great sense of caring and her wisdom of keen listening into my own practice. Mary was my grandmother.

A woman's life can really be a succession of lives, each
revolving around some emotionally compelling
situation or challenge and each marked
off by some intense experience.

—WALLIS SIMPSON

GIRL TALK #85: Today I will make changes to enhance my health. My plan is to be proactive and prevent stress and illness if possible.

Many wise people, from doctors to shamans, have said: "Physical symptoms are superficial. Change the way you live if you want to get better."

So today I'm making it my business to avoid illness and to keep myself healthy. Here's how I'm doing it:

- I'm spending time outside, at least an hour a day (unless it's freezing). I'll watch the birds or smell the flowers or walk in the snow.
- I'll work out for thirty minutes a day, three times a week. I'll walk a mile every day.
- I'll practice healthy breathing, which can regulate my heart rate and keep my blood pressure down, my circulation up and my digestion working properly.
- I'll do a little yoga every day, stretching my tight muscles.
- I'll meditate for ten to twenty minutes at least once a day, twice a day if I can.
- I'll keep a journal to help me understand my feelings on any given day. It will help me connect with myself.

I'm going to enhance my health because I like myself. How about you? Think about promoting your health, whether you are well or ill. Give yourself a gift; the rewards will be many.

To enjoy life we must touch much of it lightly.

—VOLTAIRE

GIRL TALK #86: Today I will think about how negative behavior is such a drag and positive behavior is such a pleasure.

Those of you who remember Art Linkletter will recall what a wonderful talk show host he was. The segment I loved best was when he interviewed the children. So you can imagine my delight when we were both invited to be keynote speakers at a conference in Atlanta. He listened to my talk attentively; then it was his turn. He spoke of teen drinking and drug abuse and reminded us how times had changed.

"When my sons were little I'd send them to their rooms," he said. "After a while they'd repent and change their ways."

Then he said that now, as a grandparent, that simply doesn't work.

"When I send them to their rooms, they've got Nintendo, a computer, a television, a telephone and a virtual toy store," he said. "So what's the punishment?"

Then he added, "About the only deprivation left is that they can't bring their girlfriends into the room with them!"

We all laughed at the truth he spoke. And we all took home a thought for the day.

> *What most of us want is to be*
> *heard, to communicate.*
>
> —DORY PREVIN

GIRL TALK #87: Today I will remember my last trip to Disney World in Florida. I think it may be time for a return visit.

Walt Disney and his magical characters and kingdoms have touched the lives of my family many times over the years. My photo albums are filled with pictures of my kids with Mickey Mouse.

The rides and shows are fun, but the evenings are extra special with the bright lights against the warm, dark Florida sky. Of course, part of the adventure is the bonding between parent and child, sharing the magic together. Add to that the flowers, the music, the marching bands, the fountains, the dizzying rides. It truly is a land of make-believe, where the worries of everyday life disappear and happiness rules.

As a special treat, we recently offered to meet everyone in Disneyland for a family reunion. Amazingly, and to my utter delight, everyone accepted—coming from as far away as Alaska. The whole family that once numbered five was now together again. This time our ranks had swelled to fourteen. But I was much too busy having a good time to count.

I never lose sight of the fact
that just being is fun.

—KATHARINE HEPBURN

GIRL TALK #88: Today I'll start a list of things I'm thankful for. When I have a difficult day or a painful loss, I will come back to my list to replenish my grateful soul.

There is a wonderful Hasidic parable about the power of gratitude in changing the course of destiny. It's about the length of time it takes to say "thank you."

When we offer thanks to God or to another person, we transform our lives. It's easy to be thankful when times are hard, when you are ill or in debt, or when your heart is aching. Those are the times when it's best to think of what you do have, not what is missing or hurting.

Every day is a gift. Even when we feel as though we're falling apart, there is something to be thankful for. In those trying times, small acts of kindness can heal our pain. The deepest lessons are revealed through joy and happiness. Some days bring more, some bring less. Then a day will come along that will amaze you with its goodness.

Whenever we say "thank you," we increase our ability to recognize the gifts that we have and develop the healing quality of gratitude.

> *If you can't be thankful for what you receive,*
> *be thankful for what you escape.*

> —ANONYMOUS

GIRL TALK #89: Today I will evaluate the difference between my "want to" purchase and my "need to" purchase.

We often confuse money, expensive trinkets, designer clothing, huge homes and luxury cars with who we are as people. We identify with the outside trappings instead of looking to our soul for a sense of self.

The more-is-better philosophy leads to a false security. We look for inner contentment in outer possessions. It all stems from conditioning, where we learn early in our childhood that a new bike or popular toy will make us happy. That leads to high-tech toys like computers and big-screen TVs and expensive, trendy goodies like cars, diamond-studded watches, gold jewelry and fashion-plate clothing.

But instead of bringing freedom and self-esteem, those pricey trappings entrap us. What if someone steals your jewels or car? What about insurance? How can you leave home when someone may break in? You need an alarm and more insurance.

My question is: Do you *need* it, or do you *want* it? There's a huge difference. Is your self-worth high enough that you don't need to flaunt extravagant baubles to feel good about yourself?

Good! That's the answer I was hoping you'd give.

No one can make you feel inferior
without your consent.

—ELEANOR ROOSEVELT

GIRL TALK #90: Today I'll remember my twenties and see what I learned from that time of experimentation and maturation.

One's twenties are a time to test our choices. Those formative years are usually a time of education or training for a future occupation. It's likely that a life mate will be chosen. For most young people it is a time of financial insecurity, and also the first blush of independence.

This decade will also bring internal conflict. It's frustrating and frightening being on one's own. It's also an exciting time to learn about books, movies, hobbies, new foods and making new friends who grew up in faraway places and have different religions, attitudes, backgrounds and cultures. It's a time to chart a personal course of development and to stay true to one's spirit.

Looking for other options and experimenting with different decisions will help each of us define the road ahead. There is internal and external activity, much like an internship for the larger responsibilities of a growing family and financial pressures.

How we long for someone else (like Mom or Dad) to pay our car insurance or dental bills, or have dinner on the table when we come home dog-tired from work.

The choices we make during this decade will have a new sense of importance and shape our destiny in ways we cannot even imagine.

We should be careful to get out of an
experience only the wisdom that is in it, and stay there,
lest we be like the cat that sits down on a hot stone.
She will never sit down on a hot stone again, but
she will never sit down on a cold one either.

—MARK TWAIN

GIRL TALK #91: Today I will not play the fool; instead I will reflect on the Twelve Steps to recovery and see if any parts of my life can use some cleaning up.

April Fool's Day comes only once a year. But too many people spend their lives playing the role of a clown. These sad cases are so wrapped up in their own hang-ups that they cannot be taken seriously by others and they have no respect for themselves.

Originally the Twelve Steps to recovery were used by Alcoholics Anonymous. However, their universal appeal have made them appropriate for many other support groups. Years ago a friend came up with a "shorthand" version. Here they are:

1. Saw a problem.
2. Heard there was help.
3. Decided to trust help the best I could.
4. Took a good look at myself.
5. Shared that "look" with another person.
6. Practiced trusting God.
7. Asked for help from that God.
8. Thought about those I'd hurt.
9. Said I was sorry whenever I could.
10. Gave myself regular checkups.
11. Grew in trusting God.
12. Tried to live by these steps and help others when and however I could.

There are some things you learn best
in calm, and some in storm.

—WILLA CATHER

GIRL TALK #92: Today I will look at how my pas-
siveness causes problems for me and make a decision
to become more powerful. Using my strength and
courage, I can make many wonderful things happen in my life.

When Gloria Steinem founded *Ms.* magazine, women
were struggling to gain acceptance in society and in
the workplace. I knew from firsthand experience
what it felt like to be treated as a second-class citizen, and I
learned about sexism when trying to get a loan to start my first
business. I went from bank to bank and was turned down at each
one. My credit was perfect; my salary was higher than many men
I knew. The problem was that I was a single woman.

Finally I found a private individual (a man) to lend me the
money at an exorbitantly high interest rate. Plus, he demanded
a piece of my business as his reward for lending me the money.
Eventually I paid him off—and then I had to buy back a piece of
my own business!

Ms. magazine was a great support and comfort to me in those
days. Gloria Steinem encouraged women and gave them an
emotional boost. She made us feel that we were important, and
she gave us ideas on how to conduct ourselves in a professional
manner.

While maintaining her own femininity, she suggested that
women enter politics and become part of the world's decision-
making process—a revolutionary new idea at the time.

From Gloria Steinem I learned the pitfalls of passivity and the
power of collective strength. She made the word *radical* a positive word for women.

> *Some of us are becoming the men*
> *we wanted to marry.*
>
> —GLORIA STEINEM

GIRL TALK #93: Today I will think about my life and all that I have to appreciate. Maybe I'll slow down my pace and take in all that is around me.

Appreciation means being able to drink in the beauty that surrounds us—fluffy white clouds, kaleidoscopic flowers, lush green meadows, an azure sky, diamonds sparkling on a lake. It means being able to enjoy soothing music or even rock-and-roll, and savor foods, whether spicy, bland, hot or cold. Thankfulness means being able to accept things that are different without prejudgment.

There are so many gifts in life: the birth of a child or grandchild, a first kiss, a partner's love, family, friends and even one's health. I pray that I never become indifferent to the wonderful things that life gives me. And I always try to remember to say thank you.

As we learn to appreciate more, we find ourselves more satisfied with what life offers. We can stop searching for something we don't have—and probably don't even need.

Be not afraid of life. Believe that life is worth living and your belief will help create the fact.

—WILLIAM JAMES

GIRL TALK #94: Today I will look at the relationship between my mother and myself. It is important to evaluate what is real and what is imagined.

The mother-daughter connection can be the most traumatic and painful relationship in a family. Or it can be the best—filled with love and understanding.

Some believe the reason for the high emotional level is that the mother is the first female role model. She is the standard by which all female children measure themselves. Secretly she compares her own looks, popularity, body and talents to her mom's.

Memories of mother can be filled with warm moments, laughter and good times. Or they can be charged with anger, ridicule and unreasonable rules. There can also be a mix of feelings, which will cause confusion.

Unresolved emotions keep us hostages of our past. One of my clients, who was sixty-five years old, was still feeling inadequate and unhappy because she was fearful of trying new things. In exploring the mother-daughter bond, she realized her older sister was always considered the accomplished one. My client had simply given up. But she still harbored anger and resentment and guilt. She had become a prisoner of her own thoughts.

Today is a good day to start unraveling the mystery of your relationship with your mother. It might take years, even with professional help. But today is the first day of the rest of your life. It's not too late to start.

> *Love cures people—both the ones who*
> *give it and the ones who receive it.*
>
> —KARL MENNINGER

GIRL TALK #95: Today I will try to define what money means to me and how much value I will give to spending or accumulating it.

We've all heard the saying, "Money is the root of all evil." That erroneous belief (the actual Bible verse from I Timothy 6:10 NKJV says "For the love of money is a root of all kinds of evil.") can cause unnecessary deprivation. It's not the money that is evil; money is neutral. It's people who do bad things. Money is actually a wonderful way of making our lives fuller, richer and more varied.

It is important to value the freedom and security that having money can bring. Money can make life easier and more comfortable. One of the greatest rewards is that you will have choices. When there is no money, the choices are few. Your time and energy are directed to making it. But when you have slightly more than you need to take care of your bills, you can relax a bit and enjoy life without the constant worry.

Very few people grow up with a clear idea of how to relate to money. In a sentence or two, can you define your relationship to money? Think about the value you place on acquiring it, the motivation you have to earn it, the discipline you have to keep it and how you like to spend it—on yourself and others. We'll come back to this later in the book to see how you're doing.

> *Although the world is full of suffering, it is also full of the overcoming of it.*
>
> —HELEN KELLER

GIRL TALK #96: Today will be a serene day for me. Perhaps something sacred will present itself.

Weekends are a welcomed time for relaxing. My daily activities keep me busy from dawn to dusk. So today I took advantage and went back to sleep for an hour. I dressed down in sweat pants and a shirt and a pair of comfy old slippers. After slipping a CD into the player, I settled down in the closet to reorganize my clothes, shoes and miscellaneous other items. Once that was done I tackled my desk.

Did I say this day would be serene? Well it is, in a way. I'm by myself, enjoying my nest, working at my own pace and not trying to please anybody but ME.

After a lunch of chicken noodle soup, I went through old catalogs and magazines, tossing out the old ones. Later, I'll settle down on the couch for some much-needed meditation time. All of this girl stuff—the puttering and cleaning and curling up with a good book—is comforting and yet productive.

When one's surroundings are clean and organized, and when one's home is quiet and peaceful, it's easier to find the God-place in each of us.

We should all plan to set aside one weekend a month for ME time, when we can put our space in order and take a few moments to commune with our Higher Power. Just say "no" to friends and family and settle in alone for some quality time with yourself.

> *Our grand business is not to see*
> *what lies dimly at a distance, but to do*
> *what lies clearly at hand.*
>
> —THOMAS CARLYLE

GIRL TALK #97: Today I will act joyous. If it doesn't feel natural, I'll keep doing it until it does.

Dancing is my joy. After conquering two serious illnesses, dancing helps me return my body to optimum health, and the music makes me feel alive.

"Real joy comes not from ease or riches, or the praise of men, but doing something worthwhile," said W. T. Granfell. So when I dance I am happy. It may not be earth-shattering, but it is my expression of joy.

Nature also cheers me. The first early blossom in spring—which is right around the corner—then the warm summer rain. Even the dynamic colors of the leaves as they get ready to fall, fill me with magic. When my grandchildren come for a visit, gladness lifts my spirits, and even spending a quiet evening at home gives me inner peace.

Connecting with my Higher Power allows my hope to rise and my vitality to be strengthened. The light and joyful heart has a better grasp on the ups and downs of daily life. Problems are easier to deal with. Most of them work out without worry.

Joy may not feel natural to you, especially if you have lived in a chaotic or abusive house—or if you are in one now. The first thing to do is get rid of the toxic people in your life and move into an environment where you can nurture your spirit.

Genuine joy will quickly bring into focus what is important and what is not.

If people only knew the healing power of laughter
and joy, many of our fine doctors would be out of business.
Joy is one of nature's greatest medicines.
Joy is always healthy. A pleasant state of mind tends
to bring abnormal conditions back to normal.

—CATHERINE PONDER

GIRL TALK #98: Today I will think of pregnancy; there is a reason why it does or doesn't result in a baby.

When you become pregnant, a whole new reality sets in. Your body is carrying a new life. You may have already guessed, since your breasts are full and your stomach is queasy. You may be depressed or have the feeling something about you has changed.

As the trimesters progress, there are conflicting emotions. Some women are told they are beautiful, their hair has a healthy shine and their cheeks have a rosy glow. But the woman herself feels fat and bloated. Sleep is difficult with a round tummy, and bending over to tie one's sneakers is out of the question.

When the time comes for delivery, the pain and exhilaration are blended into an unforgettable few hours. Luckily for most women, the pain is soon forgotten and only the magical moment remains—the exact point in time when she takes her place in history as a mother. Nearly every mother can tell you the exact time that her son or daughter came into the world.

But a pregnancy that does not result in a baby is a painful blow. It may seem trite to say that everything happens for a reason, but most doctors will agree that babies whose mothers do not carry them to full term were not ready to be born. It's nature's way of caring for everyone concerned.

Whether or not a pregnancy comes to fruition, all women share an invisible thread that binds us together. Supporting each other is what is ultimately important.

> *To everything there is a season,*
> *a time for every purpose*
> *under heaven.*
>
> —Eccles. 3:1 NKJV

GIRL TALK #99: Today I will do whatever is necessary to correct a situation that is wrong.

Sister Mary Thomas was the principal of the Catholic grade school I attended. She was an angry, overbearing and irritable nun. Today she'd be accused of child abuse, but back then it was okay to punish boys with a leather strap and the girls by smacking their hands with a wooden ruler. We'd cringe when Sister Mary came near, but nobody would confront her. It simply wasn't done.

Upstairs in the library was a porcelain basin that Sister Mary used to wash the hands of all 160 students. She never changed the water and she wiped all of our hands on the same towel. If you were at the end of the line, your hands were probably dirtier than if they hadn't been washed at all.

I had a reputation as a bit of a troublemaker. So in eighth grade I decided to write an anonymous letter to the Board of Health describing Sister Mary's unsanitary practices. A few days later four men showed up unannounced. They interviewed Sister Mary as well as several students. The next day she was gone.

We were overjoyed. No more Sister Mary. But she returned several weeks later, a changed nun. Gone was the bowl of water. Gone were the beatings and ruler rappings.

I'll never know what happened to her during that time, but it was a blessing for everyone.

> *All great reforms required one to*
> *dare a lot to win a little.*
>
> —WILLIAM L. O'NEILL

GIRL TALK #100: Today I'll think of the Easter message and what it means to me. Then I will make whatever plans I need so that when Easter arrives I'm ready.

The end of winter brings the resurrection of our spirit and our Lord. We wake up to the warmth of the earth, to color and change. It's a time of renewal and revitalization. When we pay attention to the Easter story and the message God has given us, we can relate that to our own lives. Are there relationships that need to be renewed? Are there dreams that should be brought forth? Everything is possible, even that which appears impossible. It's time to spruce up—from our attitudes to our clothes.

Whether we are religious or not, the essence of the Easter story is relevant to us all. The message is: Light is more powerful than dark; life wins over death.

Easter is a symbol of victory—the connection of the Higher Power to each and every one of us.

The distant strains of triumph
Burst agonized and clear.

—EMILY DICKINSON

GIRL TALK #101: Today I will reflect on hard work and who or what inspires me to put forth such effort.

Right from the beginning, I was impressed with Rosalynn Carter. She was the President's working partner and still remained a respected autonomous person during her four years in the White House.

Rosalynn was a first-born child, and she demonstrated many of the classic traits. During her early years, she helped her mother. When her father died in her teenage years, she took over the sewing and housekeeping duties, as well as the care of her three siblings. After completing high school, she enrolled at Georgia Southwestern College at Americus. There she met Jimmy Carter.

After their first date, he said to his mother, "That's the girl I want to marry." She was only seventeen at the time, but they married a few years later and had three children. Amy was the only daughter; there were also two sons.

Even though she is a shy woman, Rosalynn helped her husband with his business, then used her quiet strength and power to help him run for office. Once he was elected, she attended cabinet meetings and major briefings.

Rosalynn took an active interest in the mentally ill, the elderly, the poor and the handicapped. But perhaps her greatest demonstration of her selfless spirit has been shown since they left Washington, D.C. Even now she dons jeans and takes a hammer to lend a hand to Habitat for Humanity, the non-profit program her husband helped found to build homes for hard-working families who could not otherwise afford a house of their own.

From Rosalynn I have learned that hard work is not something you seek, but something that comes with life. Instead of running away or shirking one's duty, she has shown how to attack hard work head on, and with class.

*Life begets life. Energy creates energy. It is by
spending oneself that one becomes rich.*
—Sarah Bernhardt

GIRL TALK #102: Today I will listen. I will also stop talking when I feel nobody is listening to me. Sharing and listening are too important to treat halfheartedly.

Listening is a skill we should all practice. Most of the time we are so preoccupied with our own concerns and interests that we only listen with half an ear. When that happens, both people lose. The speaker feels frustrated and unimportant. The listener has missed an opportunity for a meaningful connection.

Not hearing can damage a loving relationship. It can also ruin a parent-child bond. When a parent stops listening, the child clams up and refuses to share. The bond of trust is broken and in many cases can never be repaired.

True intimacy comes when we hear each other with an open mind and active ears. By detaching from our own petty concerns, we can really hear what our friends, family members and coworkers are saying. We never know when a kernel of new truth or a different approach to life may be given to us. We might miss a better solution to a problem or a more efficient way of solving a situation.

Listen with wholehearted attention, using eyes, ears, heart and emotions. Watch facial expressions and postures, which often convey messages without words. Tune in to sense and feeling.

One thing is for certain: if you do not listen, you will not hear!

You should not have your own ideas when you listen to someone. To have nothing in your head is naturalness. Then you will understand what he says.
—SHIUNRYU SUZUKI

GIRL TALK #103: Today I will see if anything good can come from a bad decision.

If I had gone to college right out of high school, things might have been different. But I was employed and independent. Maturity came early. My dating was not with college boys, but with men who were usually older than I. In some ways it was exciting. They were worldly and seemed to have much to offer.

Shortly after my twentieth birthday, I became engaged to a man who was thirty-one. His world seemed very settled. He was financially secure, a successful company man, and we enjoyed each other's company. We were married six months later.

If I knew then what I know now, that marriage never would have taken place. I was simply too inexperienced and our ways of seeing the world were too different. We were never able to bridge the gap and after twelve painful years, the marriage ended.

As difficult as those years were, I learned to be gentle with myself. It was important not to feel as though I was a failure. I did not take the blame, although the choice I made to marry may have been the wrong one at the time.

But from our union came three wonderful children, who have given me the most wonderful grandchildren. So in looking back, I accept that while the marriage may not have flourished, a whole new generation was born.

> *There are two ways to meet difficulties: you can alter the difficulty or you can alter yourself.*
>
> —PHYLLIS BOTTOM

GIRL TALK #104: Today I will say a prayer for the angels who have come into my life when I needed them most.

There is a magical moment when someone is there for us and we feel safe and protected. During those graceful moments we have truly been touched by an angel.

Our Higher Power commands angels to watch over us to prevent loneliness and pain. Since they honor and cherish me, I must learn to honor and cherish myself, too.

Angels also come in the form of mentors and teachers. Mentors support us and share their wisdom. Teachers challenge us; they push us to struggle until we find the truth.

Throughout history people have had different notions about God. But they can relate to angels. Here is a reference from the Bible.

Behold, I send an Angel before you to keep you in the way and to bring you into the place which I have prepared.

Exod. 23:20 NKJV

God answers prayers by sending people.

—ANONYMOUS

GIRL TALK #105: Today I will honor all that I am worth and make at least one financial decision on behalf of myself.

Since I grew up in an impoverished home, when I reached adulthood I had a difficult time spending money on myself. When I became a public speaker, it was imperative that I had nice clothes. Since I traveled extensively, I needed a wardrobe for every occasion.

I found a red cashmere jacket. It cost a fortune (or so it seemed to me), but it was perfect and I loved it. After only three wearings I was 30,000 feet in the air, on a plane bound for Chicago, when I realized I'd left it on the connecting flight. I was heartsick. Then these thoughts crossed my mind: (1) I loved the jacket and the way I felt when wearing it; (2) if I made a few sacrifices I could buy another one; (3) I was worth it!

When I reached my destination, I wasted no time before heading back to the store where I got the jacket and buying another one. I wore it for many years and felt wonderful every time I put it on.

The lesson is that when self-worth dictates a decision that increases your self-worth, money is simply a medium to facilitate that process. So don't be stingy with yourself.

> *There's a period of life when we swallow a knowledge of ourselves and it becomes either good or sour inside.*
>
> —PEARL BAILEY

GIRL TALK #106: Today I'll think about my ability to adjust to circumstances.

During the years I lived in the Black Hills of South Dakota, I lived in a beautiful log home in the hills. The house was designed to sleep eight guests in private quarters, while my husband and I had a private suite at the opposite end. Our business manager, Larry, was a frequent guest since he lived out of town. Usually this presented no problem.

But there came the occasion when all bedrooms were full and Larry needed a place to stay. We offered the sofa bed, even though it was embarrassing to ask the president of a large and successful firm to sleep there.

On the day Larry came, I had hand-washed some items. Since it was raining, I hung them around my bedroom. Soon the guests began arriving and spread throughout the house. By the time Larry showed up, the house was humming with activity. Since he needed some quiet time, my husband offered him our bedroom, completely forgetting my personal things that were strewn about. As we stepped into the room I was struck with the humor of the situation—three powerful people, two of them presidents of companies and two nationally known speakers—surrounded by damp laundry.

"A real professional does what has to be done," someone once said. How true.

> *Problems have only the size and the*
> *power that you give them.*
>
> —S. H.

GIRL TALK #107: Today I will make plans to keep my suitcase ready in order to make traveling easier for myself.

Traveling has been part of my lifestyle for as long as I can remember. Sometimes it's an overnight stay, at other times it's a month in a foreign country.

To make life easier I bought a pull-suitcase that fits under an airplane seat. Then I bought duplicates of the items I use every day: nightclothes, underwear, makeup, soap, toothbrush, toothpaste, hairbrush. With all the basics ready, all I need is a few minutes notice and I can be on my way.

Here are some tips from a traveler who knows the drill:

- Ask for electronic ticketing. It's faster and you don't have to worry about misplacing tickets.
- Check expiration date on frequent flyer miles. Don't lose out on free travel.
- Always check the weather for your destination so you know what to pack—warm clothes or cool.
- Before leaving make sure your flight is leaving on time. Save time and energy if it's delayed.

Is there anything as horrible as starting a trip?
Once you're off, it's all right, but the last moments are
earthquake and convulsion, and the feeling that
you are a snail being pulled off your rock.
—ANNE MORROW LINDBERGH

GIRL TALK #108: Today I will give myself a message of appreciation for my body.

Increasing your self-worth can be as simple as accepting who you are at this moment. If it's a major change that you want—like a nose job or losing a certain number of pounds—first ask yourself why it's important. Then ask how much time and money you are willing to spend to make it happen. Then come to a conclusion and make plans to do whatever needs doing.

Once that is done, move on to other aspects of your life. Stop focusing on your body. Pay attention to your career or job, hone up on your parenting skills, learn a new hobby. All of these can be sources of self-worth.

The next thing is to set your own personal standards for how you look and stop worrying about how the cosmetics and fashion industries want you to appear. Those are idealistic standards that nobody but glamorous models can achieve. Know that your body and mind can be tangible sources of feeling good about yourself. Accept who you are.

Wealth is not what we have but what we are.

—ANONYMOUS

GIRL TALK #109: Today I'll plan an outing and have a new and different experience.

Waking up at 5:30 in the morning to go for an early horseback ride was not my idea of the best way to start a summer morning. But fifteen of my friends had planned the adventure and I wasn't a "poor sport." So I pulled on my jeans and cowboy boots and headed out the door into a bright orange and yellow sunrise.

At Hart Ranch in Rapid City, South Dakota, I was assigned a horse named Buttermilk, who had a sleek, smooth, tawny coat with matching mane and tail. We mounted and lined up to ride along the trail leading into the ponderosa pine.

Under the magnificent South Dakota sky, there was not a sound, except the steady clip-clop of the hooves as they wound through the shaded path. When we stopped to dismount, I was delighted to look out over an expanse of spectacular land. Around us were birds, butterflies and small woodland critters. A deer walked out and stood by the path, watching us intently as we filed past in single file. What a Godly place!

At a chuck wagon set up in the woods, the smell of hot coffee and sizzling bacon welcomed our growling stomachs. The horses were released to find their way back to the corral, while we wolfed down pancakes and more coffee.

"It doesn't get any better than this," said one of my friends. I couldn't agree more wholeheartedly.

Perhaps nature is our best assurance
of immortality.

—Eleanor Roosevelt

GIRL TALK #110: Today I'll think about my own transformation. Are there qualities I need to develop? Have I chosen guides to help me?

Transformation does not happen overnight. We change over time through a complex mosaic of interactions with other people, our environment, our work, our living, our loving and our spiritual experiences. During the process, we are making choices triggered by what happens around and within us. Transformation means that we keep the essence of who we are but we add to that.

The evolution of a person means developing qualities that invite growth and change. Some of these traits are:

- Ability to resist conformity
- Willingness to invent a new lifestyle
- Desire to create personal goals
- Living in the present
- Accepting pain as a necessary part of growth
- Having a solid value system
- Decisiveness
- Courage

Mentors and teachers can help the process since guidance is important for the traveler on the road to spirituality. Each person has a unique path to self-realization, but learning can also come from others. All options should be made part of the growth and development process.

Perhaps as we approach the year 2000,
the future will develop from the "survival of the wisest"
rather than the "survival of the fittest."

—ANONYMOUS

115

GIRL TALK #111: Today I will choose one item from the list to do today and one to do tomorrow.

One of our greatest sources for personal healing is the child inside of each of us—that part of ourselves that reconnects us to our childhood and youth. By going inside and touching this youngster, we can return to a time when we had more free time and fewer responsibilities. There are many ways to tap into that bright-eyed energy:

- Smell the flowers.
- Bake cookies.
- Paint your finger- and toenails.
- Blow bubbles.
- Play or walk in the sand.
- Walk in the snow.
- Put on a record and dance.
- Swing on a swing.
- Play hopscotch.
- Color with crayons.
- Jump rope.
- Bounce a ball.

There are hundreds of others. Think about when you were a kid and bring back a recollection or two. Then do it.

> *But above all things put on love,*
> *which is the bond of perfection.*
> —COL. 3:14 NKJV

GIRL TALK #112: There is a reason for everything, so today I'll reflect on my feelings about babies being born.

Childbirth is a major passage in life. I remember the tiny bundle the nurse handed to me when my son was born. First I counted his fingers and toes, then I ran my fingers over his velvety cheeks. This miracle of smells, noises and smiles was repeated when each of my daughters was born.

Every aspect of life changes with a newborn. Sleep is gone for quite a while. There are new appointments for shots and pictures. Company is nonstop for a while, until the newness wears off, and the days of spontaneous outings end. Every move must be planned with an infant. You need diapers, wipes, blanket, bottles, baby food, toys, extra clothes, a baby seat and the ever-present pacifier.

A child usually brings out our maternal side, and also a spirituality we did not know existed. The marvel of giving life to another human is truly miraculous. The protection and love we feel for the helpless and vulnerable babe bind us to him or her in a way that can never be broken. That child's welfare is ours until the day one of us dies.

Having a baby is a two-way gift. The parent's gift is the child and the child's gift is the parent. And blissful are both that can share it equally.

Blessed be childhood, which brings down
something of heaven into the midst
of our rough earthlings.

—HENRI FREDERIC AMEEL

GIRL TALK #113: Today I will commit to taking care of all aspects of my health.

ood health is more than the absence of illness. It's an approach to life that keeps one in the best optimum condition possible. Here are some of the things it includes:

- Physical fitness: good nutrition, no addictions, plenty of exercise
- Mental health: a realistic approach to life, a creative imagination and ability to play
- Emotional well-being: the willingness to face and express true and honest feelings
- Social interaction: the ability to make and maintain relationships
- Spiritual strength: an understanding of your place in the universe
- Vocational vitality: the willingness to make choices and decisions to push you to attain higher goals

The quality of your health expresses how well you integrate with the world. Healthy people go with the natural flow of things; they don't obstruct it. They embrace that which improves and maintains their well-being and they stay away from toxic environments, situations and people. They develop a balance of body, mind, emotion and spirit that brings a lifestyle of high health and low stress.

When health is absent, wisdom cannot reveal itself,
art cannot manifest, strength cannot fight, wealth becomes
useless, and intelligence cannot be applied.

—HEROPHILUS

GIRL TALK #114: Today I will remind myself that it's never too late to become a woman of distinction.

When I entered the aerobics room at the fitness center, I hoped I wouldn't feel out of place. The instructor, Estelle, quickly welcomed me and put on the music. From that moment on, all thoughts of awkwardness were forgotten.

Estelle was in perfect shape and her personality filled the room with sunshine. She appeared to be the ideal blend of balance, strength and endurance.

After that first session, I looked forward with excitement to the next one. Those three mornings a week became a top priority for me as I lost weight and toned up under Estelle's careful guidance. She offered us health tips about nutrition and shared her favorite low-fat recipes.

The energy and brightness of this woman still inspire me. Her smile and inside lightness radiate warmth and pleasure. I didn't realize it at the time, but when I began taking lessons with Estelle she was already eighty-two years old! And even now, years later, her energy is amazing and her capability inspires awe in those who meet her.

If I can be like Estelle at eighty-two, I will consider myself truly blessed. Even if I'm not, I am grateful to have known this gifted and beautiful woman.

*One is not born a woman,
one becomes one.*

—SIMONE DE BEAUVOIR

GIRL TALK #115: Today I will remember that serious illness and death are big deals. Everything else is a little deal.

L ife is much simpler when we learn to separate the big things from the little things. I'll share an anecdote to illustrate my point.

One day a letter came in the mail through which I learned that a trusted colleague had betrayed me. She had taken some of my ideas and published them as her own. My day was filled with anger and I was preoccupied with my own hurt feelings.

Later that same day I received a phone call from a friend who said her husband had been diagnosed with a terminal illness. That put everything into focus immediately.

So now I do my best to separate the piddling from the powerful. All my day-to-day activities, which keep me occupied from dawn to dusk, are immediately set aside when a family crisis arises. Some things must wait. Priorities are those things that can't—like offering comfort to a friend who will shortly lose her husband, even though I'm distressed over losing a colleague's support.

When I save my fretting for the big deals, it makes my life more serene and less stressful. The small things take care of themselves so I can deal with the big ones.

> *You gain strength, courage and confidence*
> *by every experience in which you really stop to*
> *look fear in the face.*
>
> —ELEANOR ROOSEVELT

GIRL TALK #116: Today I'll think about when I might have enabled someone, preventing them from taking responsibility for themselves.

In 1975 I was involved in the first successful treatment programs for nicotine addiction. While looking for a permanent center in which to house the program, we were using an old convent. One of the nuns there became the caretaker. She was kind and understanding and quickly gained the trust of the clients.

At the end of one treatment session, the forty people involved took up a collection for Sister and bought her a color television. It was quite a splurge at the time. She put it in her bedroom and often commented on how much she loved it.

Six months later I happened to visit her room and noticed the TV was gone. "Where is it?" I asked.

"I had to sell it so I could buy a smoke-eating machine."

"Why did you do that?"

"I hated to see those people have to go out in the freezing winter to smoke by the old Dumpster," she said. So she installed the smoke-eater in the stairwell so the people in the nicotine addiction program could smoke in comfort!

Needless to say, I felt it was time to explain about how when we help someone in that way, we enable them to continue harming themselves instead of learning what it takes to get well.

Enablers are the worst enemies of the people they love the most.

—CARRIE R.

GIRL TALK #117: Today my thoughts will be with the angels and I will think about when they have been in my life.

One night I was driving home from class when I decided to take a shortcut. The bad part of town I was going through was only about four miles long, and I figured I could shave off fifteen minutes from my trip. Ten blocks into my shortcut my tire blew and I was traveling on the rim. I pulled over into a dark, deserted residential street.

Off in the distance I could see a building with a light on. It was ten o'clock at night, and as I walked toward the beacon I prayed for safety and help.

From the porch, I could see some scary looking men inside. But what was I to do? So I knocked on the door.

"Yeh, what do you want?" said the man who opened it.

I explained that my tire had blown out and I needed help. He looked at me strangely, then asked if I wrote books. Surprised, I answered that I did.

Amazingly, he went to the shelf and pulled out one of my books. My photo was on the back cover.

"Hey, we'd be happy to help a lady like you," he said. "We're an A.A. group and your books have been a mighty help to us."

An hour later we stood around my car saying a serenity prayer together!

You never know when angels will be coming into your life, so be ready to receive them when they do.

Wherever there is love, there is
an angel nearby.

—Anonymous

GIRL TALK #118: Today I will think about mother-hood—the ideas and feelings. I will honor whatever those emotions mean to me.

When I chose to become pregnant, I was not aware of what a lifelong decision I was making. Yet I couldn't wait, and the whole experience of blooming and wearing maternity clothes was wonderful. Being pregnant meant I was now a grown-up, entrusted with a new life. The birth itself was a miracle, and when I held that little six-pound bundle in my arms, I felt like a new life had begun for me. My relationship with my son is as special now as it was then.

That blessed experience was repeated again and again. My daughters have been like finding a treasure chest full of miracu-lous gifts, and my six grandchildren are more precious than any-thing I will ever own.

If we are lucky, our decisions are positive and enrich our lives. Becoming a mother was the most important choice of my life, and I'll always be grateful I made it.

Your children are not your children.
They are the sons and daughters of life's longing for itself.
They come through you, but not from you.
And though they are with you, yet
they belong not to you.

—KAHLIL GIBRAN

GIRL TALK #119: Today I will meditate on the pain that I occasionally feel and be proactive in trying to prevent the pains from returning.

Pain is your body's way of letting you know something is wrong. It may be physical or it may be emotional. Both can produce tangible pain. Too often we reach for a pill to dull the ache. It may offer temporary relief, but the pain will return if we don't find out the cause.

Many illnesses are time limited. That means the body will heal itself if we only give it a chance. Since we live in a high-tech medical society, we can partake of the most miraculous cures. However, instead of running to a doctor for every twinge or throb, we can direct our energy to self-healing whenever possible. After all, we have more power to make ourselves better than we give ourselves credit for having.

When you feel pain coming on, ask yourself these important questions:

- What's happening in your life that may be contributing?
- Is there a change of behavior that will reduce the pain?
- Are you willing to make those changes?

Let not your heart be troubled.

—JOHN 14:1 NKJV

GIRL TALK #120: Today I will practice solitude. I will commit to five minutes until it becomes natural to want to commit to more time. Slowly, I will find out what solitude means to me.

Solitude is the state of being alone. It does not mean being lonely. Instead, it means being able to be isolated from others for the purpose of nourishing the soul in peace and quiet. A soul in solitude experiences a blissful state. A soul in loneliness feels empty and painful.

When I was a child I played alone for hours. The world was mine. With my imagination in high gear, I would create any kind of world I wanted. Each passing hour brought more possibilities. Even as a teenager, I found time to enjoy books and music, watching clouds and just thinking. As a mother, my times of solitude were few and far between. I managed a dip in a warm tub or a few minutes of reading before falling asleep.

Now that my children are grown and my responsibility is less, I take long walks in the mountains, meditating on my life, finding insight and an escape from stress.

Too often we find that quiet time feels unfamiliar. It makes us fearful. So it's good to start a little at a time. Five minutes to begin with; you don't need the television blasting all the time. Be with you—alone. Eventually, you will welcome as much solitude as you can carve out of your busy life.

The stillness of solitude allows a greater contact with your inner self as well as with your Higher Power.

Language has created the word loneliness
to express the pain of being alone, and the word aloneness
to express the glory of being alone.

—PAUL TILLICH

GIRL TALK #121: Today I will choose five people to remember with a May Day basket. It will be fun to plan these special treats for five special people—and won't they be surprised!

As a young girl, May Day was very special to me. We'd make up baskets from things we had around the house, like pipe cleaner sculptures, candies, homemade cookies, notes and flowers. Then we'd leave them on the porches of our friends and neighbors. I thought these fun gifts had become a distant childhood memory until last year.

The doorbell rang and a man in a uniform asked me to sign for a package. When I opened it, I realized the date was May first, and it was a basket from the wife of my business manager. When I called to thank her, I learned that it's a longstanding tradition to send them, and that she has well over 100 people on her May Day basket list.

So I'm now back in the basket business and today's the day to send them out. It feels good to be giving to others and to be renewing an old family tradition.

We make a living by what we get.
We make a life by what we give.

—Paula L.

GIRL TALK #122: Today I will reflect on marriage. Do I want the intimacy that a union provides? Am I willing to work at making it successful?

Marriage is a coming together as a pair. This coupleship is as fragile as a newborn baby in the beginning. It must be nurtured and coddled until it grows into its own strength and maturity. Only then can it overcome the many obstacles that are sure to be thrown in its path.

Coupleship means a passionate, spiritual, emotional and sexual commitment between two people. It matures if both partners maintain a high regard for the value of the other. The intimacy that springs from the union will depend on the conscious decision and loyal commitment of both parties. A couple must protect itself from any invasion or threat, including self-defeating behaviors like gambling, drugs, infidelity and outside forces or people that threaten the sanctity of the union.

Before marriage, spending important time together helps each party learn about the feelings, opinions, behavior and beliefs of the other. Exploring sexual attitudes will also show whether or not the couple is compatible. There are many facets of learning how the other person operates in life and what values are held sacred.

Becoming a couple is one of the first major passages in life. It is the time a person stops being I and becomes WE. It is a time of excitement, mystery and surprise. It takes work, keeping the lines of communication always open and struggling through disappointment and disagreement.

Is it worth the effort?

For me it has been. But each person must make that important decision for him- or herself.

> *Forming a happy, joy-filled partnership*
> *is one of the greater challenges.*

—SHARON WEGSCHEIDER-CRUSE

GIRL TALK #123: Today I will think about my age and what I have gone through to get to this point in my life. I will welcome each day and each year and plan to get the most out of the time that remains.

Mary's hair is completely gray. She's a bit young to have a snowy top, but she admits she's earned every last gray hair.

"They stand for wisdom and experience," she says.

Mary learned about hardship early on, when she was only a child and her father died. She married and gave birth to five children, sank into the hellish world of alcoholism, recovered by using her strength of spirit, and raised her children to the best of her ability with a husband who was rarely home.

With her beautiful unlined face, striking clothes and soft gray hair, one might expect Mary's life was privileged. But it was not.

"Now I look forward to my twilight years," she says quietly. "We older gals have special gifts and I hope to put mine to good use in the time remaining."

In her purple blouse and skirt—her energy color—Mary inspires me to be proud of my age. Like her, I hope to appreciate each passing year and take from them all the lessons and pleasures life has to offer. Mary is an inspiring friend.

Undoubtedly, we become what we envisage.
—CLAUDE M. BRISTOL

GIRL TALK #124: Today I will take this list, add to it my own ways of relaxing and call it my "Stress Reduction List."

We are surrounded by stress—at home, on the road, at work and at play, and with our children, spouses, lovers and jobs. Stress can make us physically ill if we cannot control it—if we let it control us. So here are some tips for managing stress:

1. Sit quietly in a dark room, breathe slowly and deeply.
2. Listen to your favorite CD.
3. Keep a book of jokes handy. Read a page or two every day.
4. Exercise for fifteen minutes every few hours.
5. Pray.
6. Scream into a pillow.
7. Take a short nap.
8. Cuddle your pet.
9. Go out to the garden and weed or plant.
10. Do a spontaneous favor for a friend.
11. Go to a movie.
12. Write a letter.
13. Take a hot bubble bath.
14. Take a walk.
15. Curl up on the couch with a good book.

If there's something special you like to do to unwind, add it to this list, then photocopy it and post it on your refrigerator. When you are overwhelmed, pick one and do it.

Live in peace in times of stress.

—Anonymous

GIRL TALK #125: Today I will meditate on nature and how I have a unique place on Earth. We are all part of a whole and I will do my best to protect and care for all God's creatures.

At the northern end of Kauai, one of the Hawaiian Islands, there is a special place where one can watch the whales play.

The sun was just past its peak—with the promise of a gorgeous sunset—when we arrived at the lookout point at the top of a hill. Soon the water became a moving whirlpool. Then suddenly, a powerful and immense shape moved out of the water and back into it. With grace and power, the whale played (if "played" is the right word) with seven of its friends.

The awesomeness of these huge mammals was inspiring, and I felt honored to have the opportunity to watch the mightiest of God's creatures. It also reminded me just how small I am in comparison.

We are all part of nature, the large and the small. We owe it to each other to co-exist in peace and harmony. For without it, the world as we know it will no longer exist.

The whales of Kauai are a symbol of the wholeness of the universe. And as I watched them swim south, my spirit was lifted and my hope renewed that we can all make this universe a better place.

Though we travel the world over to find the beautiful,
we must carry it with us or we find it not.

—RALPH WALDO EMERSON

GIRL TALK #126: Today I'll think of unusual situations I've been in, how I got there and what they meant.

In my career as a public speaker, I have found myself with movie stars, politicians and other celebrities. So I wasn't surprised when the wife of a famous man asked me to coach her for an important meeting. "I've never spoken in public before," she confessed. "I could use some help."

We arranged to meet at her house, but when I arrived she had some construction workers there, so we went to her neighbor's house—a former United States president and his wife. They welcomed us and gave us a quick tour of their lovely home. Just as we began to practice, the former first lady said that she had a dresser in the bedroom that we could use as a lectern. Thinking it would be more like the real thing, we accepted.

So there we were, the famous man's wife giving her speech, me coaching, the former first lady and my husband acting as an audience. And then the former president came in, wearing his socks and looking for his shoe. Down he went on hands and knees as he poked under the bed for it. The scene struck me as hilarious, and I broke out into a fit of laughter. We all did. It felt as though we were in an Andy Warhol painting.

He found his shoe, put it on, apologized and left. My student finished her speech, the "audience" applauded and we called it a day to remember!

> *Like the body that is made up of different*
> *limbs and organs, all mortal creatures exist*
> *depending upon one another.*
>
> —HINDU PROVERB

GIRL TALK #127: Today I will think about my friends and appreciate them. Maybe I will make an effort to connect with some of them and let the rewards of friendship be an important part of my daily life.

I have always had wonderful female friends. They come in all shapes and colors, and we've done many exciting things together. Although we don't always have everything in common or share the same values, we have spent important moments of our lives together.

One of the gifts of being a woman is that we can bond almost immediately—usually within a few hours. It doesn't take me long to learn a person's history. That's how women are.

When emotional traumas occur, women friends help heal each other. We confide our deepest secrets and share joy and pain in equal measure, never shying away from that which hurts. Finding time to nurture relationships with female friends is one of the best investments we can make in our own happiness. Our roles as mothers, wives and workers demand time and energy. With friends, we can share a cup of coffee or a glass of wine, kick back and relax. People with friends tend to be healthier, happier and less anxious than those without.

My friends enrich my life immeasurably. I am reaching out today to touch one or two. How about you?

Trouble is part of your life and if you don't share it,
you don't give the people who love you
enough chance to love you.

—ANONYMOUS

GIRL TALK #128: Today I will think about the family I came from and be grateful I was given the gift of life. What I do with it is my choice.

Years ago when I was in therapy, I came to realize that my heritage was both painful and happy at the same time.

My maternal grandmother made my world a safe and loving place. Although she was poor, we never experienced poverty or loss.

With my mother and father, however, who were parents long before they were ready, there was pain and insecurity. A catastrophic fire, loss of home and business, struggles with addiction and financial insecurity all contributed to my own feelings of self-doubt. Add to that mix other siblings, both of whom shared my parents' affection. I must admit, I grew up needing far more than I received.

Looking back, I can see that my family did the best it could under the circumstances. My parents had the best of intentions but they had so many needs of their own, they simply could not fill mine.

I suppose I could hold the feelings of loss and deprivation against them. But it serves no purpose. So I choose to recall them with love and respect. If only they were still here and I could tell them in person. But they are not. So I keep those thoughts close to my heart and say a silent prayer of thanks every day for the gift of life they gave me.

> *Life can only be understood backwards,*
> *but it must be lived forwards.*
>
> —SÖREN KIERKEGAARD

GIRL TALK #129: Today I will select at least two timesavers and make them part of my daily routine. Then I'll use that saved time for myself.

Saving time on little things adds up to hours, days, months and even years. So I'm always looking for shortcuts. Here are a few of my time-saving tips:

- I don't get out the sewing kit for one thing. I wait until I have a few items and then do them all at the same time.
- Same goes for hand-washing lingerie.
- I set aside one morning for a complete cleaning, instead of taking an hour here or there.
- If I'm watching television I sort photographs, do hand-mending or work on other projects that don't require my full and undivided attention.
- I make only one trip a week to the grocery store. To make several trips only wastes my precious time.
- When I get gas I fill up. That way I don't usually have to stop to refuel more than once a week.
- If I'm working on a project, I buy extra supplies so I don't have to stop and run to the store to buy more.
- I conduct as much business as possible over the telephone. Getting in the car uses time, energy and gas.
- I never go out for just one item. I wait until I have a list of errands, then figure out the most efficient and cost-effective way of getting them all done.

Work is love made visible.

—Kahlil Gibran

GIRL TALK #130: Today I will set aside a place in my home to store decorations to celebrate the special holidays that come throughout the year.

I am a holiday addict. I love the special decorations and all the fuss that we put into celebrating those special days. The colors are especially wonderful—the orange and black of Halloween, red and green of Christmas, pink and yellow of Easter, and red, white and blue of the Fourth of July. I love the rituals and getting together with friends and relatives.

Over the years I have accumulated a variety of decorations, and each year I add more. When I get into that accumulation mode it's impossible to stop. Wherever there is a sale, I stock up. And I know I'm not alone in this compulsion.

When my closets fill to overflowing, I dig in and spend some time rearranging. God forbid I should get rid of anything! No, I can always manage to squeeze in a few more items. Let's see, the next big event is the Fourth of July. I'd better start looking around for anything in red, white or blue so I'm sure I'll have everything I need!

Keeping all the old decorations adds to the fun and makes memories.

In violent and chaotic times such as these,
our only chance for survival lies in creating our own
little islands of sanity and order, in making
little havens of our homes.

—SUE KAUFMAN

GIRL TALK #131: Today I will remember my high school years, the pleasure and the pain. If there are any classmates I want to connect with, now is the time for a call or letter. We shared a bit of history and it might be nice to remember that time together.

High school is an impressionable time. Most people can remember a great deal about those four years. Perhaps it's because we were in transition, changing from children to adults. Our vulnerabilities seemed to be visible to all, but our friendships were true. Some have lasted a lifetime.

Although we had a small senior class at Comfrey High, there were a number of cliques—the class heroes and the lost children. The same people always seemed to run student council.

When I went to my class reunion after five years, very little had changed. At dinner the old friends sat together sharing stories and catching up. When I recently attended my fortieth class reunion, things had really changed. There was more mixing and mingling. The cliques had finally dissipated. There were a few deaths, a few widows, some had changed careers, others had retired. There were photos of grandchildren and more in-depth discussions than ever before.

Roaming the halls of the old school the next day, I was flooded with bittersweet memories of gym, class and the lunchroom. The students who had shared those times with me seemed a bit older, a lot wiser and more accepting. Perhaps wisdom does come with maturity.

Then is then. Now is now.
We must grow to learn the difference.

—KATIE N.

Today, Mother's Day, I want to remember my mother. She died too soon—just two days after her sixty-seventh birthday.

She had been in and out of hospitals for several weeks with heart disease. She seemed to know the end was near because she wanted to go home. When she arrived home, she walked around touching everything, especially the photographs of the children and grandchildren. Then she touched the dishes, and the pillows and quilts she had so lovingly made. She went into the bedroom and touched the bed she had shared with my dad. All of the special things in that house received her personal blessing.

Her death a few days later left a hole in our family. We tried to mend the wound, knowing that she was no longer suffering. We comforted ourselves knowing that Mom would have hated to sit around and let old age take its toll. She was always spunky, with a great sense of humor.

Mom was never famous but everyone in town knew her. In her malt shop, and later at the food drive-in, she prepared countless meals for the folks in town. And when she lay in her open casket, they filed past to pay their last respects. People came with their hearts filled with love.

Her children and grandchildren are her legacy, her story, her masterpiece. We carry the best of her within us. From her we learned how to be loving, compassionate, humorous, courageous, giving, strong and trustworthy. Not a bad inheritance from one woman.

Life is not a brief candle. It is a splendid torch that I want to make burn as brightly as possible before handing it on to future generations.

—George Bernard Shaw

GIRL TALK #133: Today I'll think about myself and whether or not I have developed the quality of enthusiasm. If not, I'll practice it daily.

Vince Lombardi, the great football coach, would tell his team that if they were not fired up with enthusiasm they would be fired from the team—enthusiastically!

Enthusiasm means to be inspired or possessed. It's zeal, fervor, zest, zing. You can hear the energy in those words. It uplifts ourselves and others. It's contagious. Think of the times in your life when you were zealous about something and how wonderful you felt.

Whenever I commit to doing a new workshop, I wait for that moment of inspiration. Then the enthusiasm surges through me and I become inspired, excited, ardent, as I pick a topic and select appropriate music and props. My energy is then transferred to the audience and they, in turn, are filled and give their vigor back to me.

Children are almost always charged with enthusiasm—even if they're only making mud pies or playing on the swings. When we observe people whose lives are filled with passion, we know that anything is possible. And anything IS possible when you are enthusiastic.

Enthusiasm is the yeast that makes your hopes
rise to the stars. Enthusiasm is the sparkle in your eyes,
the swing in your gait, the grip of your hand,
the irresistible surge of will and energy
to excite your ideas.

—HENRY TOR

GIRL TALK #134: Today I will get out my health care policy and become familiar with my benefits and limitations.

Health care is a major expense we all must deal with. Even with the best insurance coverage, finances can go down the drain when a serious accident or illness occurs. For this reason, it's best not to take anything for granted. Instead, learn about your policy and where it may fall short. Learn about the medical system, and if you don't have insurance, make some plans to get covered.

Study the Explanation of Benefits section or ask the customer service representative to explain it to you. Don't wait until an emergency arises and you find yourself at their mercy. If you're in a managed care network, an HMO or a PPO, get an updated list of approved doctors and hospitals.

Speak to your primary care physicians about negotiated fees. Doctors will often work with you. If you have no insurance, make sure your doctors know this. They can adjust the bill downward or leave out tests you might not need.

It's important to have a list of doctors, dentists, hospitals, clinics and emergency numbers near each phone in the house. The time to prepare these lists is before you need them.

> *Wisdom consists of the anticipation*
> *of consequences.*

—NORMAN COUSINS, M.D.

GIRL TALK #135: Today I'll think of the women I know who have faced the challenge of breast cancer. I will honor the memory of those who have been lost and celebrate the victory of the many survivors.

I have not met Dr. Susan Love in person, but she's been a major factor in my life since I was diagnosed with breast cancer.

"Get a copy of *Dr. Susan Love's Breast Book*," my oncologist suggested. "It's the bible for anyone who has breast cancer."

When I learned I had it, I was shattered. Nobody in my family had experienced this kind of cancer. There were so many decisions to make and my mind was not working properly. My emotions had taken charge. My fear, of course, was that this was the end. Since I didn't know the specifics of the disease, I could only imagine the worst.

Reading the book was an education. Dr. Love wrote about the very emotions I was feeling: shock, anger, vulnerability, and finally, the desire to "get on with it." Her book let me know what had happened and what would happen. It answered questions too personal to ask anybody, even the doctor. As I read further, my hopes grew, and by the time I was finished, I felt as though I had a good chance of a full recovery.

From her suggestion, I joined a support group and later started one of my own. I began networking with women just like myself. For all of us, Dr. Susan Love is God-sent. She has shared her skills and her compassion to help ease the trauma of this dreaded disease.

Concern should drive us into action,
not into a depression.

—KAREN HORNEY

GIRL TALK #136: Today I'll remember the turning points in my life. Nothing is permanent and possibilities are always available, whether I make the decision to explore them or not.

With my children in school full-time and the freedom of a few hours every day, I made the choice to begin college. I had to start from scratch, with the required courses. Registration itself was a challenge, as anyone who has tried to figure out the maze of course selection, payment and sign-up will attest to.

During the 1960s, college campuses were overrun with hippies. Coming from a quiet suburban neighborhood, the mother of three, I was totally unprepared. My classmates wore ripped jeans, long hair and psychedelic T-shirts. I had every hair in place and was impeccably dressed in a matching powder-blue outfit. The discomfort was great, but the excitement of learning was greater. It only took a week for me to put on jeans, let down my hair and stir up my political sentiments.

Our culture was changing radically. Assassinations were common and it was time for me to choose a lifestyle that fit my values, not the stereotype I had become. It became imperative for me to define my significance in the world and act upon it. Suddenly it was not enough to be a quiet little homemaker, hiding from the big bad world. I wanted to be part of everything, in the thick of it, along for the ride.

Although I started college late in life, I've never for a second regretted it. In fact, it was one of the most positive changes I've ever made.

You can't turn back the clock but
you can wind it up again.

—BONNIE PRUDDEN

GIRL TALK #137: Today I will meditate on what I really want for myself and what choices I have to make to get what I want.

Thinking in new and refreshing ways can bring you personal freedom. So many mothers would like to stay home with their young children but feel they can't afford to. Yet I see them living way over their heads, with huge mortgages, driving expensive cars—which means large payments and top-dollar insurance. If you want to cut down your full-time job to a part-time one, or if you want to stop working all together, take a close look at how you live. Then make adjustments.

- Can you save money by brown-bagging lunch?
- Can you buy less expensive clothing or carpool to work?
- Can you use your talent to work at home?
- Can you cut down on your extra activities if they are expensive (like a boat or pricey ski vacations)?
- Is there a way to live on one income?
- What corners can you cut at home to reduce your overhead?

There are ways of making money without sacrificing your motherhood. Think about your options. I trust that you'll figure out a creative solution that will make you happy.

Ah . . . there's nothing like staying home for real comfort.

—JANE AUSTEN

GIRL TALK #138: Today I'll explore my life to see if the Twelve Steps can help me face some issues in my life that need attention and healing.

Bill Wilson and Dr. Bob may have been the greatest social architects of this century. They were the men who put together the original Twelve Steps of Alcoholics Anonymous. Now these steps are being used at support groups for eating disorders, gambling and nicotine addiction, drug and sexual addiction, and for workaholics, among others. Hundreds of thousands have found transformation and inner peace through these twelve steps.

THE TWELVE STEPS OF ALCOHOLICS ANONYMOUS[2]

1. We admitted we were powerless over alcohol—that our lives had become unmanageable.
2. Came to believe that a Power greater than ourselves could restore us to sanity.
3. Made a decision to turn our will and our lives over to the care of God *as we understood Him*.
4. Made a searching and fearless moral inventory of ourselves.
5. Admitted to God, to ourselves and to another human being the exact nature of our wrongs.
6. Were entirely ready to have God remove all these defects of character.
7. Humbly asked Him to remove our shortcomings.
8. Made a list of all persons we had harmed, and became willing to make amends to them all.
9. Made direct amends to such people wherever possible, except when to do so would injure them or others.
10. Continued to take personal inventory and when we were wrong promptly admitted it.
11. Sought through prayer and meditation to improve our conscious contact with God, *as we understood him*, praying only for knowledge of His will for us and the power to carry that out.
12. Having had a spiritual awakening as the result of these steps, we tried to carry this message to alcoholics, and to practice these principles in our affairs.

2. The Twelve Steps are reprinted with permission of Alcoholics Anonymous World Services, Inc. Permission to reprint the Twelve Steps does not mean that A.A. has

By identifying with other people who have some of the same struggles and possibilities, we reduce our feelings of isolation and fear. It's healing to hear how others address and resolve problems.

This is the miracle of healing circles.

If you have knowledge, let others
light their candles at it.

—MARGARET FULLER

GIRL TALK #139: Today I will examine my life and evaluate my activities. Everybody needs something that makes one feel good, and it's a bonus if it also contributes to the well-being and happiness of others.

On Wednesday mornings, Summerlin, Nevada, becomes a sacred place when 100 women come together to tap-dance. They range in age from fifty to eighty-five. Some have been Rockettes, some have entertained soldiers in USO shows, some have danced all their lives and some are just beginners. The talent is abundant, with comedy stars, singers, costume designers and show people.

When I took up tap dancing I had no idea what fun it would be and the benefits I would derive—not only from the physical exercise, but from the sharing and sincere friendships. We support each other through trauma, grief and illness. The group accepts invitations to perform all over Las Vegas and donates the money it makes to charity to improve the quality of life for others less fortunate.

So on Wednesday mornings, when single women, wives and widows come together to care, to laugh, to share and to dance, the studio becomes a special place. And I am honored to be there with this exceptional group of ladies.

> *Life is 10 percent what you make it and*
> *90 percent how you take it.*

—IRVING BERLIN

GIRL TALK #140: Today I'll cherish picnic memories and make a commitment to update those memories with an old-fashioned picnic this weekend.

Each of the summer holidays is a wonderful time for a picnic. But before I pack my basket, I like to take a look at each of them and see what meaning they hold for me.

On Memorial Day we remember those who are no longer here on earth, but whose memory lingers on. Originally, Memorial Day was to honor the veterans who fought in the wars. I remember watching bands and soldiers marching in parades when I was a child. Today we've expanded the theme to honor all those who have died. Death is a part of life and remembering is a way to keep them alive.

The Fourth of July is a time for fireworks, music, parades and celebrations. The red, white and blue is a sign of victory—that we live in a free country and can enjoy the benefits of democracy. Labor Day says summer has come to an end and we'll be shifting into fall and then winter.

But what ties these three holidays together is the hunger for a picnic—the smell of grilled burgers and hot dogs, the cold beer and iced tea, pies and watermelon, potato salad, lush tomatoes and corn on the cob.

Throw in a baseball game, a Frisbee, a circle of friends and the twilight hours as fireflies come out and the sun goes down. At picnics we are all kids, enjoying the wonders of life.

The one fact that I would cry from every housetop is this:
Good life is waiting for us here and now.

—B. F. Skinner

GIRL TALK #141: In meditating on the relationships I have with people in my life, I will choose a few ways that I can improve the quality of those relationships.

Families who want to be strong and endure the hard times need to learn some bonding tools. Through my years as a therapist, these are a few I have come up with to make families closer.

- Develop family traditions and rituals.
- Check in with other family members at periodic intervals to keep the connection solid.
- Build memories by collecting family photos and putting them into albums. Make small ones for other relatives.
- Don't let anger and resentment poison relationships. Talk openly if a problem arises.
- Attend family functions even if you have something else to do. It makes others feel important and needed.
- Celebrate all birthdays together.
- Be someone who can be counted on when problems arise.
- Call home and let your family know when plans change.
- Always let someone know where you'll be, especially when traveling.
- Allow everybody their space and respect their privacy.

Children do not know how their parents love them,
and they never will, till the grave closes over
those parents, or till they have
children of their own.

—Edmund Vance Cooke

GIRL TALK #142: Today I will make at least one decision and take one step toward supporting that decision.

Inner emptiness may feel like a spiritual vacuum. When this happens, there is a restlessness that nothing can calm, compulsions that nothing can fix. We feel as though we have an emotional flu—we call it the blahs. This emptiness will persist until a spiritual awakening touches us, filling us with purpose and clarity.

Spirituality is a quality that infuses life with meaning. It energizes our lives and ultimately provides us with a rationale for life. Science and technology can tell us how to effectively and efficiently use our bodies and minds. But they offer little help in the sensitivity department.

To help put you in touch with your spiritual side, there are three things to think about.

1. Sin is whatever holds you back from your potential.
2. Sorrows are stepping stones for greater things.
3. Frustration arises when you give your power away.

Remember, nobody can take your power; you relinquish it, then suffer the consequences. But when you accept that you must take the first steps down the spiritual path, your emotional void will begin to fill up with your efforts, actions and positive forward movement.

Slow and steady wins the race.

—Aesop

GIRL TALK #143: Today I will remember a special place in the country, like my aunt's farm in Minnesota.

My aunt and uncle's farm has filled me with so many happy memories that I will always be thankful for being allowed to spend time there. Fresh eggs, home-cured bacon, milk straight from the cow, a cold, dark cellar filled with mouth-watering vegetables and fruits. Potatoes, squash, zucchini, apples, green beans. I can still remember the taste of them all these years later.

There was constant activity—planting, fertilizing, harvesting, milking cows, tending the piglets, baking bread and cakes, making homemade lemonade. Everybody had a role to play and everything was important to make the farm function smoothly. There was a natural rhythm and balance. Each evening, when work was done, we all sat around the table saying a prayer for our blessings.

As a little girl, one of my great pleasures was to make a meditation place in a grove of trees. It became my refuge, especially during my teenage years.

The farm is still there, where it's always been. And although my aunt is many years a widow, she still lives there, flowers blooming all spring and summer. Whenever I can find the time, I return to visit her and to remember the wonderful memories that will stay with me forever.

Happiness is not a place to travel to.
It's a way of getting there.

—ANONYMOUS

GIRL TALK #144: Today I'll examine my goals and ideas to see if now is the time to bring out some old plans and make them work.

When determination is lacking, most good ideas remain nothing more than passing thoughts. People without fortitude may want the rewards that a completed job or project brings, but they either never get started or they stop before finishing it. Stamina is needed, and an inspiration to accomplish something. When we are truly determined, each of the steps toward the goal is meaningful. The process becomes as important as the end.

True tenacity unleashes creativity and energy. There is much discipline and hard work required. The reward is the rainbow—whether it is money or a pat on the back, a raise or promotion, or world fame.

The two areas in my life that require this maximum focus are writing books and planning family gatherings. Both demand planning, preparation, research, a final goal and determined energy to make them work without too much stress or financial strain.

As the saying goes, "Anything worth doing is worth doing well". To which I add, everything worthwhile takes determination and effort. Amen.

> *What we do upon some great occasion*
> *will probably depend on what we already are;*
> *and what we already are will be the result of*
> *previous years of self-discipline.*

—H. P. VIDDON

GIRL TALK #145: Today I will think about money and time as limited treasures to be used on my own behalf.

When we go to work, we trade our time and energy for money. Even if we inherit money, we give our time and energy to lawyers, accountants and trustees. It is important to understand this since it helps us make choices.

Time and energy are a limited commodity. We only have so much in life. If you are forty, your average life expectancy is 37 years. If you are sixty, that figure drops to 20.5 years. It's a trade-off when we give up time and energy to obtain money.

So let me ask you a few questions about this concept:

- How much time do you want to spend working—hours per day, days per week, years until retirement?
- How much do you need to support yourself in comfort and contentment?
- What do you need to make your life richer and fuller? And how much will it cost?
- How much money is enough?
- What do you ultimately want to achieve?

Once you've answered these questions honestly, you will have some idea how much time and effort you have to trade off to get what you want. Spend the rest of your time and energy on yourself.

Life is a series of problems. Do we want to
moan about them or solve them?

—M. Scott Peck, M.D.

GIRL TALK #146: Today I'll think about when I was in my thirties.

If the twenties were a time of choice, the thirties may be called the era of speed and effort. If one's education is finished by the age of thirty, then it's time to put that knowledge to use. It's a time to climb the corporate or professional ladder. The thirties are an age of commitment to reach one's goal.

Relationships can be a struggle. The blush of early marriage is gone, and more time and extra attention are required to make the union work. It may be difficult to jockey time to nurture a mate and also children. These are busy years.

During this time it is important to keep a running inventory —how are you shaping up as a parent, partner, employee or boss? The wisdom that comes with experience often leads to the first stirring of dissatisfaction and restlessness. We may feel restricted by the choices we made in our twenties. It may feel as though life is all work and no play. The nagging becomes a slow drum roll as the thirties approach forty. There is a constant beating inside that says, "I want more."

Either choices must be made or commitments deepened and renewed. Sometimes action will bring an inner calm, but with it will come a great deal of soul searching. Choosing to act upon these imagined possibilities probably will not happen until you reach forty—or even later.

> *The race is not always to the swift*
> *but to those who keep running.*

—Pastor

GIRL TALK #147: Today I'll think about reading. Maybe I need a good book to jump-start the process again.

When my children were young I read to them regularly. We would discuss books and share them. By the time they were in high school, they devoured magazines by the dozens. Daily discussions of newspaper articles bonded us as a family. This love of reading was passed from my offspring to their offspring.

Books open a world that can be shared by everyone.

"What will change you most in five years will be the people you meet and the books you read," said Benjamin Franklin.

Reading can lead you to discussion groups, book clubs and even bookstores, where you can meet people who have similar interests. It's a fine way to network. My son belongs to a group of people who pick a book to read, then once a month get together for a potluck dinner and a discussion.

Books can take away the blues when you are alone, or give you a rib-tickling belly laugh when you're down. They are informative, entertaining and mentally stimulating. Books are one of life's ultimate pleasures.

Do yourself a service, and make a promise to visit the library or bookstore tomorrow and get a good book to read.

Nothing in life is to be feared.
It is only to be understood.

—MARIE CURIE

GIRL TALK #148: Today I will get five boxes, mark them and organize my bills, letters and notes.

In both my personal and professional life, I have an over-whelming amount of letters to be answered and bills to be paid. So I need to be organized, but I have to work at it and be clever in how I arrange my things so I can find them when needed.

First, I purchased five letter-size boxes and numbered them one to five. Then I began sorting. Items with top priority went into box #1. Those one step below on the priority chart went into #2. Box #3 was for things that needed my attention, but not right now. Into box #4 I put things I'm not sure I even want to deal with. And finally, box #5 gets the letters or notes I just can't decide whether or not I want to save or throw away.

Once a month I go through boxes #4 and #5. Usually I toss out everything in them. That's the easy part! The rest of the boxes are dealt with on a regular basis so I don't get behind in my correspondence, and the bills are paid on time. This system works perfectly for me, but you've got to decide what works best for you.

> *Your work is to discover your work and then*
> *with all your heart to give yourself to it.*
> —GAUTAMA BUDDHA

GIRL TALK #149: Today I'll meditate on the memories that bring me joy and decide to let go of any of them that I don't want to keep.

Just like a tree that grows strong, it is important to know our roots. We feel grounded, connected, if we know where we came from. So it's vital to go back in time now and then, not to pine for old times, but to learn about our past as a way to enjoy the present and appreciate the future.

My journey is taken with my photo albums. Any time I choose I can go back in time—to the high school, to gaze upon old classmates—and even beyond, to when I was a little girl.

Before some of my older relatives died, I visited them to learn about my roots. Not only did it help me understand my heritage and my medical history, but I learned about family dynamics, which has helped me know myself better.

I once saw a poster that read, "God gave us memories so we might have roses in December."

We can choose to remember the best of the past or we can let go of those memories that are painful and harmful. Letting go may not be easy, but it will become more so as we grow older. That's the beauty of maturity.

> *Memory is the power to gather*
> *roses in winter.*

—ANONYMOUS

155

GIRL TALK #150: There are many people in my life I appreciate. So today I will send a card to recognize them.

Appreciation is the glue that binds a relationship together. A counselor I knew once said that he wished he had the same relationship with his adult children that he had with his friends. He said none of his friends would store their belongings in his basement or garage. They wouldn't ask for loans which they never intended on repaying. They wouldn't stop by without calling first.

Letting people know we respect their time and space is a way of showing appreciation. Here are a few more:

- Say thank you, for big things and small.
- Say something positive once a day.
- Hug family members and good friends whenever possible.
- Surprise people with a note, card or treat.
- Let loved ones know you love them.
- Receive compliments with a simple thank you.
- Celebrate important days by sending a card or calling.

We all want to feel important and appreciated. When we let others know how much we care two things happen: first they feel good about themselves, and second, they are likely to reciprocate—which will make us feel good about ourselves!

When you feel grateful for something others have done for you, why not tell them about it?

—ANONYMOUS

GIRL TALK #151: Today I'll think about my garden and someone named Sue.

Sue is a small woman who loves to garden. She hauls dirt and fertilizer; she turns over soil and works like a woman twice her size. She has plots for flowers, vegetables and squash vines. As soon as warm weather comes, she's outside transforming her world into a riot of color.

Spring and early summer are hard-working times, with not much to show for the effort. With pruning and preparing the soil and planting seeds, many long hours are spent with no return. But patience is one of the lessons I learned from Sue.

In gardening, as in life, there is much preparatory work before anything of real value is produced. The second lesson I learned is that after the initial planting, there are weeks of nurturing. Water and sunshine are needed, weeds must be pulled. And some believe that plants need encouragement from their gardener. It's very much like raising children—everything good is worth waiting for.

When midsummer rolls around, the results start to show: Roses bloom, lilies burst forth, morning glories blossom and a myriad of other flowers show their colorful faces. Mornings are special, with home-grown raspberries and strawberries

When fall sets in, she will turn the pumpkins into pies or jack-o-lanterns for Halloween. Then Sue will lovingly put her garden to rest for the winter by clearing out old roots and weeds, setting in mulch to nourish the ground during the winter and saying good-bye to her plot of cherished land for the long months ahead.

From Sue I have learned that there is no glory or blossom without preplanning, commitment and love. Gardening is like relationships. We all respond to love, care, nurturing and affirmation. And, like a garden, we all need a rest now and then. Sue is my sister.

Give her of the fruit of her hands, and let her own works praise her in the gates.

—Prov. 31:31 NKJV

GIRL TALK #152: Today I'll dream a little. Then I will make an effort to make my dreams a reality.

"Stop dreaming and get to work!" How many times have you heard that? Little did our teachers and parents know that the creative juices are stirred up when we daydream.

"Nothing happens unless it's first a dream." The poet, Carl Sandburg, said that.

"If you can dream it, you can do it," is a sign at Disney World. Before we go into action, we need a dream.

In my program there was a wonderful man who was in a crisis, and he was unsure how to move forward. For a while he was incapable of doing anything, even though he wanted to. Then he visualized his dream; after that he was able to vocalize his plan. Finally, he moved forward and changed his life for the better.

"Life is a daring adventure or it's nothing at all," said Helen Keller. Regardless of the outcome, when we follow our dreams we have the satisfaction of knowing that we tried. And when we put forth the effort and have faith in our ability to make those dreams come true, chances are they will. Dreams are gifts meant to stretch our capabilities.

We have seen too much defeatism,
too much pessimism, too much of a negative approach.
The answer is simple. If you want something very
badly, you can achieve it. It may take
patience and very hard work. Faith is a
prerequisite of any undertaking.

—MARGO JONES

GIRL TALK #153: Today I will look to see if there's someone in my life who gets depressed. Maybe I can help by being available to listen.

In my many years as a therapist, clients often came to me saying they were depressed. This often occurred around holidays.

One December so many women were calling for appointments that I couldn't keep up with them. So I developed a workshop that could accommodate ten at a time.

I rented a retreat center and set up a "depression kit" near each bed, consisting of a heating pad, tissues, a book of cartoons and a nightshade for their eyes. Their first task upon arrival was to put them on and take a nap.

This was followed by a lecture that I called "How Awful Life Is at This Time of Year." Then they were instructed to cry as much as they could. After that they picked a partner to unload on and were instructed to cry some more. That night they were to read the book of cartoons and get a good night's sleep.

The following morning ten enthusiastic, rested women walked into the lecture room and said they weren't depressed any more. So instead of another lecture, we went for a hike and then went to see a movie. Everyone left the retreat with one new friend and a lighter heart.

Sadness and depression usually come and go in an ebb and flow. At those times we need a shoulder to cry on and an attentive ear. But most of us are resilient, and we spring back from these minor setbacks better than before.

> *Every holiday I hope for the best*
> *but expect the worst.*
>
> —Anonymous

GIRL TALK #154: Today I will think about my inevitable death and the deaths of the people I love. At some point it will be important for me to make plans and be prepared to help my loved ones take this final step.

Our culture denies death. We hide it behind the walls of hospitals and funeral homes. Death, however, will touch each and every one of us. It will affect us individually and as a family unit. To write a book on the subject takes great courage and understanding.

Elisabeth Kubler-Ross was the person to take that bold step. Her willingness to break the taboo surrounding the subject has had immeasurable results, especially for doctors, nurses, terminally ill patients and the families of those people who have died. She tells us how to express our feelings, she outlines the stages of grief and of dying. She says that when we accept our death, we are then free to face our passing with honesty and courage.

"Death," she says, "offers each of us a chance to discover the true meaning of life."

The day I finished reading her book *Death, the Final Stage of Growth,* I was finally able to plan my memorial and give instructions to my family. It was truly liberating.

From Elisabeth Kubler-Ross I have learned that to talk about death is to share an intimate subject without the need to be frightened or embarrassed. Instead it makes one free.

> *Death is an absolute natural necessity*
> *in the scheme of things.*
>
> —Sigmund Freud

GIRL TALK #155: Today I will think about how I connect with my Higher Power. I'd like to find a special place to contemplate my own spirituality.

In my early years as a wife and mother, I belonged to a group that met on Sunday nights to discuss what spirituality meant to us. We tried to find ways to incorporate our beliefs into our hectic lifestyles with children, work and spouses.

Under the guidance of Father Burke, we took the first of many pilgrimages to Burkliff in the northern part of Minnesota. His family owned a rustic log cabin that was perched on a rocky cliff above Lake Superior. We talked, ate, laughed, cried, planned and explored the "why" of our lives.

This poem sprang from one of those spiritual retreats. I felt compelled to write about what I was feeling.

Burkliff

As one watches the force of the waves
Beat upon the cliffs
One respects the awe of this dramatic display.
One cannot miss the tranquility
Of the tiniest blossom
Satisfied with its small contribution
To the beauty of the shoreline.
The elegance of the mighty cliffs reminds me
That I am small and mortal
The cliffs will last far longer than me
And I feel humble.
Stars, how bright, how meaningful.
I am reminded of a mystery.
We do not know or understand all things.
The beauty and serenity of pine and birch trees
Remind me of what is real, what is beautiful
The cabin itself, strong enough to protect
And gentle enough to comfort
A rare combination of roughness and softness.

Most of all I feel the presence of God
In a community of work, laughter, tears, food and talk
I feel whole and alive
I am a part of something more powerful than myself.
If I can put into action the respect, satisfaction
Humility, mystery, appreciation and confidence
That have touched me at Burkliff
I will have found God
And I thank him.

> **. . . *a life of simplicity, independence,***
> ***magnanimity and trust.***
>
> —HENRY DAVID THOREAU

GIRL TALK #156: Today I will find a place in my home where it's easy to display photos of special people and events.

I have put countless holes in the walls of every home I've ever lived in to hang up my family photos. It's important to have these portraits around me, easily seen, for I derive a great deal of support, strength and pleasure from the memories shared with these family members and friends.

A few years ago I figured out a way of not putting so many holes in my walls. I bought a corkboard, which I put up near my desk. Now I can tape or tack up at least forty photos at a time without a single nail mark. Each day, as I glance at my wall of photos, I am reminded of all the people in my life that I love and with whom I share fond thoughts.

There is a special energy and magic that take place when we can gaze at the faces of those special people in our lives. At work, at home or on the road, there are always photographs nearby to comfort and guide me.

We shape our dwellings and afterwards
our dwellings shape us.

—Winston Churchill

GIRL TALK #157: Today I will give myself a breast self-exam, looking for anything unusual or lumps. If I need a mammogram, I will get one.

One in eight women will get breast cancer. If it's not you, it will be someone you know. Since I've been there, I'd like to share my experience with you.

At the time of diagnosis, a woman feels an overwhelming combination of fear and disbelief. Early detection is the most important factor, since there are more options and a much better chance of a full recovery. With the technology of mammograms, there's no excuse for not staying aware of your state of health.

If a malignancy is found, you must not hide under the covers and hope it will go away. It will not. You must act and act fast so it doesn't spread to other organs. If you feel your doctor isn't working in your best interest, find someone who will. Your good health and your recovery depend on a satisfactory relationship with your medical professionals.

Being a breast cancer survivor isn't my primary identity. However, I am proud to be one. And grateful, too. Today I lead a perfectly normal, healthy life. So this information is coming from somebody with firsthand knowledge. There is no cause for terror, helplessness or a defeatist attitude. You can conquer this dreaded disease and wear a smile on your face and in your heart, knowing you have looked death in the face and triumphed.

In every problem there is an opportunity.

—Virginia Satir

GIRL TALK #158: Today I'll take a risk and ask someone for help.

When I was a single parent, I came to believe that God had a special place in heaven for anyone who had gone through this phase of life. My fantasy was that there would be an extra pair of hands to help, a few extra dollars to spend, a loving, caring baby-sitter, a car with a tank of gas and an ear willing to listen when I needed to share. But that was a fantasy.

In real life, to dwell on those thoughts takes too much time and energy, especially when there is so much to be done. On the plus side, as a single parent I was totally in charge, not only of my own life, but of my children's lives as well. I didn't have to compromise or argue points. I found support from others when I needed it, and I learned to find creative solutions to problems others may have found overwhelming.

That stressful time as a single parent let me share experiences with others in a way I could not have done as a married woman. In the long run I had the opportunity to connect in a giving, sharing way.

So if you're a single parent, struggling to make ends meet and wishing you had more time and energy, know that someday you will be grateful for the experience. It will make you stronger, wiser and more self-sufficient. You will understand that you are a capable and courageous woman who knows how to handle the complexities of life and survive.

What is life but one long risk?

—DOROTHY CANFIELD FISHER

GIRL TALK #159: Today I will appreciate my skills and what I have to offer. I will believe in myself and never let anyone make me feel small and unimportant.

Billie was a therapist. Her dramatic clothes and abundance of jewelry made her seem outrageous. But she worked magic with her clients.

During one summer, Billie was facilitating a group of professionals who were in therapy for their own addictions (eating disorders, nicotine addiction, etc.). Ten people sat in a circle introducing themselves. One of the group members was offended by Billie's hot-pink dress and the silk flower she wore in her flaming red hair.

"What are your credentials to be my therapist?" the woman demanded.

With quiet dignity Billie replied, "I was handpicked by Sharon to be your therapist, whereas you are the patient in this group. Shall we begin?"

Later in the week that therapist approached me and said she learned much from Billie and was now able to improve her life, both professionally and personally.

Billie and I had a good chuckle over that. Perhaps this is an "in" joke for therapists, but there is a lesson: You never know who your next teacher will be.

Fortunate are the people whose roots are deep.

—AGNES MEYER

GIRL TALK #160: Today I'll think about my values and how I honor and protect them. If challenged, am I willing to be clear about my position?

During the 1960s, the war in Vietnam was causing unrest, especially on college campuses. As a small-town girl, it felt odd to be caught up in the political protests that raged nonstop.

One student in my class was studying for the priesthood. He was quite vocal about his feelings on the war. Frank's intentions were honest, and they were based on deep spiritual beliefs of right and wrong. We became friends and I agreed with his philosophy. Then I read about his arrest for burning his draft card. I was surprised, saddened and filled with conflict. For me, he had broken the law. My values were being challenged and I was unsettled.

Frank went to jail; there was nothing I could do. But I did visit him in the federal prison. He was a model prisoner who believed he was right in the position he had taken; he accepted the consequence of his actions. But his life and his choices challenged me. Would I be willing to stand up for what I believed? Would I go to jail for my values?

To this day I don't know. But whenever I have a decision to make and support, I think of Frank. Nobody is threatening to throw me in prison, but I would like to think that if I truly believed in a cause, I would be as true to my values as Frank was to his.

I realized a long time ago that a belief which does not spring from a conviction in the emotions is no belief at all.

—EVELYN SCOTT

GIRL TALK #161: Today I will become more flexible as I work to take the stress out of my life.

Attitudes produce stress. They clutter our lives with conflict. When we get rid of strong opinions and learn to go with the flow, life truly does become easier. Here are some attitude adjusters that may help you have a more relaxing time.

1. Drop your pretense. Be natural, be yourself.
2. Try not to worry. It's a useless emotion.
3. Learn to enjoy daily routines, even if they are dull.
4. Try not to live in fear that there's not enough. There is plenty to go around. It comes when you need it.
5. Think of a day as twenty-four silver dollars. Spend them wisely.
6. Accept the fact that change is good and steadfast habits are self-defeating for personal growth.
7. Act promptly—avoid procrastination, which is a major stress factor.
8. Workaholics must learn to slow down. You are worthwhile even if you're not producing every minute.

There. Now have a relaxing day. Take a few of your silver dollars and go shopping. Buy yourself something nice or try something new and different.

Adjust your attitude—surprise someone.

Explore daily the will of God.

—CARL JUNG

GIRL TALK #162: Today I will begin to keep track of where my dollars, quarters, dimes and nickels go.

Sexuality was the topic of a seminar I was conducting a few years ago. Halfway through the lecture, a woman raised her hand and asked me a question about money. I answered, then moved back to my material. Apparently the question sparked the interest of the audience, and soon queries about money began to multiply. When I asked why they were so interested, the women said they could learn about sexuality elsewhere, but they wanted to know how I managed to achieve financial independence as a woman.

The rest of the seminar was on finances.

I told them I began keeping track of every dime I spent. For ninety days straight I logged all incoming and outgoing money. I found out quickly that money goes out faster than it comes in. Impulse spending was my worst problem, and I had to learn to budget my cash more prudently.

It's a very good idea for every one of us to keep track of our funds, at least for three months, to see where and how it is spent. And don't forget the little things like tolls, tips, magazines, packs of gum and snacks.

Once you see the pattern, you'll be able to set a budget so the income outweighs the outflow. Then you'll be on your way to financial independence.

I do want to get rich but I never want to do what there is to do to get rich.

—GERTRUDE STEIN

169

GIRL TALK #163: Today I will think about my health and plan to take a daily walk. If it's a hardship to make it on a given day, that's okay. But I will strive for regularity.

Some days are windy, others are cold. Still others are perfect, with clear skies, crisp air and a sun that is neither too hot nor too cold. No matter what the weather, I try to take a daily walk. I'm up to three miles now, which seems to take forever when the wind is blowing. When it's misty, there is a feeling of mystery. And on sunny, bright days I am inspired and filled with awe at the glorious mountains in the distance and the small, colorful flowers at my feet.

I've put together several walking tapes that keep me entertained during my special meditation times. There are no phones, no pagers, no faxes or letters to read. This is my own personal time.

Some days I walk with no music at all. I let my mind relax and unwind, playing itself like a worn-out record. Yet I always come back home with my problems resolved, and my soul nourished.

'Tis peace of mind, lad, we must find.

—THEOCRITUS

GIRL TALK #164: Today I will reflect on where I am at forty. Am I going up the mountain, at the top, or coming down? What does midlife mean to me?

The decade of one's forties can be viewed as reaching life's midpoint. There is no momentous celebration for this transition, yet each of us feels it in some way. The questions that came to my mind when I reached that point were:

- What have I done up until now?
- Am I in a relationship or job I want to stay in?
- How can I better use my knowledge and resources?
- Do I want to try another path and see what is out there?

The forties start the process of serious thinking about our future; deadlines seem more real and a bit closer. If you've waited to start a family, the biological clock is ticking faster. Professional careers are reaching a point where major decisions must be made.

Physically speaking, we begin to notice changes. Gray hairs are sprouting, the skin is showing small lines on our arms, legs and face. There is a thickening at the waist, no matter how hard we work out at the gym. Menopause is around the corner and hot flashes may have already begun, or the dreaded night sweats. It's the end of growing up and the beginning of growing old.

On the other hand, this is the most optimistic time of life. The knowledge and wisdom you have gained can be put to good use. If you've had children, they are on their way toward independence and your time is your own. Chances are you have a wide network of friends and coworkers. If you are really lucky, you have a spouse or partner with whom you can share quality time.

Taking care of your body and keeping a positive mental outlook during your forties can make this the prime of your life. Put worries aside and concentrate on the goals that you set for yourself in your thirties. Enjoy your children and your loved ones. Take one day at a time and know the best years still lie ahead.

The hero is no braver than the ordinary man,
but he is braver five minutes longer.

—RALPH WALDO EMERSON

GIRL TALK #165: Today I will examine some of my comfort rituals.

Comfort is something we all need. Sometimes it's plentiful, at other times it seems scarce. I need it most at the end of a long, hard day; when I am depressed or lonely; during a time of transition such as a move, a divorce, or a job change.

Comfort rituals help us take care of our needs and nurture ourselves on a regular basis. Each person has their own idea of comfort but I'll share some of mine.

- In the morning, when I don't have to rush off, I have coffee and toast in bed while I read the paper. But every day, no matter what my schedule, I spend a few minutes with my meditation angel who says, "A day hemmed in prayer is less likely to unravel."
- During the day if I need a pat on the back, I go to my comfort trunk, which contains little gifts to myself: books by my favorite authors, a box of chocolates, choice CDs, a few inspirational items and a bottle of fragrant lotion. I close my eyes, stick my hand into this grab bag and treat myself.
- At bedtime I take a hot bath with aromatic oils or a scented candle nearby. I have a small waterfall fountain that I turn on (or you can leave the faucet running). The sound of moving water is relaxing.

Taking responsibility for ourselves helps us connect with our inner self and the spirit that keeps us going.

If you can imagine it, you can achieve it.
If you can dream it, you can become it.
—WILLIAM ARTHUR WARD

GIRL TALK #166: Today I will address an impossible situation. Maybe I will be able to solve the problem this time.

Experiential therapy is a type of powerful psychodrama that is used to allow people to reenact a part of their lives that they consider to be unfinished business. There is a lot of role playing, and we often use props and costumes to help move the action along.

At our treatment facility in the Black Hills, we had a prop room with a variety of costumes—Easter Bunny, Santa Claus, military outfits—as well as a mix of outrageous female garments, most of which I am embarrassed to admit were mine at one time or another.

It was the last day of April and we were dressed in shorts and T-shirts, setting up a new program. We were totally unprepared for the blizzard that swept down from Canada and blanketed the roads, making travel impossible. There was nothing else we could do but hunker down for the night. The facility had extra toothbrushes, pillows and blankets. But no one had clean clothes. Then we remembered the prop room.

Needless to say, after we showered and cleaned up, we reassembled in the main room, and what a sight we were— Santas, bunnies, vampires, 1950s guys and dolls, farmers and a five-star general! It was an evening nobody will ever forget.

Life is what happens to you when
you're making other plans.

—John Lennon

GIRL TALK #167: Today I will meditate on the dynamics of my family and take an honest look at the connections. I will make a commitment not to play into unhealthy situations.

My father was my hero. It's a common phenomenon for a "Daddy's little girl" to worship him with awe. Sometimes a father even diverts some of his affection and attention from the mother to the daughter. It does not take long before the little girl realizes the power she has over Daddy and sometimes uses it to manipulate the family. In the early stages, everyone's needs are met. But as time passes, problems begin to arise.

Mother begins to feel left out. A subtle, covert resentment can develop toward both father and daughter. She can act out this anger in coldness rather than words. Sometimes the quality of the marriage relationship lessens. The daughter may act like a mini-wife. She may also rebel against the responsibility placed on her shoulders, but not know what sets off her hostility.

The father then has two angry women on his hands, so he either withdraws from both or takes turns supporting one, then the other. Everyone gets hurt.

The power structure is also askew. Siblings are left out of the "inner circle," and family business is conducted from father to daughter to mother, and lastly to the siblings.

On Father's Day, take a moment to reflect on your own father and the dynamics of your family. There may be many unresolved issues still brewing inside you. Outside help may be required to untangle the web that has been woven.

That's the risk you take if you change, that the people you've been involved with won't like the new you. But other people who do will come along.

—LISA ALTHER

GIRL TALK #168: Today I will think about special places. In particular I will recall the good times I've had at Rutlen's Bed-and-Breakfast.

My aunt and uncle in Colorado run an unusual bed-and-breakfast inn. It's not for the public; it's strictly for family and friends to share.

The home is a spacious five-bedroom, four-bath, two-story structure nestled in a large yard of full-grown trees. There is a porch, deck and patio. Just beyond lies a golf course and inside is a welcoming fireplace. The home is always filled with the aroma of cooking.

The house is special, but it's because of the people who live there. They have offered their home to generations of family and a wide variety of friends. At certain times in our lives my mother, my grandmother, my son and I all lived with this aunt and uncle. There are guests almost every weekend, summer and winter.

There's an extra car in the garage and plenty of food in the freezer. Conversation always includes catching up on family news and discussions of world events. It's fascinating to hear so many ideas and beliefs being tossed about and accepted without hard feelings by anyone. We are always grateful for a chance to gather at this sacred spot in the Colorado mountains, where love and sharing are the first order of business.

Today I will believe that as I give to the world, the world will give to me.

—ERNEST LARSEN

GIRL TALK #169: Today I will look at the qualities of a spiritual warrior and assess whether I am one or not.

To live one's life means making choices. The decision to go forward and care for oneself, by necessity, becomes a spiritual journey. Those who are successful have a few traits in common:

1. They don't try to fit into the lifestyle molds of others.
2. They march to their own beat.
3. They are willing to change, if necessary, and make improvements.
4. They take risks and learn from their mistakes.
5. They trust in themselves.
6. They live in the present, not the past or the future.
7. They don't get bogged down in things they cannot change.
8. They accept pain as a valuable lesson.
9. They lead simple lives.
10. They shed excess emotional baggage as quickly as possible.
11. They make choices and set boundaries.
12. They accept their own goodness and know their self-worth.
13. They appreciate the effort of others.

Those who go through the war of life take responsibility to live as fully and as richly as possible. These spiritual warriors find the rewards are plentiful.

> *Plant your own garden and decorate your*
> *own soul, instead of waiting for*
> *someone to send you flowers.*
>
> —VERONICA SHOFFSTALL

GIRL TALK #170: Today I will look at my body and decide to take a proactive part on behalf of my own wellness. If there are any problems, I promise to seek professional advice.

Over the past few decades, research has proved there is a mind/body connection when it comes to certain diseases. In other words, the mind can help make the body ill, or it can help make it well.

A personality profile of a cancer patient often includes unexpressed anger, pessimism about life and a feeling of helplessness and lost hope. Major stress or grief can trigger the onset of diseases, including cancer. And a person who becomes focused solely on caring for and about others runs the risk of developing a cancer-prone personality.

In time the physiology of this person changes. The immune system becomes weakened, T-cell activity is decreased and there is an abnormally high hormone secretion.

Optimism and hope are two primary factors in healing. It's important to express anger and to take charge of one's life. Avoid toxic situations and people. To help avoid the onset of illness, act assertively and give up feelings of lost power and hope. Laugh your cares away.

Meeting the challenge of cancer produces
wisdom and strength.

—A CANCER SURVIVOR

GIRL TALK #171: Today I will get my finances in order. Money makes money and I am responsible for seeing that my money is used in the most profitable way.

Have you heard about the Beardstown Ladies? If not, let me tell you about this remarkable group of women who pooled their resources and talent to make a bundle of money.

Each of them put in twenty-five dollars. Then they used their savvy and common sense to invest that money in the stock market. The gamble paid off. Not only did they make a huge profit on their investment; they wrote a bestseller about their experiences and sold well over 300,000 copies.

The Beardstown Ladies inspired me to take a closer look at my own investments and also to write this piece. Here's their advice for investing:

- Organize your own club.
- Develop a plan.
- Find companies and research them.
- Become informed.
- Choose a responsible broker.

I'd like to add one more. Get a copy of their book, *The Beardstown Ladies' Common-Sense Investment Guide.* Then live by their motto: "If we can do it, you can do it, too."

It is good to have an end to journey towards,
but it is the journey that
matters, in the end.

—URSULA K. LE GUIN

GIRL TALK #172: Today I will start an album of photos. My efforts will be to keep that album current.

My family and friends have spent many wonderful hours recalling the good old days by leafing through my photo journals. I am proud that I've kept them up to date. Too often we postpone recording special events until we have the time to do it perfectly. Then it simply doesn't get done at all.

I always have an empty album ready for the photos when I get them back from being developed. I put in a short description of the trip so we can all remember. If I have more time I embellish with anecdotes.

History comes alive when we sit down and look at the pictures. The albums are treasures, worth far more than their weight in gold. When my grandchildren come for an extended visit, I order triple copies of all the pictures we take and make a mini-album for each family. Long before children can read, they can begin to treasure memories through photos. These books have bonded our families together.

It is not that I belong to the past,
but the past belongs to me.

—MARY ANTIN

GIRL TALK #173: I think I'll learn to accept when I make mistakes and not be so hard on myself.

The first addition to my Black Hills home was a meditation room and an indoor hot tub. It was a wonderful treat to soak in the tub, especially after a grueling day.

We had a revolving group of therapists from the center visiting at our home. Some were newcomers and others had been there a while. All the therapists would gather in the water to share the events of the day. On one occasion three gals and one guy were in the tub wearing their bathing suits when a new counselor arrived. He strolled around the room looking at the photos, then slipped a tape in the player and got in the tub. He was totally nude and completely at ease.

One of the women came rushing to my husband. "I don't know what to say to him and I don't know where to look!" she pleaded. My husband brought him a cover-up and suggested a walk. He asked him why he was nude. He said that in California, where he came from, they don't bother with bathing suits.

My husband lent him a pair of trunks and he returned to the group. We all shared what we were feeling and the counselor learned the Midwest is a bit more conservative than the West Coast.

All growth is a leap in the dark, a spontaneous
unpremeditated act without
benefit of experience.

—Henry Miller

GIRL TALK #174: Today I will lessen my fears of change and begin to believe that my destiny is unfolding as it is meant to. I will remain secure in the process.

Turning points come when we least expect them. They may be as gentle as a moment of clarity that nudges us in a different direction. Often we don't understand what is happening. We only know we have been touched and re-directed. If we follow our hearts and intuition, life unfolds in an exciting and wondrous way.

Or turning points can be like a smack in the face: a profound and serious jolt like an accident, illness, job loss, divorce or death. In those cases, the path we are led to may not be one we would have willingly chosen. We are challenged to question our beliefs and the meaning of life.

My earliest turning point was the realization that both my parents were alcoholics. Through this insight I learned to care for myself at an early age. My father's suicide helped me develop inner strength. My daughter's serious illness made me face my fear and develop a new kind of compassion. And my most recent trauma with breast cancer helped me conquer my own anxiety about death.

These pivotal points in our lives help us grow and learn. We can fall victim to their negative power, or we can harness it and turn it into a positive learning experience. We can resist and fight or we can surrender and welcome the gift of change.

The years forever fashion new dreams when old
ones go. God pity the one-dream man.

—ROBERT GODDARD

GIRL TALK #175: Today I'll think about my family and the families of my friends and our stepchildren. I will learn to be especially sensitive to everyone who is trying to adjust to new relationships.

Having a baby gives us a chance to incorporate a child into our lives gradually. But having a child, even a young one, enter our world through marriage is quite another matter.

These little human beings come complete with attitudes, feelings and personalities. Sometimes they mesh with ours, sometimes they clash. Finding acceptance and a common meeting ground is a major passage that all parties must go through.

When communication is open and trust is offered, the transition can be smooth. When there are secrets and manipulation, everyone expects the worst. They are rarely disappointed. Too often there are no winners.

The birth parent feels guilty and angry that his or her spouse is not being received openly and fairly by the existing children. The new spouse feels rejected and hurt. The children are confused and want things to be the way they once were. But some things that are broken cannot be fixed. They are forever altered, and everyone must learn to work with the new configuration.

It takes a great deal of openness, flexibility, effort and adaptability to make a stepfamily work in a positive way. These are complex times and this is a complex dynamic. But it can be done. It has worked in my case and it can work in yours. It takes determination and set limits, especially in terms of what is expected of the children.

Fear makes strangers of people who should be friends.
—SHIRLEY MacLAINE

GIRL TALK #176: Today I'll exercise some patience. It might be a struggle, but now is the time to try.

Patience is a worthwhile quality for which to strive. With insight and practice, it can become a regular habit. When we try to be tolerant, our lives are more peaceful.

Driving can be especially trying for me. When I am behind the wheel I am not always the calm, cool, collected Sharon people know. Certainly I'm not the only one who becomes impatient when traffic moves too slowly. When I feel impatient, I do my best to be extra courteous on the road.

A trainer once suggested that to develop patience I let someone with fewer items go through the grocery checkout line before me. I've tried it on occasion and it not only surprises a perfect stranger, it lets me know that I can be tolerant.

Projects are another trying period for me. I know they take time but I want instant gratification. Of course, I know that doing things well does not mean just getting the job done. It means taking care to craft it carefully.

So whether we are doing projects, working on relationships, planting a garden or whatever, patience is a quality to cultivate patiently.

> *Have patience with all things but*
> *first of all with yourself.*
>
> —Saint Francis de Sales

GIRL TALK #177: Today I will think about mothers and daughters.

There are many reasons a mother might not be around to support a daughter. Sometimes the mother is not emotionally capable of dealing with the endless problems of child rearing. More commonly, the mother is drug- or alcohol-dependent, depressed or mentally ill. When the mother detaches from the child physically or emotionally, that child is frightened, lonely and unhappy. In extreme cases abuse is present, and trauma is so deeply inflicted that it will take years of therapy to release the demons and heal the wounds.

Children are amazingly resilient. They have the ability to rebound, mature and become productive members of society and healthy, happy individuals. Outside agencies are important for impacting the child in a positive way. The National Association for Children of Alcoholics is an excellent resource.

When a mother dies, the loss is staggering. When the bond is close, the child stands the best chance of emerging from the trauma with the ability to love again. A caregiver must allow the child to grieve in order to recover fully. There is no time limit for grief. But if the mother/child relationship is not good, the child will be filled with guilt and remorse that will require professional help to heal.

All that applies to the absent mother applies equally well to absent fathers.

She wanted a happy world
and everyone in it happy, but she was at
a loss as to how to accomplish this.

—ANNE EDWARDS

GIRL TALK #178: A trip to Hawaii is something I will think about today. It is a place to replenish the spirit.

No trip to Hawaii is complete without a walk through a dormant volcano. It's like being on a foreign planet as we walk along Devastation Trail, through areas where lava has pushed through foliage and frozen in time under a crusty, hard shell. Where the areas were inhabited, the lava covers stop signs, benches and anything else that was in its path. The black obsidian, a dark volcanic rock resembling glass, sparkles in the sun.

Lava reminds me that nature and creation continue no matter what stands in their way. At the active volcano site, eruptions give warning that lava is coming. It flows steadily but slowly, warning everyone in its way to get out!

Whenever my soul needs refreshing, I head for Hawaii, where the splendor and majesty of nature is unparalleled. There, I always find a little sapling or flower that has somehow managed to push through the glass-like lava, as though to say, "I won't die!"

It's an important message. We can survive even the most destructive of nature's forces. What it takes is courage, tenacity and strength.

> *The sign must come like dawn.*
> *You cannot see its arrival, but you*
> *know when it is there.*
>
> —DIANE W.

GIRL TALK #179: Today I will care for myself in the way I need. Can I protect myself from stressful relationships and situations?

I met Grace Gawler after one of my lectures when she handed me a copy of *Women of Silence*. "I've come all the way from Australia to meet you," she said.

During the many discussions that followed our initial introduction, we connected at a very deep level. We shared stories about breast cancer patients we had both known. And we agreed that more research needs to be done to fully understand the impact of this disease on a woman's psyche.

We recognized that women need to fight back and never give up. "They need fire in their souls and passion in their hearts," Grace said.

"They need to release the negative emotional energy that is bottled up inside and eats away at them," I added.

Grace believes that women who cannot say no to others are prime candidates for becoming cancer victims. "Say NO to cancer!" she states emphatically.

From Grace I am inspired to care for myself in new ways. I have taken her suggestion seriously and now say NO when I don't want to do something. I stay away from caustic people. I am the only one who is responsible for my well-being. I intend to see that I stay healthy and my happiness remains intact.

I like living. I have sometimes been wildly, despairingly,
acutely miserable, rocked with sorrow, but through
it all I still know quite certainly that
just to be alive is a grand thing.

—AGATHA CHRISTIE

GIRL TALK #180: Today I will think about giving back to the world in a positive way.

While we're on the subject of cancer, one of the best ways to give back to the community is with a fundraising walk. I join the Race for the Cure for Breast Cancer, but there are many others you can join. And you don't have to be a cancer survivor to be part of the cause.

Each year more than 3,000 walkers get together early on a Saturday morning for a three-mile walk. The breast cancer survivors wear pink headbands to proclaim their victory. Others have pink armbands or other signs with the name of a survivor or someone who didn't make it. The walkers come in all ages, both genders and varying states of health. There are elderly ladies, young mothers pushing babies in strollers and a legless man in a wheelchair. Some are fresh from chemotherapy, with no hair as their symbol of success.

Whatever your cause of choice, community events like this feed the soul. And when you sign up, remember Helen Keller's courageous words:

> *I put my hand in yours and together we can do what we could never do alone. No longer is there a sense of hopelessness. No longer must we depend upon our own unsteady will power. We are all together now, reaching out for power and strength greater than ours. And as we join together, we find love and understanding beyond our wildest dreams.*

Courage is grace under pressure.
—Ernest Hemingway

GIRL TALK #181: Today I will prepare myself for the things I want in life because I'll never know for sure when I'll get the chance to shine.

For many years I was on the road nearly nonstop. Although I was weary and wanted to return home, it would cause a crisis if I canceled a sold-out workshop. The demands were heavy and the stress level high. It was obvious I had to train a replacement, just in case I couldn't "go on with the show."

Two women were chosen to come with me and learn how I presented a workshop. We had reached the point of being ready to send these women out on their own. They knew the content; all they needed was the experience.

In Oklahoma City, I checked into the hotel with one of the ladies. When I awoke the next morning I had the flu. I simply couldn't get up. The sponsors said 200 participants expected me. We were all in a fluster, until I had a brilliant idea. My trainee was about my size; she even looked a bit like me. She knew the material and, quite frankly, we had no choice.

An hour later she was Sharon Wegscheider! The workshop was a success, and the participants were overjoyed at having met me—until she told them the truth, that she was posing as Sharon Wegscheider. Surprisingly, they took it quite well and, in fact, told her they enjoyed the workshop immensely. When I recovered I wrote a personal note to all 200 participants, thanking them for their acceptance of my replacement and for having such a good sense of humor.

Fortune and love befriend the bold.

—OVID

GIRL TALK #182: Today I will think about kindness and how it can help others feel good. From this day forward I will make kindness part of my style.

Kindness is a quality of goodness. Those who volunteer their time to help others, caregivers, and those who relieve stress by running errands, baby-sitting, typing a letter or making a meal all exhibit a kindness of heart.

A good friend in Chicago drives children to the local prison so they can visit their mothers who are behind bars. Another friend sings and plays his guitar to children in hospitals. Still another visits nursing homes and helps the patients write notes and send cards to loved ones. I keep bags of treats on hand for children who visit and small cards of inspiration to mail to those who need support. These acts of kindness make the world a better place in which to live.

From our earliest years we can practice goodness. There are thousands of ways, even without actions—a word of support or encouragement will accomplish the same thing.

It's not hard to be kind. It costs nothing and it means so much. If you can find two situations a day in which to show a bit of goodness toward others, every day will be worthwhile.

Three things in human life are important.
The first is to be kind. The second is to be kind.
And the third is to be kind.

—HENRY JAMES

GIRL TALK #183: Today I will look back at the moves I have made.

Some of my friends and family live in the same town where they were born. They have never moved. Others have lived in so many places that I've lost count.

Moving can be a frightening and exciting experience. You leave your roots and the people you've grown up with, but you go out into the world and meet new friends. At seventeen I moved from a tiny town to a major city. It was a monumental change in my life, establishing myself with new doctors, a dentist, a bank, an accountant, dry cleaners, grocery stores and so on.

Those in the military and many corporate executives take moving as an everyday part of life. It's no big deal. But for most of us it is a challenge of tremendous proportions—not only the actual, physical packing and transporting of household goods, but the search for a suitable place to live at the other end. Then getting accustomed to the local customs.

Moving is a wonderful way to become more open and accepting of others. Geographic moves produce personal growth and a broader frame of reference, both of which are positive attributes. And it's marvelous to see other parts of the country and the world.

Fortunately psychoanalysis is not the only way
to resolve inner conflicts. Life itself still
remains a very effective therapist.

—KAREN HORNEY

GIRL TALK #184: Today I will be captain of my own ship and chart a journey that will bring me to the destination of my choosing.

I was in California one summer feeling misunderstood and overwhelmed. Then a friend talked me into going to hear Terry Cole-Whitaker, who was lecturing at a church service. Although I didn't want to go, I have been eternally grateful that I did.

Terry's basic premise is that we are born perfect, with unlimited potential. Through negative circumstances we learn to limit our own development. Terry contends that we all have the power of choice and the freedom to take charge of our lives. From Terry I learned the difference between real and false guilt.

Real guilt stems from intentionally hurting someone else. False guilt is when others try to manipulate us into feeling bad about ourselves. From Terry I also learned to take risks—to go beyond my comfort zone.

"If you are to reach your potential, you must live life to the fullest," she said. "And behind every risk is the opportunity to learn from your mistakes."

At the time I heard Terry speak, I was frozen with fear. Through her words I came to understand that I am the captain of my own ship, and where I choose to take myself is where I will end up. So now I know and I'll pass that on to you: Every woman's journey is of her own choosing.

When one is a stranger to oneself, then
one is estranged from others, too.
—ANNE MORROW LINDBERGH

GIRL TALK #185: Today I will plan a few small vacations for the rest of the summer and let myself be refreshed.

July Fourth is the official kickoff of the summer vacation season. This is the time when Americans pack their suitcases and camping gear and look forward to a change of scenery and a relaxing time. Others like to kick back, stay at home and do nothing special, or nothing at all. No matter what you do, the main thing is that you return to your regular routine refreshed, reenergized and contented.

If money is a consideration, look around your hometown. Usually there are many things to do within a twenty-mile radius. You can even spend one night away, in a different town, exploring the shops and museums, if there are any. Have a leisurely dinner, take a stroll, go to a movie. Have room service bring breakfast the next morning. You'll feel as though you've been gone for a week by going away for one night!

If you're planning to fly, book as far ahead of time as possible to get the best price. Airlines also have tie-ins with rental car companies, so always ask for their discount.

Camping is another low-cost way to get back to nature. If you don't have the equipment, you can rent it or borrow it so there's no huge investment. There's nothing as refreshing as waking up to the sounds of nature. So have a great summer vacation, and have fun without going into debt!

> *Vacations stir up the blood, expand the chest,*
> *electrify the nerves, clear cobwebs from the brain,*
> *and rejuvenate the whole system.*

—ANONYMOUS

GIRL TALK #186: Today I'll worry less about clothes if I'm invited somewhere. It's enough just to be myself.

I was invited to be the opening speaker at the annual conference on Addiction and Families, which was held in Colorado Springs, Colorado. I received an invitation to a special country-western gala after the program. I was looking forward to wearing a new cowgirl outfit that had been given to me by some Texas friends. The genuine outfit garb included a denim hat with a colorful pheasant feather band, a jeans outfit and beautiful navy boots with turquoise snakeskin inserts. Since it was difficult to fold—especially the hat and boots—I packed my presentation clothes and wore the cowgirl outfit on the plane. Before the flight was over, I'd been dubbed "Loretta Lynn."

So you can imagine my horror when I arrived at the airport and found my luggage was missing. It would not arrive until the next day. The only clothes I had were on my back and I was due on stage in an hour. Since there was no time to buy a new outfit, and since the hotel wasn't in the clothing rental business, I ran a comb through my hair, freshened my makeup and decided to make the best of it. The audience was appreciative and, in fact, gave me a standing ovation.

And here's the lesson: It's not the clothes that count, but the woman inside them!

> *When you do something you are proud of,*
> *dwell on it a little, praise yourself for it.*
> —Mildred Newman

GIRL TALK #187: Today I will pay attention to my worries for fifteen minutes. Then I will stop wasting my time with them the rest of the day.

Worry is a waste of time that interferes with daily living and takes away from the enjoyment of life. It keeps us awake at night and distracts us when we drive. Excessive worry interferes with our health and our relationships. But it accomplishes nothing!

Therefore, it makes sense to set aside no more than ten minutes a day and get it over with. Keep a pad or Post-it Notes near your "worry spot" and document all those things you are troubled with. If you really want to be productive with your worry time, try to find a workable solution to your dilemmas.

Once the ten minutes are over, leave your worry spot and do not think about any of those things until your next scheduled appointment.

Worry does nothing constructive. So if you feel you must fret over something, select a time and a place and just do it. Then let it go and move on with your life!

It is those who have a deep and real inner life
who are best able to deal with the
irritating details of outer life.

—EVELYN UNDERHILL

GIRL TALK #188: Today I will have a little chat with God through a prayer. It may be short and simple— a reconnection with my Higher Power that feeds my soul.

Prayer is simply talking to God. Prayers come in all shapes and sizes, in all languages and lengths. The Lord's Prayer is one of the most famous, and it was helpful for me when I was growing up.

Worship brings people together in a spirit of support and love. This is the Serenity Prayer: "God grant me serenity to accept the things I cannot change/Courage to change the things I can/And the wisdom to know the difference."

Most of us wait for a catastrophe to pray for guidance or help. But we don't need a special connection. In fact, a simple thank-you invocation at the end of each day will help you feel a spirituality that might be missing in your life. For whatever problems you may have, there are a thousand things to be thankful for.

Talking to God or Buddha, or whoever is your Higher Power, will help you unburden yourself and give you courage to face the day. So start today, say a prayer. You don't need anything longer than the one set out above. You can use that until you develop your own.

> *Without prayer, I should have been*
> *a lunatic long ago.*
>
> —MAHATMA GANDHI

GIRL TALK #189: Today I will address the type A part of my personality and make small changes that will bring me more relaxation and comfort in my life.

Studies have shown a link between coronary disease and certain types of behavior. The type A personality is fast-moving, aggressive and competitive. In work and relationships there is a pattern of joyless striving. Emphasis is on future goals, gaining status and financial rewards. This person tends to hold anger and resentment. Grievances pile up and multiply, for there isn't time for this person to work anything out. Type As are referred to as workaholics.

Type A people cannot relax. So their blood pressure rises, their hearts beat faster and there is vascular constriction. Eventually the heart is damaged and it breaks down.

Pressure-reducing activities are a priority for type A personalities. The best stressbusters are exercise, optimism, yoga, hot baths, breathing exercises and reading.

If you are a type A person, photocopy this page and tack it to the refrigerator as a reminder to slow down. If you know someone who fits this description, send that person a copy. You might save a life—it may even be your own.

Don't be afraid your life will end, be
afraid that it will never begin.
—GRACE HANSEN

GIRL TALK #190: Today I will get my financial affairs in order.

Over the years, and through hard work, I have been able to get ahead financially. Here are some of my tips to help you reach your own level of economic security and independence.

1. Pay off credit cards. Charge only what you can afford.
2. Eliminate debt as quickly as possible. Reduce interest payments.
3. Keep a minimum balance in your checking account to avoid service charges, which can add up to a whopping $200 per year.
4. If you can take public transportation, use it.
5. Repair and keep an older car instead of buying a new one. This will also save on insurance.
6. Eliminate frequent trips to the store. Shop once a week to save time and money.
7. Be good to yourself so you don't get sick. Doctors' bills, medicine and time away from work all cost money.
8. If you are living comfortably, stay put. You don't really need a bigger, fancier house, do you?
9. Use the library for books.
10. Limit impulse spending—in other words, stay away from the mall! If you need something, shop wisely and compare prices.

A penny saved is a penny earned.

—Old Maxim

GIRL TALK #191: Today I will honor the rituals in my life, even if they might seem strange or odd to others. It only matters that they have meaning to me.

R ituals can become habits that may seem odd to people at times. Take my husband, for instance. Whenever we fly anywhere together, he grasps my hand at takeoff and holds on tight until we level off. He knows this gives me a great deal of comfort and he is more than willing to comply.

Business often takes him on trips that do not include me. And rituals become strong habits that are hard to break.

He was on an airplane seated next to a businessman in the first-class cabin. As the plane started down the runway preparing for takeoff, he automatically reached out and grasped the man's hand. He held it a minute before the man pulled away and asked, "What are you afraid of?"

Through his embarrassment, my husband explained my nervousness at takeoffs and how he held my hand as solace.

"My wife holds my hand, too," said the stranger, laughing.

The rest of the ride was uneventful, but it can be comforting to know that there are others who share a similar ritual.

They love the best who love with compassion.

—ELLEN ANNE HILL

GIRL TALK #192: This is the day to think about the special projects I've been putting off.

Teaching at the local university was a second job I had while raising my three children. The extra income went a long way with helping me stay within my tight budget. During that time I put together several handouts containing original material about family dynamics and the topics we were covering. It cost quite a bit to photocopy, so I decided to put them together into a little booklet and sell them to the students and anyone else who was interested.

Since time was short, I gave the job of finding a printer and distributing the booklets to my daughters, who were fourteen and sixteen at the time. I paid them a salary to complete the job.

Over the next eight years, the Nurturing Networks company expanded and grew. My daughters learned how to print, market and distribute the booklets through bulk mail services. They worked for NN throughout their college years and sold thousands of booklets.

From this invaluable experience we learned it was possible to start from scratch, and that three women could run a successful company. It took time, determination and focus. It also shows that you can do whatever you want when you put your mind to it.

The pessimist sees the difficulty in every opportunity, the optimist sees the opportunity in every difficulty.

—L. P. JACKS

GIRL TALK #193: It's time to reflect on gratitude. Today is a good day to start plans and take care of unfinished business.

In the 1980s, adults who had grown up in abusive and dysfunctional homes began to meet in support groups to share things they had kept secret for years. At the first national conference held at the Princess Hotel in Scottsdale, Arizona, it was my honor to be chairperson. Nearly 2,000 people filled the large conference area. The crowd emanated fear, excitement, trust and hope.

This was a historic moment. Never had this many people joined together to share their painful stories with others. It was the first step for many of them in healing the past and moving on with their lives.

As Whitney Houston sang "The Greatest Love of All," we stood, held hands and sang along. The love and optimism were overpowering. That moment will stay with me forever, and I'm certain that every person in that auditorium will remember it also.

We don't know how lucky we are.

—ANONYMOUS

GIRL TALK #194: I will mark all important dates on my calendar today. I will also buy a box of greeting cards to use for special occasions.

One of the greatest bonds that link people is sending and receiving greeting cards. Cards do not have to be limited to birthdays, anniversaries or special occasions. They can be sent for colds, for fun or for no reason at all. I try to sit down on the first day of every month and write out the cards that I'll need for birthdays and so on. Then I put a stamp on and mark the date it is to be mailed.

When I know a friend or relative is going through a bad time, I pull out a generic card or a blank card and write my own thoughts inside. I can even generate them on my computer.

The post office loves me since I send out so much mail. And it gives me a tremendous feeling of satisfaction knowing I am brightening someone's day. If you like to receive cards as much as I do, try sending some. What goes around comes around, and you'll soon find your mailbox full of cheery greetings.

> *When people are loving, brave, truthful,*
> *charitable, God is present.*
> —HAROLD KUSHNER

GIRL TALK #195: Today I will celebrate the stage of maturity where I am and wait to see what the next stage will be.

I thought I was mature when I got my driver's license. A whole new life opened, filled with responsibility and freedom. I thought I had reached full maturity on my wedding day.

Other milestone times included the birth of my children, college graduation, the formation of my own professional company, the first book I published, the painful time of divorce, the joy of finding a soul mate, the joy of becoming a grandmother. With each of these happenings, I thought I had reached a new level of maturity. But now I know that although maturity means being fully developed physically, mentally and emotionally, we never really stop growing. There are deeper insights and new levels of understanding to be reached at different stages of our lives.

As long as we are willing to expand our minds, we will continue to mature. But just as peach trees don't blossom in the fall or bear fruit in the winter, we cannot rush the process. There is a time and a purpose to every level we reach. There is no way to rush ahead of the process, nor should we try. Gain every bit of experience from the stage you are in now. Learn and grow wise, then use that knowledge when you pass into the next phase of your life.

Maturity: a state of full development.

—Webster's Dictionary

GIRL TALK #196: Today I will vow to honor turning fifty with bright colors and a message of congratulations for earning that distinction.

The selection of birthday cards for fifty-year-olds is depressing. The over-the-hill and other gag cards make me angry. Why do people see it as a negative thing? Turning 50 and growing to 100 can be the best years of our lives.

The fifties are a time to reap the benefits of our hard work and enjoy the many friends we have made. If you are lucky, the fifties will bring you grandchildren, as they did for me—seven times over!

During my fifties I came face to face with my own mortality when I learned about my catastrophic illness. It made me slow down, evaluate my life and take a good look at what was important and what was not. I learned to simplify.

The fifties are a time for an attitude adjustment. You can either grow old gracefully or live life to the hilt, jamming every minute with projects, travel and pleasant company. The fifties can be greatly rewarding years, but it is also a time to make an absolute commitment to maintaining your health and exercising. With these two essential ingredients, the prognosis for the future is optimistic indeed.

The principle of life is that life responds by corresponding, your life becomes the thing you have decided it shall be.

—RAYMOND CHARLES BARKER

GIRL TALK #197: Today I will look at my relation-ships and pay attention to the needs of the individual and the couple.

Coupleship is a term I have coined for being more than just a couple. It's not you and it's not me. It's WE. Couple-ship is passionate, spiritual, emotional, sexual commit-ment between two people that nurtures both people and maintains a high regard for the value of each person.[3]

In my years as a therapist, I have found that most couples fall into one of four categories:

1. The fulfilled couple. Affectionate and sexual, good friends, similar values; mutual agreement on decisions that affect both parties.
2. The satisfied couple. Polite, convenient relationship, share hobbies, children, church; have many outside individual interests.
3. Low-energy couple. Once close, but no longer, many resentments and unresolved hurts; they stay together for the sake of the children.
4. Spiritually dead couple. Depressed, hurt, angry feelings have led to separate lifestyles; the relationship is non-sexual and with many secrets.

It is important for every couple to identify itself and then work on the coupleship—putting part of each person into the relation-ship and keeping part for each as individuals.

Above all, the soul, the self and the union must be nurtured and nourished individually.

It is the right of two committed people to form a relationship and build a life together.

—SHARON WEGSCHEIDER-CRUSE

3. Sharon Wegscheider-Cruse, *Coupleship* (Deerfield Beach, Florida: Health Communi-cations, 1988), p. 23.

GIRL TALK #198: I have passed through many stages in my life. Today I will think about where I am going personally and professionally.

After my divorce, guilt and sadness hung over me like a black cloud. I had little support from family and only a tad more from friends. For a while I lived in a world of loneliness, which was slowly but surely destroying me. Then I happened to pick up Gail Sheehy's book entitled *Passages*.

Through her words I learned about the power of true love. Her descriptions of caring, commitment and trust were filled with wisdom. From her I was able to understand the dynamics of my first marriage in a whole new way. I saw that it was not my fault that it didn't work. Thus, finally, it became easy to forgive myself for getting a divorce. I was also able to pat myself on the back for having the courage and insight to act on my feelings and stand up for what I believed to be right.

Sheehy puts into words what countless people think and feel. In her book *New Passages,* she suggests we shouldn't try to fit into old molds. Instead, we should customize our own lifestyle and life cycle. She challenges our old ways of thinking and behaving.

Her work is refreshing and inspiring to anyone who is struggling with guilt, self-worth issues, depression or love. She opens a world of new possibilities for us all to consider.

> *A bird does not sing because he has an answer.*
> *He sings because he has a song.*
>
> —JOAN WALCH ANGLAND

GIRL TALK #199: This is the day I'll check to see whether or not I really am an optimist. If I find I'm not, I'll turn myself around so I will be.

Not only do optimists live longer, they have fewer illnesses and more fun. They see the glass as half full, not half empty.

Nobody knows if people are born to be optimists or if it's a quality that is developed. But if you find that your view of the world is pessimistic, you will have to make a concentrated effort to change that way of thinking.

- Take the word *never* out of your vocabulary.
- Listen to your language: Is it positive or negative?
- Make a list of things you like about yourself.
- Add two more things every week and keep the list handy.
- Be kind to yourself.
- Learn from your mistakes, don't punish yourself for them.
- Be good to yourself.
- Try to see the up side to a situation, not the down side.

When life becomes promising, the world is a happier place in which to live. So dust off those rose-colored glasses and put them on. It's much more fun being an optimist.

> *Even if it is not fully attained, we become better by striving for the higher goal.*
>
> —VIKTOR FRANKL

GIRL TALK #200: Today I'll remember that asking people to see things my way may not be the right approach.

One of the projects I was involved with was the creation of an alcoholism treatment center in Austin, Texas. It was to be a first-class facility that would be housed in an old landmark house that would be restored to its original beauty. That meant raising money.

At that time alcoholism was still a closet secret for most families and individuals, especially in that area of the country. The woman who wanted to start the center knew quite a number of influential people in Dallas, so she threw a black-tie fund-raiser at her lavish apartment. She noted on the invitations that there would be entertainment.

Of course, everyone thought it would be a band or a singer. Were they surprised when they finished a five-course dinner and the lights dimmed. The hostess stood up to introduce the entertainment, and a spotlight shone on ME. I must admit I looked quite spectacular that night, in a white designer gown she had bought for me, complete with all the accessories.

Instead of being disappointed that there was a lecture instead of music, the audience stayed tuned in to my speech and applauded me with gusto at the end. They even left sizable donations for the project. I guess it's not what you say, but how it's said that really counts.

> *We all live in suspense, from day to day,*
> *from hour to hour; in other words, we*
> *are the hero of our own story.*
>
> —MARY McCARTHY

GIRL TALK #201: Entertainment is my goal for today, even if it's only reading the comics.

Entertainment is an important part of our lives. And it doesn't have to be expensive. Matinee movies are less expensive than at night, but if you have a large family, rent one for only a few dollars and make your own popcorn.

Want company? Throw a potluck dinner. Everyone comes out a winner, trying new dishes and enjoying good conversation.

Try the library for CDs, videos and books, all at no cost.

You can entertain yourself with a long, refreshing walk outside, or a bike ride, or sitting by the ocean, a lake or on top of a mountain.

Hobbies can be relaxing—knitting or crocheting, making miniature houses or putting together a puzzle. Playing cards alone or with a friend is also a good way to relax, and so are board games like Monopoly, Trivial Pursuit and Scrabble.

There are endless ways to entertain yourself. Don't wait for an invitation or sit at home feeling left out if the phone isn't ringing off the hook. Many of the suggestions above can be done alone. And if you want company, make a few calls and throw the potluck dinner. Whatever you do, just make sure to have fun doing it.

Performance: intended to amuse or divert;
recreation, pastime, sport.

—WEBSTER'S DICTIONARY

GIRL TALK #202: The soul has gifts, so today I will see if I can find what they are.

We hear the words "soul food," "soul music" or that a person "has soul." What exactly do they mean?

Experts say the soul can be defined as essence, vitality or spiritual force. Soul has passion that can be heard when a musician is totally immersed in his or her work. When my sister's garden blooms, it shows her soul. An old man sharing his life's stories is giving a part of his soul to others.

When we encounter a soulful experience, it touches us deeply.

Soul has nothing to do with wealth, power or education. It is the ability to express oneself with awareness and purpose. Spiritual sharing eventually becomes spiritual power; it shows a close link with God or with a Higher Power.

We all like to think we have soul. To determine whether or not we do takes long hours of introspection and commitment to becoming one with the universe. Sharing on a personal and positive level is the key. Soul food is prepared with love and devotion. Soul music offers one's spirituality in a musical format. Having soul is one of the best compliments a person can receive. I'd like to think I have soul. Do you?

It is never too early or too late to care
for the well-being of the soul.

—THOMAS MOORE

GIRL TALK #203: Today I will look at my image and be honest about what I see. I will not become part of the culture striving for ultra-thinness at the expense of my health.

The anxiety about being fat is a condition known as *anorexia nervosa*. Women can starve themselves to death in an effort to conform to what they perceive as society's obsession with thinness. While this is a real disease, the core of the illness is self-image.

The disease begins with anxiety about how one looks and escalates into an obsession. At the heart of the matter is extreme control over the food one eats (or doesn't eat). The anorexic derives her self-worth from being able to forgo food; she feels superior to those women who have to eat to survive.

Sometimes anorexics exercise to the point of exhaustion. Others gorge, then purge, adding *bulimia* to their list of unhealthy accomplishments. This killer disease destroys the body's delicate balance of vitamins and minerals, and it destroys organs, which are meant to process—not regurgitate food. Tooth enamel is decayed as stomach acid washes over the teeth when food is expelled.

This insidious disease can turn a slender, healthy woman into a sick, weak person. She becomes the opposite of what she wants to be. Wise is the woman who knows when to stop.

My darkness has been filled with the light of intelligence,
and behold, the outer daylight world was stumbling
and groping in social blindness.

—HELEN KELLER

GIRL TALK #204: I will commit myself to my work today and protect myself from professional abuse.

You can imagine my excitement when a national publisher approached me and asked me to write a book about family therapy. It was quite an honor and I was flattered. Then came the work. For eighteen months I wrote nonstop, even on flights and in strange hotel rooms where I was booked for speaking engagements.

At the time, I was an employee of an agency whose policy was that anyone planning to be published needed the approval of the company president. When the manuscript was ready, I presented it to him proudly. A great deal of time and effort had gone into making it just right.

"Rewrite it," he said. "I'm not happy with the copy."

I was shocked. But I did as I was told and presented it to him a second time. To my amazement, he said the same words to me again! So I asked other professionals to take a look at the book. Each one of them said it was ready for publication. So I returned for a third time to the president and asked him why he was being so obstinate. He told me that he didn't want my book published but if I was so determined, he'd give me a choice. I could keep my job or publish the book. Period. The decision was monumental. I needed the job, but a golden opportunity lay at my feet.

The rest is history. I left the job and published my book. It was the best thing I could have done for myself. The book became a bestseller and received many awards.

Success is to be measured not so much by the position that one has reached in life, as by the obstacles which were overcome while trying to succeed.
—BOOKER T. WASHINGTON

GIRL TALK #205: I'd like to make plans to do something special for two of my friends. Today is the day I will start.

W hen our friends go through rough times, we'd like to feel useful. There are many things we can do to make a difference. These are a few that I use:

1. Send a balloon or flower basket with an appropriate message.
2. Send a letter or colorful note.
3. Cut out cartoons or interesting articles and mail them regularly.
4. Deliver homemade or store-bought chicken soup.
5. Bring a video, a few books, little gifts or a complete dinner when visiting. Every bit helps.

When I was ill after my surgery, I loved it when friends brought dinner and stayed to share it. The company was as nourishing as the food. When I was well enough to go out again, my sister came over and took me out for ice cream and to the hairdresser for a cut and shampoo. Both treats lifted my spirits more than anyone can imagine.

So if you have a friend or relative who is ill or down in the dumps, get out there and be a pal. Use any of my suggestions or create your own. Just do it!

Always remember that no matter what the problem may be, there is an infinity of solutions.

—MARION WEINSTEIN

GIRL TALK #206: I'd like to think about the ways I can change my attitude. So today I will think about my approach to life and whether I've developed class.

When we hear someone say, "That person has class," or "She's a class act," what does that mean? A mentor of mine once said, "Class is the ability to face both the joy and pain of life with hope and love."

These are the things I believe constitute class:

- Being able to laugh at yourself
- Not accepting defeat
- Being sensitive to the needs of others
- Going beyond what is expected of you
- Acting appropriately in any situation
- Showing high quality and excellence at all times
- Remaining dignified even when embarrassed

There are hundreds of ways to show class. These are only a few. We should all examine our behavior from time to time to see if we are being classy or classless. As for me, I try to be the former and pray I'm never the latter.

Many persons strive for high ideals.
And everywhere life is full of heroism. In the noisy
confusion of life, keep peace with your soul.

—Desiderata

GIRL TALK #207: Airports are usually filled with stress. Today I will see them as an adventure.

As you have gathered from reading this book, much of my past twenty-five years has been spent in airports. Everywhere I look there are stories, some happy, some sad. One of my favorites happened a few years ago on a West Coast-to-Minnesota flight, with a stopover in Chicago. I boarded in Los Angeles. Across the aisle were four women in white nurse's outfits, each holding a beautiful Vietnamese baby. When we landed in Chicago, the flight attendant asked us to depart quickly since these babies were to be picked up by their adoptive parents.

After I deboarded, I watched the babies as they met their new fathers, mothers, siblings, aunts, uncles, grandparents. Cameras flashed, balloons soared overhead; there was a fever pitch as the flurry of motion went into high gear. Tears flowed, my own included. It was as if four babies were being born, all at the same time, in the middle of an airport! The hand of God was with us at that exquisite moment of joy, measured four times over.

When the excitement subsided I headed over to my departure gate, only to find that the plane had left without me! Despite the inconvenience of having to find a hotel and book new reservations, I felt it was a small price to pay for such a once-in-a-lifetime experience.

He who distributes the milk of human kindness
cannot help but spill a little on himself.

—JAMES BARRIE

GIRL TALK #208: Entertaining is one of my joys. So today I'll set up my entertainment center.

For those of us who like to entertain, it's important to streamline our setup to save time and energy. I have designed and built a special cupboard in my garage. Over time I have collected Oriental serving bowls, chopsticks, spoons and bamboo mats. I have pasta bowls and Chianti wine. There is a fondue pot with forks. I also store fortune cookies, special nuts, candies and other treats like caviar, smoked oysters and party crackers.

When I want to have people over, I can order Chinese or Thai food, set a pretty table and add tea and fortune cookies. Voilà. For an Italian feast, I can boil the spaghetti, get out the Chianti and serving bowl, add a loaf of fresh bread, and my party is on its way. Cleaning up is easier, too, when there is a place for everything and everything goes in its place—the party shelf in the garage.

My bar glasses, cocktail napkins, stirrers and nut bowls also have their special niches. I store liquor in an easy-to-reach cabinet. If entertaining isn't fun and easy, we tend to avoid it. So if you enjoy having friends over, make life uncomplicated by making an entertainment center for yourself.

Hospitality is one form of worship.

—The Talmud

GIRL TALK #209: Today I will listen for the voice of my Higher Power and I will keep my eyes, ears and heart open, expecting a miracle.

A miracle is defined as "an event that appears unexplainable by laws of nature and so is held to be an act of God." During my years as a family therapist, I have seen many acts that I consider miracles.

A woman found a daughter she had given over for adoption years before. An infertile couple conceived while in therapy. An adult son and his father were able to bridge years of estrangement and move forward with their lives.

There is also the miracle story of the little boy who was attending a concert by the famous Polish pianist, Paderewski. Before the concert began, the child slipped out of his seat and onto the piano stool, where he started playing "Chopsticks." The audience booed and hissed. Overhearing the commotion, Paderewski rushed on stage, walked to the piano and improvised a wonderful harmonic variation. As they played he whispered to the boy, "Don't stop."

At that moment Paderewski became the messenger from above, encouraging the youngster to nurture his talent. And the miracle was that it happened at all.

*Someday, after we have mastered the wars,
the waves, the tide and gravity, we will harness for
God the energy of love, and then for the second
time in the history of the world, man
will have discovered fire.*

—PIERRE TEILHARD DE CHARDIN

GIRL TALK #210: Remarriage is a risk and a challenge. Today I will think about my remarriage and how it contains all the components for renewal and belief in the future.

When a marriage ends through divorce, desertion or death, one partner is left alone. Some choose to stay single, others remarry. Yet the whole notion of tying the knot again is filled with challenges and possibilities. Here are some of the questions that need answering before you try again:

- Do you stay in your place or move into your partner's?
- Do you keep finances separate or pool your resources?
- Do you keep your possessions? Do you keep his? Do you start anew?
- Do you keep your friends?
- Do you keep your job? How does he feel about you working?
- What happens with the children? How do you work out the arrangements?
- Do you want (more) children? Does he?

Remarriage is not for sissies. It requires commitment, effort and an overwhelming amount of trust and acceptance. Both parties come into the union with unfinished business, emotional baggage and an insecurity about trying again.

On the other hand, there is hope of a new connection to heal the old pain. There is also a chance to be close to someone in a loving and meaningful partnership. A new union may be tenuous at first, but it will grow stronger. It is a chance to remake your life and make it better.

> *The tragedy of life is not what men suffer,*
> *but what they miss.*
>
> —Thomas Carlyle

GIRL TALK #211: Today I will meditate on nourishing my relationships.

When our lives get busy and stressful, we may forget to set aside time and energy for our most valued relationships. When you are a couple, there are always forces tugging you apart. Finding the time to be together can become a burden instead of a pleasure.

My husband and I have tried hard to make our marriage work. These are some of the tips we have found helpful:

- We use movies or videos as stressbusters.
- When things get hectic, we take a walk and hold hands.
- We share the same bedtime so we can spend a few quality minutes talking or cuddling before we go to sleep.
- We meditate together fifteen minutes a day.
- When we fight, we do not demean each other.
- We set aside together time, when neither of us has commitments to other projects or work.

Relationships are like plants. They need to be watered and nourished regularly. If they become dry for too long, they die. One does not fall in or out of love.

One chooses to grow and deepen love,
or one chooses to ignore the needs of love,
and love withers and dies.

—ANONYMOUS

GIRL TALK #212: There are opportunities all around me. Today I will see if I can take advantage of any of them.

Virginia Satir was a wise and talented woman. During my college years I found a book she had written called *Peoplemaking*. It was an enlightening study on family dynamics, with a common-sense approach to a comprehensive subject.

We were obviously destined to meet, since the story of our initial contact was nothing short of amazing. I was stranded one evening with car trouble. I walked to the nearest house and asked to use the phone. The people were in a hurry to leave and when I asked where they were going, they said to a workshop given by Virginia Satir!

She was all I had expected and more. At another unexpected and unplanned meeting with her, she invited me to attend an intensive month-long training session with her in Mexico. During that informative trip, she gave me the basics I needed for becoming a family therapist. She inspired me to develop programs of my own. In essence, this woman shaped my twenty-five-year career as a therapist.

My thanks to this wise and wonderful spirit who nourished so many souls, including mine. And thanks to my car for breaking down when and where it did. (One of those Higher Power gifts.)

It's important to know that words don't move mountains.
Work, exacting work, moves mountains.

—DANILO DOLCI

GIRL TALK #213: Eliminating clutter is my goal for today.

T he best way to simplify your home and your life is to unclutter it. That can mean removing junk from garages and closets, or simply getting an answering machine to pick up your calls when you are busy.

To help you get rid of clutter and stress, here are some tips that work for me:

- Ask yourself, *Do I need it?*
- Keep boxes and shopping bags so you can discard used clothing and books easily.
- Do not answer the phone when you are in the bathroom, bedroom or kitchen. Callers will leave a message or call back.
- Leave work at the office; don't bring it home.
- Leave family problems at home; don't bring them to work.

This is only a start. Build and tailor the list to take care of your own personal clutter. Once you streamline your time and home, life will appear much less burdensome.

> *Only a very exceptionally gifted mind could cope*
> *singly with all the problems which present*
> *themselves in the perfecting of a home.*
>
> —ARNOLD BENNETT

GIRL TALK #214: If there is a project I want to start, today is the day to do it.

During my early years as a therapist, my attention was directed primarily toward young children and adolescents. There were virtually no programs at the time devoted to helping these youngsters.

At the time I was employed by an agency that was housed in a professional building—a lovely, quiet setting that catered to adult services. But my practice had four- to eighteen-year-olds racing up and down the halls and into the bathrooms. They bothered the other clients and the employees as well. My boss called me into his office one day and said something had to be done; he didn't want them in the building.

Not wanting to give up this portion of my practice, and knowing the desperate need for it, I rented space elsewhere for the weekends. From Friday night to Sunday night I helped these kids get a new start on life. Within three months there were over a hundred youngsters enrolled.

Looking back at the times when I was forced to make major decisions, that ranks as one of the highlights. Little did I know then what a major role I was playing in fulfilling a tremendous need. I listened to my heart and have never regretted it.

Large streams from little fountains flow.

—DAVID EVERETT

GIRL TALK #215: There's often more than meets the eye when it comes to stress. So today I'll probe a little deeper.

My husband is a clever guy. He carries a picture of Pride furniture polish and Joy detergent in his wallet. Whenever he's in a long line and people around him are grumbling, he asks if they want to see his pride and joy. Then he whips out the photo and everyone has a good laugh.

From this gesture I've learned that we are usually too busy to connect with people. A break in the routine can lift the spirits and break the tension.

Once, when I was angry at being mistreated by a sales clerk, I asked, "Are you having a bad day or is it me?"

She answered that her child was sick at home and she wanted to be with her. My anger was instantly replaced by empathy. I would have felt the same way. She apologized for her behavior and we parted with a better understanding of one another.

Nowadays when I am treated poorly, I usually explore what's going on. Most of the time the situation turns into a win-win affair instead of a no-win predicament.

> *Relationships are only as alive as the*
> *people engaging in them.*
>
> —DONALD B. ARDELL

GIRL TALK #216: Today I will begin putting away gifts to give on special occasions. I will keep them in a safe place until I am ready for them.

Giving gifts is one of my favorite hobbies. Remembering birthdays with a card gives me great pleasure. I try to stay aware of the people in my life and when they have special occasions. When I see a sale or something unusual, I buy it right then and there. That way I am prepared and rarely caught short.

I also enjoy giving home-cooked food or a homemade present, like an album or framed photograph. The cost is low and the value is priceless. I also make my own greeting cards, either on the computer or with some of my photos.

With some imagination you can find any number of ways to make low-cost gifts for your friends and family members. Keep their sizes, hobbies and favorite colors in mind when you are out shopping. Waiting until the last minute always brings on stress. This way saves you aggravation, money and energy. I have a special closet dedicated to gifts. It's a treasure.

So be smart. Be prepared.

> *Let us imagine care of the soul, then,*
> *as an application of poetics*
> *to everyday life.*
>
> —THOMAS MOORE

GIRL TALK #217: My faithfulness to myself and others is important. So today I'll examine my affairs to see if I am honest about it.

One of the most basic virtues is faithfulness or fidelity. It demands that we are honest, sincere and trustworthy. There is no room for betrayal, dishonesty and phoniness when it comes to friends, family and God. But above all, to our own selves we must be true.

In today's society it is difficult to remain on the spiritual path and protect one's vision from the intrusions others make on our faith. We must be committed to our partners, our friends, our jobs and ourselves. It takes hard work, and there is a certain amount of loneliness that is involved when one is not willing to be swayed by popular opinions.

However, we are never truly alone. By believing in our inherent goodness and virtue, we know that good things will come our way if we are patient. It is not a cloud of darkness over your head but a misty cloud of change and protection.

Having the strength to endure during difficult times will bring a rainbow across our path. Faith is peace and hope as well as goodness of spirit, honesty and integrity.

True virtue is its own reward.

Adventure is something you seek for pleasure.
But experience is what really happens
to you in the long run.

—KATHERINE ANNE PORTER

GIRL TALK #218: Am I a cheerful person? Today I will examine my attitudes and behavior to see whether or not I am.

Cheerful people are the ones I am most happy to see. Being lighthearted is a way of facing life, and it's a choice any of us can make. Like all habits, it can be improved and made stronger. Granted, all of us have days when we feel blue, and it would be phony to act otherwise. But when we choose to be optimistic and make it a part of our personality, our physical and emotional health improve. We also brighten the lives of others.

A dear friend of mine lost her husband at the young age of forty-two. This tremendous loss made her angry and lonely, and filled her with grief. But in time she was able to set aside her unhappiness and bring back her wonderful sense of humor. She never laughed at the enormity of the situation, but she did lighten her heart and the hearts of those around her by being the cheerful person we had always known. Her grief was relieved by her positive attitude.

Cheerfulness spreads quickly, like a fire ignited. We all have lessons to learn and contributions to make. Being upbeat is the best way to inspire others.

The soul is dyed the color of its thoughts.

—Marcus Aurelius

GIRL TALK #219: Today I will tap into my own personal power.

People with power lead the most satisfying lives. In order to tap into your storehouse, write the statements below onto index cards, three per card. Then tape a card to your bathroom mirror and make the statement twice a day for a week. Then change the card and put up a new one.

Empowering yourself is the best way to gain strength for each day, and for a lifetime.

- Great success is based on strong commitment.
- You are never defeated until you stop trying.
- You create your own reality.
- Knowledge is power.
- Self-knowledge is personal power.
- A strong spiritual system puts things into perspective.
- Passion creates power.
- Your beliefs are your choice.
- People with power can say they are sorry.
- People with power can be gentle.
- Large problems can be broken into smaller ones.
- Learn from your mistakes.
- Don't punish yourself.
- Wisdom springs from experience.
- You already have all the power you need to be happy.

Some things are very important and some are
very unimportant. To know the difference
is what we are given life to find out.
—ANNA F. TREVISAN

GIRL TALK #220: I'm always ready for a new experience, but today I will recall an old one.

Just outside Ivins, Utah, there is a small bit of heaven. It's a five-mile stretch of road that winds past the most gorgeous red rocks. The path has become the favorite hiking place of the people who visit a nearby fitness center. It's a daily goal to walk up a gentle three-mile grade and a steeper two-mile incline to touch a stop sign that perches on top of a hill.

On the way up it's hard to look around, but after resting at the top and taking a long drink of water, the walk down is spectacular.

On my first trek I wore a headset that played my special music. So when I started down, it was a sensory overload. My eyes couldn't get enough of the red rocks, the blue sky, the white clouds overhead, and in my ears was the most incredible music. The gentle sun touched my skin and my nose picked up the scent of the wildflowers along the road. I was on another planet for the four hours it took to complete the circuit.

Sometime later I repeated the trip but feared it couldn't measure up to the first. Amazingly, it did. Now I try to make Snow Canyon, Utah, an annual pilgrimage.

God is home. We are in the far country.
—MEISTER ECKHART

GIRL TALK #221: Today I will commit to getting good financial counseling.

To have your money work for you, you need to learn about investments that are safe and not diminished by custodial fees.

My early experience came from a certified public accountant whose specialty was helping his clients become financially independent. Next I met a securities broker who taught me the difference between stocks, bonds and mutual funds. Their expertise in money has helped me reach a place where I don't have to worry about finances. What a relief.

Using experts in a given field is a sound approach to increasing your net worth—which gives a boost to your self-worth. It will take expertise and commitment to reach your goals, but financial security is possible.

If you don't save on a regular basis, or if your money is not working to your advantage, you need to find competent professionals to help you make the most of your assets.

Have your money make money.
—JOHN D. ROCKEFELLER

GIRL TALK #222: You never know when something wonderful will happen. So today I'll take a risk.

I was on stage at a conference demonstrating the dynamics of a dysfunctional family. Several audience members were up there with me, acting as role players. When we finished the program, I was gathering my things when I noticed an older man sitting in his chair.

"If you can get that much accomplished by using role players, what could you do if you had all the real family members?" he asked.

I told him that it would be highly unlikely to have such a situation, since most families are in denial about what is going on in their lives.

"If I get mine together, will you work with us?" he asked.

"If you can get three generations together, I'll do it," I said.

To my amazement, he called two weeks later and said he had thirty-eight family members ready to spend five days together. When I asked how he had managed that, he told me that he owned three jets, which would pick everyone up and bring them to his Western home.

"I told them they'd be left out of my billion-dollar will if they didn't come," he chuckled.

I brought two therapists with me and we had a fantastic week. Ten people came back to the Midwest with us: six for alcohol treatment, three for drug counseling and one for an eating disorder. When we were finished, that grandpa had a healthy, happy family—one that had been given the opportunity to grow and thrive because of his wisdom and courage.

> *Progress always involves risk, and you can't*
> *steal with your foot on first.*

—MARY R.

GIRL TALK #223: Today I will make a commitment to start my day with a meditation and a prayer.

For many years my husband and I directed a treatment and training program in the Black Hills of South Dakota. People came from around the world to heal themselves from problems with addictions, compulsions and unproductive relationships.

We had more than a thousand people a year going through the facility. On staff we had sixty-five hand-picked therapists from all over the country, and teachers who came to the facility for a week or ten days to be our therapists. We lived in a huge lodge and we housed this staff at our home. We had a meditation room, complete with candles, angels and books, as well as a hot tub, bedrooms and baths.

Each morning before going to work, we stopped to meditate, asking God for strength, wisdom and courage. I have no doubt that his word was passed to our clients through this team of caring therapists. There were many healings in the therapists themselves.

Ask and you shall receive.

Meditation and contemplation may be looked upon
as keys used by a healer to open the doors to
spiritual knowledge, to turn on the healing current and
to bring into focus that which God is ready to
reveal through the use of spiritual gifts.
—AMBROSE A. WORRALL

GIRL TALK #224: I trust that there will be some sort of healing today if I am faced with a crisis. I will call on my own resources to conquer this turning point in my life.

Turning points can cause intense pain or instigate joyous celebrations. At the time they occur, we wonder why they are happening and how they will shape our lives. Later, when we look back, the reason and pattern are often clear.

Sometimes we marvel that we made it through a crisis without being maimed or killed. On those occasions we thank God or our guardian angels. With other losses we can see that it was necessary to make room for a new gift that came our way. As we reframe our history, we can see that it is all part of a divine plan to make us what we are.

I have made turning points the focal point of a workshop. As an example, I use my father's suicide to show how I was forced into independence and how I gained strength from it. I also show how facing my own possible death made me slow down and take stock of what was important in my life.

We all face pivotal events in our lives. Each has a special lesson for us. You may welcome the lesson, or you may not learn from it. That is a choice only you can make.

We wait for life to keep unfolding.
We try to understand its meaning, year by year,
experience by experience. We may control our actions,
speed up our movements, resist schedules, but in
truth life will unfold at its own pace.

—SHARON WEGSCHEIDER-CRUSE

GIRL TALK #225: Second wives often feel like second-class citizens. So today I will make an effort to support all second wives as they strive to make their marriages work.

When I became my husband's second wife, I found it exhausting trying to find my niche in his complicated family structure. The conflicts and obstacles were so overwhelming that our marriage nearly ended before it had a chance to mature. Then I picked up the book *Second Wife, Second Best* by Glynnis Walker. The book not only spoke to me, it shouted!

First, it validated my frustration at being a victim in a situation I did not create. It was THEIR problem that as adult children they didn't have enough room in their hearts to welcome me into the family. It was a great relief to know that I was not to blame. I no longer felt guilty for feeling like an outcast. These people hardly knew me, yet made no effort to know the woman their father loved and had married.

Second, I learned that wives who marry into an established family often suffer from insecurity and jealousy. It's perfectly normal. Then I read these words: "You are as much entitled to not like his children as they are entitled to not like you." That made me realize it wasn't MY problem, as I had believed. The relief I felt was enormous.

From this wonderful book, which I highly recommend, I learned that we SECOND wives are entitled to become FIRST priorities!

We will be victorious if we have not forgotten how to learn.
—ROSE LUXEMBURG

GIRL TALK #226: Today I will appreciate my unique and special qualities.

Many women are too shy or embarrassed to look at their own bodies. So this is a minor exercise for ladies only. Stand naked in front of the mirror and take a good look. Start with your feet, check your toes and instep. Move up to your ankles and study them. Look at your leg muscles and your knees, turn around and check the back. Now comes the hard part—the thighs. Move up to the gentle slope of your hips and appreciate the curve. At your pubic area think about the joy of being a woman, the pleasure of sex and the miracle of birth.

At the stomach, give yourself a break if it's not as tight and firm as it was when you were twenty—especially if you've had children. That's part of life, and of being a woman. Most men aren't as hard on us as we are on ourselves.

Your breasts are a unique part of your womanhood, whether large, small, perky, droopy or having undergone surgery. Now move to your neck, your throat and your face. There is nobody like you, you are special and unique.

Meditate on the gift of your mouth, eyes, nose and ears. Touch your hair; the color, texture and style are you.

Stand back now and look at all of you. Say, "I'll be back again soon for another lesson in being me."

I have a woman inside my soul.

—YOKO ONO

GIRL TALK #227: Today I will face a less than perfect solution with the hope that it will resolve itself.

I've already told you about my programs with children and how we had to find a separate facility because they were too noisy for my regular office. Finding staff was another struggle. These were experimental programs, and caring professionals would give up weekends or evenings to help. We had to keep our costs down but our quality up.

One evening the father of one young client said he was a C.P.A. and he knew of an H&R Block income tax office that was not used from May through December—the off-tax season. I jumped at the offer, and we set up shop on May 1. We called our services The Family Factory. By summer there were 300 children and adolescents enrolled.

For two years, except from January to April, we offered our program in the building our C.P.A. angel offered. The most important lesson I learned was that things don't always have to be perfect to work. If I had waited for the ideal situation, we may never have opened The Family Factory, and those children would still be carrying around old burdens. So if an opportunity arises, grab it. You can always work out the details later.

If we were logical, the future would be bleak indeed.
But we are more than logical. We are human
beings, and we have faith, and we have
hope and we can work.

—JACQUES COUSTEAU

GIRL TALK #228: Today I will think about being ready in case an angel reaches down to touch me on the shoulder.

The Family Factory flourished, even though we had to take a three-month break during tax time every year.

Hundreds of youngsters were being helped, and we wanted to expand and add new programs. When a reporter from the local paper called and wanted to write a story about us, I was more than ready. Finally phones began to ring and people began to take notice of the good we were doing.

One of the calls I took was from a minister at one of the largest congregations in our area. He had read the story in the paper. He said the church owned a three-story house that wasn't being used.

"If you can fix it up, it's yours to use," he said.

From the outside it looked okay, but inside was a wreck. The walls and ceiling were stained from water damage. The fixtures were rusted and some windows were cracked. Through the dirt I could see the potential, and I cried with gratitude as I accepted the gift.

Friends and neighbors, parents and strangers flowed in and out of that building like ants—fixing, repairing, cleaning, painting, sewing curtains. We renamed our business The House and it became a warm, loving, nurturing, healing place. We expanded to six days a week throughout the year, with no time out for tax time.

I have always believed that when we are ready an angel appears to answer our needs and our prayers. It certainly did with The House, and to this day I am grateful for whatever force made that reporter decide to write a story about our program.

Angels help you find courage and
open up new paths to explore.

—Anonymous

GIRL TALK #229: Today I will think of ways to streamline my wardrobe and organize my clothes.

A few years ago the rage was "having your colors done." Those of us who took up that challenge found out that certain colors make us look and feel good. They are our power colors, and they help when planning a wardrobe. In a nutshell, here are the essentials:

- Determine what colors look best on you.
- Choose basic hues that go with your best color(s).
- When you shop, buy only in these colors so everything can be mixed and blended.

To take this color scheme further, here are more tips:

- Buy only white socks, so they all match.
- For men, choose three colors: black, tan and navy.

By sticking to the basics, you can save time in the closet in the morning. In fact, you can pick out your clothes with your eyes shut. Now, that's a timesaver, all right!

Because my life has included a great deal of travel, it's been so helpful to have mix-and-match clothes and colors. I can select almost anything and know I'll have a coordinated outfit.

When we are authentic, when we keep our spaces simple, simply beautiful living takes place.
—ALEXANDRA STODDARD

GIRL TALK #230: This is a day to assess my financial situation.

If you are single, become knowledgeable about your money. If you live with someone—whether you are married or not—protect yourself financially. Do not let your partner keep secrets. Always be sure that your assets are protected and that you are not responsible for anyone else's debts. Make sure that you can survive on your income alone, without your partner. It's always best if your relationship is based on something more than financial need.

A few years ago I had a client who worked with her husband, who was a physician. She ran the office, but he had convinced her not to take a salary. Even though she felt uncomfortable about the situation, she went along with it. This woman had no idea how much her husband was worth financially and she had no sense of self-worth or financial security. Through therapy she was able to change. First she asked for full disclosure about their finances. She insisted on a salary, then opened her own savings account and IRA.

How about you? Do you know your net worth? Do you have an IRA? A separate checking account and savings account? Do you feel financially secure? Think about it. It's important.

I exist, I need, I'm entitled.

—JACQUELINE LAIR AND WALTHER LECHLER, M.D.

GIRL TALK #231: Just as a plant needs water, sun and nourishment, we need varied experiences to make sure we are healthy and growing.

Esalen is a growth center in California that was developed in the 1960s to help people share knowledge and skills in an environment that was enriching to all. The setting is spectacular, with the buildings hanging high above the Pacific Ocean on the edge of a cliff. The housing consists of rustic cabins, and meals are made with vegetables from a large garden. There are hot tubs, massage tables and a swimming pool. Colorful flowers and clean air complete this breathtaking scene.

The first time I attended was culture shock. I signed up for a workshop on counseling skills and found myself in a class with a dozen male psychiatrists. It was a bit threatening, yet a confidence builder. I learned a great deal and gained invaluable confidence as a therapist. The combination of good conversation, expert teaching, sharing, healthy meals and a serene atmosphere made for healing and nurturing.

During my many trips back to Esalen I have met wonderful people in all walks of life. Each of them has touched my life in a special way, and I am thankful.

I know how those in exile feed
on dreams of hope.

—Aeschylus

GIRL TALK #232: The passage of divorce can be devastating. Today I will think about becoming single again after being part of a couple, and I will be there for anyone who is going through this difficult passage.

With nearly 50 percent of all marriages ending in divorce, it's time for me to address this painful transition. So many things change in divorce—an act that affects everyone who touches the two parties who are splitting from each other. Children become extremely vulnerable, extended families are torn apart, friends are often asked to choose between one or the other. If both parties are in business together, more complications arise. No matter who leaves or what the reason is, divorce is never easy. It is always painful. People get hurt and yet there are two sides to every story.

While there is no such thing as a happy divorce, there are ways to reduce the hurt if each party makes a commitment to cooperate and to see the transition as a new opportunity to find a lifestyle that may be more satisfying. Instead of seeing divorce as the end, try to view it as a beginning of a better world, where peace and contentment may become reality.

In my book *Life After Divorce*, I put forth these points to help get through this passage and move on to a fuller, richer, more rewarding life:

- Accept yourself and trust yourself.
- Set realistic expectations and take risks.
- Forgive yourself and others.
- Express your feelings amd take responsibility for your actions.
- Develop new skills.
- Affirm your values.
- Celebrate your freedom.
- Surround yourself with positive energy and friends.

Live neither solely for yourself
nor solely for others.

—Margaret Wagner

GIRL TALK #233: I'll be gentle with myself today, for this may be a time when a decision must be made and I am not sure what to do. I will have faith that I'll do the right thing.

After living in Minnesota for forty years, I was offered a job in Texas. It would give me the opportunity to work in a setting that would raise my level of experience and expertise. It also paid better. With three children almost ready for college, this job would allow me to help in ways I never thought I could.

The downside, of course, was moving away from my roots. The decision was difficult, to say the least. Every time the offer was renewed I found a way to postpone giving an answer. It took six months for me to say yes. I didn't want to leave my family.

Even though my family encouraged me to go, the actual parting was devastating. Much of my car trip was blurred by tears. Although the distance forced the family into some wonderful weekend reunions that we cherish to this day, I'm not sure the job was worth the move. I might never know. But at least I did not remain frozen in time. I took a chance.

Sometimes we must leap off into the great unknown to find ourselves, or to find that what we had was better than we thought it was.

Self-forgiveness is another word for letting go.

—Anonymous

GIRL TALK #234: Today I will start a folder of things I cherish. It will be a final gift to my loved ones when I am gone.

Although funerals are usually painful, I understand it is important for survivors to come together to celebrate the life of someone who has died. Three of these occasions stand out clearly in my mind.

My grandmother, Mary, had played the organ for many years in the local church. Before she died she asked for two things: to have someone play "Mary, It's a Grand Old Name" and "Easter Parade," and have everyone sing; and an open coffin. Each of her nineteen grandchildren was to bring a farewell gift. It was quite an experience to see what was placed in the casket. There was a doughnut cutter, flower seeds, sheet music and a small bottle of wine. Family members gave the eulogies and played the music. It was truly a celebration of a wonderful woman's life.

My mother also had an open coffin, placed in a social hall. She loved good food and family gatherings. Little children ran around the coffin as grown-ups said their farewells. My sister's dog lay beneath the casket while my mother's spirit presided over the festivities.

The third outstanding memory is of a dear friend who died of AIDS. Before the funeral, we viewed photos of his life and gazed upon the items he cherished. Then we all rode to church telling funny stories. At the conclusion of the ceremony, the lights dimmed and a video was shown of him saying his own farewells to all of us. As we exited the church, hundreds of helium balloons filled the back of the vestibule. We each took two and, as a band played "When the Saints Go Marching In," we paraded outside the church and let the balloons soar upward toward the heavens.

Celebrating the lives of loved ones brings them honor and helps heal our own pain. It is important to bring closure to the relationship as well. We might all give some thought to the way we would like to leave earth and not leave those personal decisions to others. It is part of our responsibility as adults to plan for the future, including our own parting.

Some people walk in the rain, others just get wet.
—ROGER MILLER

GIRL TALK #235: Today I will take a deep breath and think about all the things I am grateful for. It will give me a strong sense of inner peace.

"All I want is some peace and quiet."

"If only I could have a little peace of mind."

Those expressions and others can mean the absence of stress or violence, or they can mean we want harmony. However we describe it, we all want it. But peace can be much more than simply a lack of noise. Perhaps peace comes to those who have come to terms with who they are and what they want from life.

When we are restless, we have trouble finding serenity. Yet acceptance of our situation can help us feel tranquil, even when life seems to be falling apart.

I recall a woman who had to care for her children alone after her husband died. Money was tight, time was short and she was always bone tired. Yet she knew she'd done her best. In her heart she found an inner peace that many find hard to achieve under ideal conditions.

When we are calm inside, we cherish the gifts of the present. When we live in the past or the future, tranquility escapes us. But through gratitude we can find the treasure in the moment and nourish our souls with the experiences of ordinary living. When all the moments of our lives are truly appreciated, we will learn the meaning of peace and quiet.

Do not lose your inward peace for anything whatsoever,
even if your whole world seems upset.

—Saint Francis de Sales

GIRL TALK #236: Today I'll consider what a "person in my position" means and make clear choices for myself.

Status is a strange thing. For many years people said to me, "A woman in your position should . . ."

What followed was a litany of things I should have or do—like drive a high-priced car, wear designer clothing or belong to certain clubs that would enhance my social position. But buying things or having status symbols was always an empty goal for me.

Each person needs to search her soul and decide for herself what she needs and how she wants to present herself. I have no need to prove myself to anyone. Do you?

When I was lecturing and in front of the public, it was important to be well-dressed. But that didn't mean I had to spend a fortune on designer clothes. My health was more important, and getting a good night's sleep, especially when I was on a hectic travel schedule.

Only you can decide what is important to you. Try not to be swayed by what other people think you should have, or wear, or buy. You know what your position in life is and how you want to be seen. Can you feel free not to prove yourself to anyone else?

*Do what you can, with what you
have, where you are.*

—THEODORE ROOSEVELT

GIRL TALK #237: If I could, I would go to South Dakota and visit Bear Butte for a vision quest. I would borrow the customs of the Native American Indians, then do it my way.

Among the Native Americans there is a strong respect for women, who have handed down stories and traditions for centuries. For twelve years I was fortunate to live in the beautiful Black Hills of South Dakota, where I learned many of life's spiritual lessons from the Lakota Sioux.

From them I learned about the vision quest. The Sioux and Cheyenne go to Bear Butte. There, atop a sacred mountain, they fast and cleanse their bodies emotionally and physically for four days. Without food they pray for a vision. During that time the vision will show the future with a clarity that helps them live better in the present. But in order to have this insight, it is important to remain open and surrender to whatever comes.

Before I left Bear Butte I walked the sacred path to the top of the mountain. There, surrounded by colorful ribbons tied to trees, I tied my own ribbon and said my own prayer. I also made a commitment to write a book dedicated to two special women: my mother and my grandmother. This is that book.

In the life of the Indian, there is only one inevitable duty—
the duty of prayer, the daily recognition of the unseen
and external. He sees no need for setting apart
one day in seven as a holy day, since
to him all days are God's.

—OHIYESA, SANTEE DAKOTA

GIRL TALK #238: Sometimes a situation happens where everything I've learned and studied will be asked of me, with little warning. Today I want to prepare myself.

When I wanted to retire from active work, I needed to leave behind some of my work. I selected two women and one man to train with me. For nearly two years we diligently covered all topics, using notes, tapes and psychodrama. It was a challenge for them to learn my techniques, but they rose to the occasion.

During one specific workshop, one of my trainees was planning to be my assistant. She was anxious but willing. However, when I awoke the morning of the session with a debilitating toothache, I had no choice but to tell her that she was on her own. She was shocked and terrified. With no time to prepare for her debut, she marched in like a trouper and took over the workshop like a pro.

Two months later the second woman came with me to assist in a presentation. Imagine my amazement when the same tooth flared up during the night and I awoke with another abscess. It was a *déjà vu*, except the trainee was a different woman.

The next day I had the tooth extracted, so I don't know what the odds would have been of it happening a third time. Some things are better left unknown. I think this was another Higher Power time.

Adversity has the effect of eliciting talents which
in prosperous circumstances would
have lain dormant.

—HORACE

GIRL TALK #239: It's never too late to learn something new. So today I will prepare myself for a new adventure.

Shirley and I were young mothers. She had two little ones, I had three. Our children were close in age, so we spent many hours together. Since I had gone into business right out of high school, I didn't have many domestic skills and often felt inadequate. Shirley, however, had learned all those household tricks from her mother-in-law. So I copied her.

And thus I learned to sew and cook. But she was always one step ahead of the game. Once our families went camping together. I brought sandwiches, fruit and cans of cola. Then I went to visit Shirley's campsite. She was grilling pork chops near a picnic table set with dishes, fresh wildflowers and long-stemmed wineglasses! I had a long way to go.

Over the years she honed her skills and I continued to learn from her. Then one day she came over to show me something. She came into my house with skirts, sweaters, pants and boots.

"I'm going to college," she announced blithely.

I was dumbfounded. I had just caught up with her and now she was heading in another direction completely. I wished her well.

Over the years my life has changed dramatically. We drifted apart, yet Shirley was often on my mind, especially when I, too, enrolled in college.

Amazingly, we now live only two miles away from each other, so we get together frequently to share dinner and swap stories of our lives. For thirty-five years, Shirley has been a true guiding light and a valuable inspiration for me.

> *Often intimacies between women go backwards,*
> *beginning with revelations and ending up*
> *in small talk, without loss of esteem.*
>
> —ELIZABETH BOWEN

GIRL TALK #240: Today I'll think about my medical and dental anxieties and how they bother me.

I grew up in a small town with no regular dentist. Instead, we had visiting dentists who came to town and lined all the residents up in a civic hall. Then they worked on one after another, with no anesthesia and a modest amount of sanitation.

While some people have a dental anxiety, mine was a full-blown phobia.

When I moved to South Dakota I needed a regular dentist. So I flipped through the Yellow Pages and found Dr. Horton, who "catered to cowards." That was the doctor for me. His office was welcoming, with teddy bears and a friendly staff. He seemed sympathetic to my phobia and the experiences that helped create it. Before he started any work, he asked what music I liked; then he supplied me with headphones, and wonderful music filled my ears. Once I was relaxed, the rest was easy and relatively painless.

Since I found Dr. Horton, my dental phobia has vanished. And that's pretty good, considering I've had numerous fillings, two abscesses, two crowns and a root canal.

It would be wonderful if all health care professionals could be as sensitive to their patients' needs as Dr. Horton was to mine. Bless him, wherever he is.

Even the severed branch grows again,
and the sunken moon returns. Wise men who ponder
this are not troubled in adversity.

—INDIAN PROVERB

GIRL TALK #241: Today I'll think about the golden years of my sixties. This will be a critical time when all my inner resources will be needed to live my life with energy and grace.

Sixty is a unique milestone for each and every one of us. Some women I know are old already. Others are vibrant and youthful.

Menopause is the transition that can make a woman give up on herself. She sees it as a signal that the end is around the corner, so she stops taking care of her body. She lets go of her sexual energy and does nothing but complain. Since her children are probably grown and live elsewhere, she feels empty and abandoned.

In contrast, there are others who celebrate their children's independence and see this decade as a way of enjoying life and sexual pleasure without the fear of becoming pregnant. Many women return to school, others take up a sport or dancing. I know many ladies who are in the prime of their lives in their sixties and seventies.

This is a time to take stock of whether we have been successful, but we must not judge by society's standards. Instead, use your own yardstick. True success comes from within and cannot be measured by awards, money or fame. It is gauged by courage, integrity and love. If you feel you've come up short, get going. There are plenty of years left to do what has not yet been done.

To be what we are, and become what we are capable
of becoming, is the only end of life.
—ROBERT LOUIS STEVENSON

GIRL TALK #242: Today I'll meditate on men. If a
man is already part of my life, I will let him know how
I feel. If I'm still waiting, I'll think about what I want.

Frog or prince? That's the question of the century. If you sit
down and list the traits you want in a man, some people
might think you're too picky. Not true. That's how you
figure out what you want in a man, so when you meet him you'll
know for certain. Here are a few of the things on my list of must-
have traits in a man:

1. He must like his work or his job. If he doesn't, he'll resent
   the fact that you like your job. He'll also be negative and
   unhappy.
2. He needs to take good care of himself. That means only
   moderate drinking, no drugs, eating properly and plenty of
   exercise.
3. He should be able to apologize if he hurts your feelings.
   He must never be abusive and he needs to learn from his
   mistakes.
4. He should be romantic and a bit sentimental. There's nothing wrong with flowers, candlelight or even tears at a sad
   movie.
5. He needs values. That means paying taxes, tipping the correct amount, respecting the law and being trustworthy.
6. He must be able to have fun, laugh, and go out and play. He
   should leave his work at work and not bring his problems
   home.
7. He must respect your individuality and choices. He must
   not open other people's mail or invade their privacy.
8. He needs a sense of humor. He laughs *with* a person, never
   at her, and he can poke fun at himself, too.

The power of a man's virtue should not
be measured by his special efforts,
but by his ordinary doing.

—Blaise Pascal

GIRL TALK #243: Today I will use my confidence to help me explore new ideas and dreams.

Confidence is derived from two Latin words meaning "with faith."

Confidence is the ability to be self-assured, to have faith that what we are doing we will do well—in whatever field we have chosen.

Recently I lived next door to a woman who was an excellent seamstress. I felt like a sewing failure when I looked at her accomplishments. So I bought a machine and asked her to teach me. She did her best, but I hated it. I had no patience and, more important, I didn't enjoy the process. When I told her how I felt, she said, "Some people love to sew, others—like you—love to write books." That's when I realized I had other skills to explore.

If we allow ourselves to believe that we are inferior to others, we are not being true to ourselves. We need to find the area in which we can shine and excel, instead of holding ourselves up to others for comparison. It may mean some deep soul-searching to find our confidence, but it's worth the effort.

Like the roses I grow, confidence blossoms with nourishment. So give it time, food, water and tender loving care. You will bloom in time and show your confidence to the world.

To be confident is to act in faith.

—BERNARD BYNION

252

GIRL TALK #244: Today I'll reflect on the saying that sometimes there are great rewards for only a little bit of risk.

In the Los Angeles area I worked in several different facilities, from hospitals to universities. No matter where I held sessions, the subject was always the same—addiction. I used a combination of lecture, teaching and psychodrama, using role players to act out a situation.

After one of my programs in a hospital, a therapist named Jack came up to me.

"I've learned so much here," he said. "And since I work with homeless, indigent alcoholics who could never afford a session like this, I was hoping you'd consider a teaching session without charging us." I thought long and hard, then said yes.

The next time I was in L.A., I called Jack and we headed to the storefront where his group met. After some hesitation, the men and women began warming up to me; we made a wonderful connection by the end of the day.

For the next three years, whenever I went to L.A., I stopped by the storefront and worked with the alcoholics and their counselors. Jack and his wife became good friends of mine and on one occasion she presented me with a lovely soft, white afghan. Whenever I cuddle up with it I am reminded of these wonderful people and the profound memories I have of Jack and his storefront counseling.

Sometimes you've got to take a chance and say YES.

The universe is full of magical things patiently waiting for our wits to grow sharper.

—EDEN PHILLPOTTS

GIRL TALK #245: Today I'll reflect on the complications of stepfamilies and how I can have a positive effect.

Blended families are an experience that demands maturity and cooperation from all parties. The TV show *The Brady Bunch* was a far cry from the reality of merging families.

Stepfamilies are built on loss—a negative reality. Whether the cause is death or divorce, one thing remains constant: everyone needs to heal. To enter a relationship with unexpressed and unresolved feelings of hurt, anger, abandonment, fear and grief is to doom the situation from the beginning. Healing is the first emotion that needs to be addressed. And it takes time for an adjustment to take place.

When a divorce is involved, there are usually unresolved feelings of anger. When a single parent remarries, he or she can start over. The children cannot. There is a "forever" connection to both parents. Siblings are usually caught in a tug of war that can be mild at best, or an emotional roller coaster ride at worst. Kidnapping a child is a common way of one parent seeking revenge on the other.

Even if all parties get along, a child is still pulled emotionally from one parent to the other. This must be understood and respected by all adults. Stepparents must understand that bonding takes time.

Now throw in half-siblings, and the situation can be explosive or joyous. Power struggles and jealousy will be part of this cocktail. Privacy is important, and each child must have a space of his or her own, even if it's only a special drawer. Each child also needs to be extraordinary in some way to the parents. Children cannot all be lumped together like a wad of clay. So while the parents struggle to make their new relationship work, they must also devote quality time to each child.

Money is sure to become an issue in some shape, manner or form. Cooperation and compromise are the key to making sure financial problems don't interfere with the melding of the individuals into a cohesive whole. Call in a financial counselor or a C.P.A. to help with money matters. Parents need to be partners, fair and equal in all matters.

If you are part of a stepfamily or are planning to marry into one, please call the Stepfamily Association of America at 800-735-0329 for information and advice.

*You may be disappointed if you fail,
but you are doomed if
you don't try.*

—BEVERLY SILLS

GIRL TALK #246: Mothers can be overly critical. So today I'll think about being a mom and whether I'm ever unnecessarily critical.

A critical mother feels she owes it to everyone to point out shortcomings, so everyone can improve themselves. If she is confronted about her lack of support, she is quick to say that it's her job to help others be the best people possible. This means she wants to help you rid yourself of all the habits she feels tarnishes the picture of a perfect you.

Some critical mothers are verbal; they never stop nagging. Others use the power of "no talk" to display disapproval. Whichever style a mother may choose, both hurt. And it doesn't help one bit to know that the mother is insecure with her own feelings of self-worth. She is trying to make up what is missing in her own life by blaming the shortcomings on others.

To get past this negative attitude, both mother and child must realize the problem lies with the mother. Next, the children must find meaningful relationships that value them as they are, to help diminish the pain of their mother's hurtful comments.

And do not forget, all that applies to a critical mother also applies to a faultfinding father.

Isn't it great, life is so open-ended.

—Brigitte Frase

GIRL TALK #247: Do I have a spirit of generosity? Do I share myself with others? Today I will find out.

Anne was born in a small farming town a few years before the Great Depression. She was a middle child, sandwiched between a brother and two sisters. She had no special place in the family. When she was sixteen, she moved in with her grandmother and cared for her until she married.

Anne's first baby was born just before her husband was drafted into the army during World War II. She rolled bandages for the Red Cross and managed to survive until her spouse returned. They began a new life, and two more babies were born. Those were the wonderful years.

She grew vegetables in a small garden behind their home, he started a business, she had dinner parties for friends. They even took in her brother-in-law and father when each needed a home. Her home was a beehive of activity. Everyone loved being around Anne, with her great sense of humor and loving, giving spirit.

On a cold winter night a fire started in their business. The water hydrants were frozen, and by dawn everything they had worked for lay in a smoldering heap. They worked to rebuild the husband's business, but prospects were bleak and money was scarce.

What hadn't changed, however, was Anne's generosity. She continued to care for her brother-in-law and to open her home for Sunday dinner. She shared what little she had.

From Anne I learned about generosity. She gave from the heart with hugs and kisses, and she gave to others what small material possessions she had.

We all need an Anne in our lives to guide us down the path of self-lessness. True wealth is not measured by bank accounts but by what is in the heart. It does the soul good to give. Anne was my mother.

Blessed are those who can give without remembering
and receive without forgetting.

—Elizabeth Bibesco

GIRL TALK #248: Today I will meditate on both the opportunities and drawbacks of inherited wealth.

The good news of a large inheritance is that it eliminates all the energy that goes into acquiring money. If the person receiving the endowment has self-esteem and feels fulfilled in his or her life, the gift is wonderful.

However, there is often a down side. And with money it can be a serious problem. Friends may want to cling because of the money factor and not out of true affection. Having a large bank account can make others feel uncomfortable and inadequate. If a wealthy person wants to work, is he or she taking away a job from somebody who really needs it? Then there is the consideration of safety, privacy and constant requests for donations.

Prosperity can be a delightful windfall or a questionable challenge.

If you are constantly wishing to marry someone with money or win the lottery, you will have some soul searching to do if your wishes come true. Wealth can be a beautiful or a painful thing. It can go either way.

> *Guilt, money and shame go*
> *hand in hand.*
>
> —ANONYMOUS

GIRL TALK #249: Today I will record whatever is important to me in whatever way works best for me.

M any people have asked me how I manage to write when I am a therapist, not a writer. My only answer is that I try to make it easy on myself. I am not a slave to a typewriter, or a computer—although it does make my job easier. My first ten books were written without the benefit of a computer.

On days when I am inspired, I can sit for hours and write. On other days, nothing comes to mind, so I go outside and ramble. I take a portable tape recorder and say whatever comes to mind. Some of my best memories and inspirations have come from the spoken word, and have been transcribed by my faithful typist, Ellie.

I also keep a pen and paper at my side at all times—even at dinner parties. I never know when I'll hear a gem I simply must have for my next book.

So I guess you could say I'm a part-time writer but full-time thinker. I consider it a gift. And somehow, throughout the years, all those thoughts and experiences and quips have melded into what we call books. I just hope the flow never stops and that you, the reader, never tire of hearing what I want to share.

Knowledge of what you love somehow comes to you,
you don't have to read nor analyze nor study.
If you love a thing enough, knowledge of it
seeps into you with particulars more
real than any chart can furnish.

—Jessamyn West

GIRL TALK #250: There is a nonverbal language that goes on between people. Today I'll tune in and see if I can learn something new.

Emanual had come from Sallanches, France, as a foreign exchange student and lived with my daughter and son-in law for over a year. He was a delightful fellow, and he quickly became more like family than a foreigner. We learned about France and he became quite Americanized.

My husband and I were planning a trip to Europe and thought it would be nice to visit Emanual's parents. After a transatlantic flight and two train rides, we met his parents in Sallanches. They spoke no English, we spoke little French. They invited us to dinner and enlisted the aid of a local priest to help us communicate. But strangely, words didn't seem to be necessary to communicate. Our eyes spoke and our hearts laughed with each other.

After a delicious dinner served by Emanual's mother, we boarded the train back to Paris. As we stood on the platform, his mother's eyes begged me to take good care of her son. My heart told her I would.

At that moment it became clear to me that there is a language larger than words. The soul speaks distinctly. It only takes a like soul to hear what is said.

Some things . . . arrive on their own mysterious hour,
on their own terms, and not yours, to be
seized or relinquished forever.

—GAIL GODWIN

GIRL TALK #251: It is important to let others know how much they mean to us. So today I'll think about the loved ones in my life—and those who have died.

Since my father was an orphan, the only grandparents I had were my mother's parents.

I don't remember my grandfather very well, since I was young when he died. I was told he lived a full life and many people cared for him. When he passed away, he was the first dead person I ever saw, but other than feeling sad for my mother and grandmother, it was not a highly emotional time for me.

When my grandmother died, it was a different ball game altogether. We had been very close. Being her first grandchild, I had been showered with love and affection. In later years, she often stayed in my home to be with her great-grandchildren.

When I received the call from the hospital, I was 250 miles away. Of course, they let me leave work immediately, and I drove as fast as the law would allow. As I pulled into the parking lot of the hospital I felt an emptiness in my heart. I wasn't ready to say good-bye. Once inside, my mother said that my grandma had slipped into a coma and death was near. It felt as though someone had kicked me in the stomach.

In the room with her, she seemed smaller. Her black hair was now snow-white, and in her pale hands she held a rosary. Through my tears I told her I loved her and rambled on about how much she meant to me. Then I saw her eyes flicker open.

"I love you, too, dear," she said. "Thank you for telling me how you feel." She smiled, closed her eyes and died a short while later.

I have always thanked God that I was able to let her know how much I cared for her before she died. It was an important connection that I treasure to this day. From my grandmother I learned a great deal about how to live and how to die.

One often learns more from ten days of agony than from ten years of contentment.

—MERLE SHAIN

GIRL TALK #252: Today I will wait. There is nothing for me to do but be myself. When there is something specific to do, it will be revealed.

Waiting is part of life. We wait for maturity, for love, for the birth of our children, and then we wait impatiently for them to grow up. We wait for spiritual gifts to be revealed, and we wait for changes to occur. Perhaps that is why the gift of patience is so important.

We can set all the schedules we want, but life is not to be hurried. Everything happens when it should. Of course, that doesn't mean we sit around doing nothing, waiting for our destiny to be revealed. We should enter into daily living with enthusiasm, shaping the circumstances to the best of our ability to bring order into our chaotic lives. At the same time, we must be ready to change directions as our turning points occur.

Some days are to be experienced to the max. Other days we lie back and see how life is presenting itself. On those days we may believe that nothing is happening, but we would be wrong. Waiting is an essential part of spirituality. If we can't wait, we interrupt the flow of destiny. We cheat the process. When we hurry, we lose. There is a loss of faith, of hope and of expectation. With those losses come fear and discouragement.

Like the cactus that blooms in the desert after a long-awaited rain, our souls will also blossom when we wait to be touched by our Higher Power.

Patience is a virtue that carries a lot of wait!
—Our Daily Bread

GIRL TALK #253: Today I shall recall the times when I've been judged in circumstances where I was innocent. It's important that I know the truth of the situation and keep my dignity.

During my training, I attended a course on Sexuality Attitude Readjustment. It was offered to medical personnel and therapists, to help sensitize them to sexual matters so they could better serve their clients. Six months after I took the course, I was invited to New Orleans to train a group of nurses.

We used three films that I had borrowed. They were in an open wicker basket, which I carried aboard the plane. As we climbed to 33,000 feet, all my tapes spilled out of the basket and slid from the front, where I was sitting, past rows of conservatively dressed businessmen, to the back. I was unaware of this until the flight attendant's voice came loud and clear over the public address system.

"Would the owner of the following films please claim them: *Sensuous Orange, Love Toads* and *Love in the Afternoon*."

I sat frozen in my seat as she repeated the announcement. Then, with all the courage and dignity I could muster, I made my way to the back of the plane and claimed my videos. Dozens of eyes followed me back to my seat.

Once on the ground I deboarded as quickly as possible. It would have been much too complicated to explain to anyone. Sometimes it's best just to flee.

I think that wherever your journey takes you,
there are new gods waiting there, with
divine patience—and laughter.
—SUSAN M. WATKINS

GIRL TALK #254: When looking beyond the obvious, there are often hidden treasures. So today I'll look for them.

Most people think of Las Vegas as the land of glitz, casinos and high rollers. But it's where I've made my home part of the year, and I can attest to the fact that there are glorious mountains, gorgeous desert foliage and tumbling mountain streams with crystal-clear water. When I look across my backyard into mountains framed by bright orange and pink sunsets, I feel as though I'm in heaven. Except for wind now and then and some blistering hot summer days, the weather is lovely.

We have the best entertainment and restaurants this side of the Rockies. My hubby and I love to dress up and enjoy the night life and glamour. It's like being on vacation—without going anywhere. It's a great place to visit and a great place to live.

When I tell people I live in Las Vegas, they are surprised at my choice. So I say, "Come visit." When they do, they love it. Many have even moved out here. We have it all, so why not?

Someone once said that when you are trying to choose between two good things and you can have both, go for it!

Risk! Risk anything. Do the hardest thing on Earth for you. Act for yourself.
—KATHERINE MANSFIELD

GIRL TALK #255: Today I will practice "power dialogue" so I can communicate better with others.

Regardless of your position in life or your status, you can positively increase your personal power by practicing certain behaviors.

- Listen to your words. Evaluate whether you sound apologetic, timid or unsure. Do you sound clear, definite and confident?
- Practice saying power words like: I believe, I want, I am.
- Learn to say NO. Set boundaries for your actions. You will be treated with greater respect.
- Give up all-or-nothing thinking. Learn to enjoy being average. It's an immense relief and more fun, too.
- Don't generalize. Words like "always" or "never" can be self-defeating. They are rarely accurate.
- Try not to be iffy. Be definite. "Should," "maybe," "perhaps" are words that imply you are not sure of yourself.

To feel as powerful as possible, clean up your speech patterns and speak with conviction, even if you are doubtful inside. Make a statement—you can always backtrack, but at least you've put yourself on the line and taken a risk. You'll feel better about yourself, and others will listen.

I am never afraid of what I know.

—ANNA SEWELL

GIRL TALK #256: Today I will clean out my collection of catalogs or set up a place to keep them.

Catalogs can be a time-saving device or a handicap. I keep a catalog basket in my office. When the mail comes, I toss the catalogs in without so much as a glance. Then, on rainy evenings or when I want to curl up in a chair and shop, out they come.

To limit my spending, I only buy items that are perfect for birthday, anniversary or holiday gifts. I also treat myself now and then to something I would have bought in the store anyway. Since shipping costs are high, I wait until I have several things to order. When they come, I store them in my gift closet until it's time to give them away.

Catalog shopping saves me from buying impulse items and saves time, energy, gas and hours in the mall. Catalogs offer a wider variety of merchandise than I could find in one place.

Catalogs also seem to have some hard-to-find items and one-of-a-kind gifts. Both my homes contain special items I've never seen in a store, only in a catalog. It's important to keep the good catalogs and eliminate the poor ones.

Tidied all my papers. Tore up and ruthlessly
destroyed much. This is always
a great satisfaction.

—KATHERINE MANSFIELD

GIRL TALK #257: Today I'll pray for wisdom.

Virginia Satir, a founder of family therapy, could say something that sounded simple, but was filled with profound wisdom.

When I first met Virginia, I was bouncing from one thing to another. Trying to hold my life together was a supreme chore. I was filled with anger at the alcoholism that ran through my family, feeling deeply hurt and lonely from my failing marriage, and I was overwhelmed with motherhood. At work I was discriminated against because I was a woman.

To others I looked as though I was functioning well. Inside I was a cauldron of boiling emotions. But instead of dealing with them, I denied and ignored them. It was as though I were driving eighty miles an hour with the brakes on.

"The only way to regain your energy and positive outlook is to make your inside match your outside," Virginia said to me. "In making changes, you will find your destiny and receive the spiritual energy to get it done." I started making big changes in my life. Healing followed.

She was right.

We all carry it within us: supreme strength,
the fullness of wisdom, unquenchable joy. It is never
thwarted and cannot be destroyed. But it is
hidden deep, which is what
makes life a problem.

—HUSTON SMITH

GIRL TALK #258: Today I will examine my fear of growing old. I'll also look at the rewards that it can bring.

Aging is a passage we will all go through. It starts when we are born and it continues until the day we die.

There are many theories about the biological changes of aging. Some researchers believe it has to do with our genes, others say DNA plays a part. All seem to agree that lifestyle is a major factor. Living healthy is also the key: being smoke-free, keeping a reasonable weight, eating right, wearing seat belts, getting adequate sleep and exercise, and avoiding addictive behavior.

Mental health plays an important part in slowing the aging process by keeping one free of stress. Attitudes of acceptance, understanding, forgiveness and patience go a long way to extending life. And a lighter heart is a healthier heart.

Growing older also brings good things like wisdom, compassion and respect. So instead of studying the lines, wrinkles and bagging skin, we should think of aging not as growing older, but as becoming wiser and more experienced.

An archaeologist is the best husband a woman can have—the older she gets, the more interested he is in her.

—AGATHA CHRISTIE

GIRL TALK #259: Today I will celebrate the riches I have earned by taking responsibility for myself.

When you think of the years that women did not hold jobs, or the early jobs at low wages, it becomes easy to understand why women have difficulty asking for their own worth in terms of a salary.

Traditionally, women's salaries are not the same as for men. Even today, many women feel uncomfortable making more money than their partners. This is a crippling belief system.

Earning and spending money are basic human rights. It is time to believe that every woman should be paid according to the service she provides. We have the right to earn whatever we want without guilt. We are worth it.

Are you getting paid what you are worth? If not, it's time to stand up for yourself. If your employer won't ante up the money, start looking for a job that pays what you feel you are entitled to be making.

One can know nothing of giving aught
that is worthy to give, unless one
also knows how to take.

—HAVELOCK ELLIS

GIRL TALK #260: Today I will focus on my history, where my ancestors came from and whether they were persecuted for any reason.

When my father returned from Europe after World War II, he was a changed man. He spoke a great deal about the terrible things he had witnessed in the extermination camps like Auschwitz. Sometimes he would sit quietly and weep. As a child I knew bad things had happened, but I didn't have any idea of the brutality that took place.

Then came the film *Schindler's List.* I sat frozen in my theater seat along with countless others, as the story of man's inhumanity to man was played out on the large screen. For hours after the film I could not speak. Steven Spielberg is a brave and insightful man for wanting to preserve the memory of this horrible part of history so it will not happen again.

Fueled by indignation over what had occurred, I went to Washington, D.C., to visit the Holocaust Museum. Immediately I was connected to those who had perished as I watched videos and heard personal testimonies. I felt as though I had been transported to Poland, where most of the atrocities took place. Although the museum was crammed with teenagers and children on spring break, the mood was somber, not joyous or noisy. The respect was awesome.

If everyone visited the Holocaust Museum, perhaps we could all commit to doing whatever is necessary to live in a world of peace.

> . . . *the silent deep abode of guilt.*
> —MERCY OTIS WARREN

GIRL TALK #261: Today I will clean out foods that are not good for me and stock up on high-fiber, low-calorie, healthy foods.

It's a good idea to shop around the edges of a grocery store, picking up fruit, produce and fresh food, instead of staying in the middle where canned, boxed and junk foods are located. To go one step further, try proactive, healthy foods like these:

- Apples with soluble fiber that helps lower cholesterol
- Fish with heart-strengthening omega-3 fatty acids
- Soybeans, which help lower cholesterol
- Beans that are high in fiber and rich in vitamins
- Garlic, which is good for everything
- Bran, loaded with fiber
- Carrots, which are high in beta-carotene
- Citrus fruits, which have vitamin C
- Potatoes, a low-fat food rich in vitamins
- Watermelon, high in calcium and potassium but low in calories

These ten foods can make breakfast, lunch and dinner and keep you lean and fit. They can be mixed and matched with other nutritious foods like peanut butter, broccoli, onions and whole wheat bread. There's no need to load up on fatty foods. Read labels and shop wisely.

I need to be able to grab a snack!

—A WORKING MOTHER

GIRL TALK #262: Today I'll look at the boundaries that keep me feeling closed in and smothered. I will take responsibility for my own space and privacy.

Some mothers are so overinvolved with their children, they don't allow their offspring to establish a separate identity. These mothers shop with their daughters, or for them. They choose their clothes, makeup, books and music. They do their daughters' homework and attend school functions as chaperones to keep a watchful eye.

A daughter in a situation like this cannot breathe. She has no privacy. Her room, her thoughts, her friends and her life are invaded by Mother. When confronted, the mother responds by saying, "You're so important to me" or "All I want is your happiness."

Mothers of this kind physically intrude on their daughters' space by hugging, kissing, fussing and going through their personal items.

There are many good qualities in mothers like this, but their daughters are smothered by the possessiveness. While she wants to be close, the offspring can only back away, which makes the mother feel abandoned. Everyone gets hurt.

One of my clients had a daughter like this. She grew up thinking it was her sole chore in life to keep her mother happy. When the daughter married, the mother extended her smothering to include the husband as well. When the daughter had two sons, the mother became the caretaker of the entire family.

Sadly, the daughter was stricken by a fatal disease in her early thirties. But Mom was there to raise the kids.

If confronted, I'm sure she would never see or admit her overinvolvement and her daughter's struggle for freedom.

> *Nothing is more difficult than*
> *competing with a myth.*

—FRANÇOISE GIROUD

272

GIRL TALK #263: Today I'll make a list of the movies that I would like to see in the theater, and I'll make another list of videos I'd like to rent.

Going to the movies is an important ritual. I like matinees, which are less expensive and less crowded. I try to skip the very violent films and focus my energy on seeing the ones with a message or a laugh.

When I go with my husband, we add food to the ritual—popcorn, Junior Mints, a soft drink. Sometimes we sneak a lunch into a noon movie. A good film is like a book—it represents a point of view. It can teach as well as entertain, and it can take us to a place we haven't been. Reflective movies pose ethical and moral questions that we may not have thought about.

Finally, it's fun to discuss the merits, or demerits, of the movie afterward. Beliefs and feelings are often provoked, and it is interesting to find out how others feel about what was presented.

Movies invite us to expand our experience and our frame of reference. They're also a great way to get away from work and worry, and simply relax.

*Good movies make you care, make you
believe in possibilities again.*

—Pauline Kael

GIRL TALK #264: This is the day I will lighten up. The little things are not important enough for me to lose my sense of humor. The big things require that I maintain a sense of humor.

The ability to see the funny side of life is a gift. If you're not born with it, then it becomes a skill that must be honed in order to enjoy living to the max.

It is too easy to become a worrier or a complainer. Just listening to the news or reading the daily paper can paint the day with doom and gloom. However, the world is full of pleasures and delights, so it becomes a matter of choice. We can succumb to the problems of life, or we can develop a sense of humor about the daily occurrences that can get us down all too easily.

When we live in a state of balance, it becomes easier to maintain a high spirit. While it is important to be serious when the situation calls for it, don't forget that laughter and playfulness can ease the tension and stress. Taking life with a lighthearted approach doesn't mean being less responsible. It only means you are moving away from the negativity that can drag you down.

So keep a light heart and learn to see the up side of any given situation.

*The most thoroughly wasted day
of all is that on which we
have not laughed.*

—Sebastian Roch Nicholas Chamfort

GIRL TALK #265: Today I will clean out my handbag and get rid of anything I don't use on a regular basis.

Whether you carry a handbag, fanny pack or briefcase, chances are it's crammed with stuff you never use. If it's stolen, everything will have to be replaced. You don't realize what's in it until it's gone. So here are some valuable tips:

- Make photocopies of your driver's license, car registration, and all your credit cards.
- Leave the insurance card in the car.
- Take out two checks and leave your checkbook at home. Note the numbers in case you want to put a stop on them (the bank doesn't charge if your bag is stolen).
- Don't carry jewelry or anything you cannot replace.
- Don't carry a lot of cash.
- Try to keep your house keys in a separate place so your home is not an easy mark for a clever robber. Remember, your address will be on your license and registration.
- If your bag is lost or stolen, report it immediately to the police. Then call the bank to put a stop on the checks, and contact your credit card companies so they can cancel your accounts and watch for illegal activity.

Fashion fades. Only style remains.
—Coco Chanel

GIRL TALK #266: Today I will commit to making healthy and wise choices about my use of alcohol. I will not drive or swim after drinking and I will not be with anyone who does.

Alcohol does not mix well with driving, boating or swimming. Hard statistics back me up on this. Sadly, too many people underestimate the danger of a few drinks when they get behind the wheel of a car or boat. When it comes to drinking and driving, there's no happy medium except to abstain completely. The idea of a designated driver is wonderful. Too bad more people don't take advantage of it.

While the media keep the dangers of drinking and driving on the front burner, they don't include prescription drugs. Even over-the-counter medications can cause drowsiness. Unless you read the fine print, you may find your reflexes are slow and your judgment is poor—the same side effects as from alcohol. Be mindful of how you react to antihistamines as well as any other medication you may be taking. If you are a passenger in a car or boat, you should also be aware of what the driver may be taking in terms of alcohol, medication or illegal drugs.

Substance abuse can be the worst offender when you are behind the wheel of a 3,000-pound vehicle. Cocaine, crack, marijuana, heroin, uppers and downers all inhibit normal reflexes and response times. So if you indulge (which you shouldn't), please let someone else drive.

It is not hard to make decisions when
you know what your values are.

—ROY DISNEY

GIRL TALK #267: I'd like to interview at least one family member today so I can learn about my personal history.

Tracing one's roots is a wonderful thing to do. It will let you know more about your gene pool so you will be aware of any diseases that run in your family. Your roots will also help give you a feeling of belonging. You may be eligible for an inheritance that you didn't even know about. Curiosity is reason enough to start tracking down your genealogical roots, just to find out if the tall tales about distant relatives are true.

Now that I've piqued your interest, here's how to get started:

1. Interview family members for facts, anecdotes, myths and stories.
2. Search public records like the Social Security Death Index, the International Genealogical Index and the Bureau of Vital Records for deaths, marriages and births. These are available in county and other governmental offices.
3. Check church records, court records, the military and cemeteries. Remember to look for "compiled information," which is data someone else has already found.

Once you get started, new ideas and avenues will open up to you. Make sure to do this while elderly family members are still alive. Take a small tape recorder, as well as a pen and paper. Dig through old photos and find out who everybody is, where they are living now (if they are alive) or where they are buried.

Once you start, it will be hard to stop until you have the whole story to share with everyone else in the family.

There are persons who have some parts like me,
but no one adds up exactly like me.

—Virginia Satir

GIRL TALK #268: Today I will think about the times in my life that I let pain sap my energy and steal my ability to care for others. I will learn to go inside and find the courage and power to face and conquer the upsets in my life.

Although Lana is quite a bit younger than I am, she has much to teach me. When we first met, her radiant spirit drew me toward her. She had married a friend of mine and faced the daunting task of being accepted by his coworkers, family and friends. Lana rose to the occasion in a way that won the hearts of everyone around her.

I liked doing "girl things" with Lana—shopping, sharing lunch, making crafty-type gifts for others. She had a never-ending ability to make the most unbelievable things. Lana was the golden girl. And then the sky caved in. She faced a personal loss. The trauma that befell her was so devastating, we didn't know if she'd survive. How does one go on with a shattered heart?

As I watched her handle this difficult event in her life, my love and respect for her grew immensely. She went somewhere deep inside herself and found a strength and courage few people could have. As she battled back from the pain, she garnered the resources inside and faced life again without resentment or malice. She became stronger and even more lovable than ever.

From Lana I have learned to be strong in the face of disappointment and hurt. She taught me that we can use our inner resources and love to overcome pain. Lana is a true inspiration.

I long to speak out the intense inspiration
that comes to me from lines of
strong women.

—RUTH BENEDICT

GIRL TALK #269: This is a day to perform a random act of kindness. In fact, I think I'll make it a weekly ritual.

Little acts of kindness allow me to reach out and touch others. For a few minutes we can connect, and both of us will be nourished. There is a national trend now to perform random acts of kindness. Here are a few I have used:

- Let someone check out before me in a grocery or department store.
- Let someone else use the stall in the ladies' room when I'm next in line.
- Leave loose change in playgrounds so kids can find the nickels and dimes.
- Give a child a quarter (always with the parent's permission).
- Pay the toll for the next person in line behind me.

Little by little we can make this world a better place to live in. Moving in the direction of caring and kindness will not be for naught. The soul is strengthened and nourished with each of these acts. Add your own to the list and see how good it makes you feel.

Try it, you'll like it!

It would all be so beautiful if people were just kind.
What is wiser than to be kind? And what
is more kind than to understand?

—THOMAS TRYON

GIRL TALK #270: Today I will clear out old attitudes and make room for increased self-worth.

Too often we are asked to give our time, as though any of us has a surplus. Even though I'm always busy, I have always tried to be available.

Throughout my life, as I have become older and wiser, I have learned to practice discernment. Simply put, that means I have learned to say NO.

"No, I'm sorry I cannot drive you somewhere."

"No, I'm not free for lunch."

"No, I don't make telephone donations."

Giving up my time and energy for someone simply because the person wants me to is unhealthy behavior. I now have a sense of my own self-worth and my services; my time and my energy have a monetary value. If I told you that a trip to the supermarket for a neighbor would take up $100 worth of my time, you might be shocked. But that's the way we should calculate the monetary value of requests from others. It makes it easier to say, "Sorry!"

Can you protect your time as though it were money? Do you put a tangible value on your energy? If not, think about doing it. Trust me, this is important for your own self-esteem and feelings of self-worth.

I am more involved in unlearning than learning.
I'm having to unlearn all the garbage
that people have laid on me.

—LEO BUSCAGLIA

GIRL TALK #271: If I am faced with making a decision today, I hope I will make the right choice.

After moving to Texas, but before moving to Las Vegas, I lived in Palm Springs, California. Nothing prepared this small-town Minnesota girl for the shock of the upscale lifestyle there. The adjustment to Texas added a bit of down-home country to my life. But Palm Springs was like being on Mars.

The people who came to my therapy sessions in the past had been ordinary, working-class and blue-collar people. But in Palm Springs, many clients wore designer clothes, and gold and diamond jewelry. Many had lost fortunes to alcoholism. Some were learning to live on a fixed income after years of wild extravagance. Their value system was completely foreign to me, and it was my task to help them find meaningful activity and relationships.

Four months after setting up the program, my husband and I were invited to the Black Hills of South Dakota. We were so touched by the beauty, simplicity and genuineness of the people that we moved again to begin a new personal and professional life. The twelve years we spent there were the best of my life.

So what did I learn? I learned that it's all right to make a choice, take a risk and give it your best shot. If it's the wrong decision, you can always fix it.

Change and growth take place when a person has risked himself and dares to become involved with experimenting with his own life.

—HERBERT OTTO

GIRL TALK #272: I will give myself permission to develop my emotional intelligence just as I develop my mental intelligence. Both are important to my being a whole person.

There was a time when mental intelligence was the measure of success. Now we know that other qualities are also indicators of a successful person. They include aspects of emotional intelligence, such as:

- Social skills: the ability to interact and manage relationships effectively
- Empathy: the ability to read and respond to unspoken feelings
- Self-awareness: knowing how you feel and how to use those emotions
- Motivation: having a zest for life and optimism in most situations
- Sensitivity: knowing how to temper feelings in order to spare someone unnecessary hurt or discomfort

Too often we give more weight to mental intelligence than emotional awareness. We might even have been taught to believe that being too emotional was to be avoided. Society, in general, tends to minimize the importance of emotions and stresses the mental self.

Yet how we handle ourselves on an emotional level determines much of our destiny. If you want to improve the quality of your relationships and feel good about yourself, the emotional side of you will need to be developed. I'm sure you know successful and highly intelligent people who are social cripples when it comes to expressing their feelings.

The best way to improve your emotional output is to share your passions with others. Yes, it's risky. You put yourself out there at the end of a limb. So make sure the person you choose is trustworthy and reliable. But it's better to "let it out" than to bottle those emotions up inside. Letting go allows you to move on and experience life to the fullest, instead of harboring grudges and living in the past.

So let go of the emotional baggage. Start right now!

> *Even a happy life cannot be without a measure of darkness, and the word "happiness" would lose its meaning if it were not followed by sadness.*
>
> —CARL JUNG

GIRL TALK #273: Today I will think of some important people in my life who would like to get a letter from me. Then I'll sit down and write them.

A few years ago my daughter and I had a misunderstanding. After several discussions we resolved the issues. Yet inside me was a nagging voice that said, "There's so much more to say." While I didn't want to open old wounds, I wanted her to know how much I loved her.

Late one summer night I decided to write her a letter. That way she could read it, save it or throw it away. It would be her choice. That realization allowed me to sit down and share with her what I could not verbalize.

Letters can be a real eye-opener and can clarify issues that are muddy when two people speak. After my mother died, I went through her papers. I was astonished at the letters she had saved. Many were from me, written years and years ago. Those letters were a great source of comfort. They connected me back to my mother when she was no longer around.

Now letters are a regular part of my life. Through them I keep family members and friends up to date. I have documented my children's growing up and my career over the years. Letters from others add to my life in countless and immeasurable ways.

With the telephone and e-mail, the art of letter writing is in grave danger. But every effort should be made to keep it alive and well. The rewards are many.

When the most important things in our life
happen, we quite often do not know,
at the moment, what's going on.

—C. S. Lewis

GIRL TALK #274: Today I will remember that when I need an angel, one will appear.

In the late 1950s I was pregnant with my first child. I was naive in matters of babies and birth, since my mother did not talk about such things. Although I didn't have much information, I was thrilled.

My son was due on the fourth of November. On the night of the third, there was a terrible storm. So I called the doctor.

"I guess I should go to the hospital now," I said.

"Are you in labor?" he asked.

"No," I replied. "But if the snow keeps falling I won't be able to get there tomorrow." I assumed all babies came on the due date.

After my favorite show I put on an attractive black dress and high heels, and fixed my hair and makeup. Off we went in a blinding snowstorm. When we arrived, it was total pandemonium. There were thirteen ladies in labor and only two delivery rooms. Those of us that arrived last had to wait in chairs in the hallway.

Looking around, I felt a bit out of place all dressed up—but once my own labor pains began, it didn't matter. It felt as though I were coming apart at the seams. But God works in mysterious ways. Even though the nurses and doctors were too busy to pay attention to me, the woman next to me was delivering her tenth child. She eased me through the pain and panic. At five in the morning I looked into my son's eyes for the first time, and was thrilled down to my soul.

Angels soften the rough edges.

—ANONYMOUS

GIRL TALK #275: Today I will stock up on chicken soup so I will be prepared for the next cold I catch.

There has never been a reliable cure for the common cold. And it appears that even with all the medications available, there never will be one. So it's best to simply accept the fact that from time to time we will experience the common cold.

In a way, the cold itself is a cure. Toxins accumulate in your body. When they reach a certain level, they need to be expelled. With a cold your eyes water, you cough up phlegm, your nose runs. If you have a fever, the sweat will get rid of more toxins and you will burn up waste products. When we really understand that colds help clean our systems, we are more willing to let the process take its natural course.

The best thing to do with a cold is get comfortable. Make a bed on the couch with lots of liquid within easy reach. Have homemade chicken soup handy in the freezer and plenty of orange juice to replenish the vitamin C. Videos or a good book will keep your mind off your misery. Sleep as much as possible so the body can heal itself.

If you allow the cold to run its course without artificial interference, it will leave you feeling cleansed and healthier than before.

A contented person enjoys the
scenery on a detour.

—Anonymous

GIRL TALK #276: Feeling safe and having a sense of belonging is my mission for today. I will make any additions or changes to my life that I feel are necessary.

We found the tiny Minnesota town of Marine on St. Croix by accident, when we ran out of food while camping in O'Brian State Park. Outside the general store was a sign indicating the population was 602. The only other buildings in town were a bank, pub, restaurant, ice cream shop, breakfast cafe, service station and town hall. I was struck by the feeling that I had gone back in time to the 1930s. The atmosphere was vintage 1930-1940, but the people and action were contemporary.

After purchasing what we needed, my husband and I drove around town admiring the scenery and laid-back atmosphere. The serenity and peace were apparent. We both turned to each other and said, "I could live here." It truly seemed like a town time forgot.

Before returning to the campground, we called a Realtor and set up an appointment. Within a week we had bought a house and were settling in, feeling much like pioneers. Soon we learned about the town politics and the town mascot (a dog named Boozer, who is now long gone). We learned that the citizens are determined to preserve the integrity of community and safe, simple living. We are proud to be summer residents of this wonderful place.

There are no rules of architecture for a castle in the clouds.
—GILBERT KEITH CHESTERTON

GIRL TALK #277: Today I will set realistic and challenging goals that will bring me comfort and abundance.

M any of us were born poor. I was. So now is the time to address our fears and our shame. We had no control over the conditions of our birth. But what is important to understand is that we have the power over our choices and our financial opportunities NOW. We know what we can do and whom we can become.

It is important to affirm the fact that we can have financial security, abundance and wealth. With affirmations, we can influence our subconscious to believe that everything is possible. Once we have faced the issue of money and addressed it, we need to let it go. If money is a constant topic of conversation and brings up unresolved feelings, stop talking about it. Instead, put your words into action. Use your mind to formulate a plan to create realistic goals that will bring the money to you.

By visualizing abundance and a bountiful lifestyle, you will let go of the negative "poor me" attitude that holds you to the past. Once you let go, you can move forward to your goal of a better, richer lifestyle.

*Do not compare yourself with others, for you are
a unique and wonderful creation. Make your
own beautiful footprints in the snow.*

—BARBARA KIMBALL

GIRL TALK #278: Relationships often suffer from misunderstandings or hurt feelings. Today I will take a good look at how I can forgive someone, or ask to be forgiven.

The loss of a relationship because of anger, guilt or a misunderstanding that leads to hurt feelings is a common occurrence and a tremendous waste. When there has been a rift between people, either they drift apart or they must make a determined effort to reach an understanding and put aside their differences. Too often the chasm becomes so wide it cannot be bridged. To avoid that kind of situation, ask yourself these questions:

1. Does the person you want to forgive show remorse?
2. Has this person tried to apologize or make amends?
3. Is this person willing to discuss the problem?
4. Was the cause of the rift enough to damage the relationship forever?
5. How valuable is the relationship?

The answers to these questions will let you know how much time and energy to invest in repairing the damage. Don't forget to look at the part you played and how your actions or words may have contributed to the problem. Then ask yourself if your pride is more important than the person involved. If not, say you are sorry.

To begin healing, be honest. Talk freely about the hurt, anger, guilt and pain. That is the only way you can clear the air and begin to rebuild what you once had. Focus on the future and learn to forgive.

We are healed of a suffering only by experiencing it to the fullest.

—MARCEL PROUST

GIRL TALK #279: There are many people I'd like to say a prayer for, so perhaps I should start a prayer table in my home.

Many years ago a wise and wonderful woman told me about a prayer table she had in her bedroom. Whenever she wanted to pray for someone, she wrote that person's name on a piece of paper, put it on the table and said a prayer. Now I do it, too. Little yellow Post-it Notes are perfect.

On the table I keep meditation books, angel cards and other spiritual items. There was a time I had the names of four infertile couples on my table. As each couple had a baby, I removed their names. As situations resolve, I remove each name.

Every morning I put on a quiet meditation tape, read from a sacred book and say a prayer for someone who needs it. While I may plan many actions and many events for each day, my morning worship gets me off on the right foot, not only for myself, but hopefully, for those who receive the benefit of my meditation.

A special bonding happens when my husband joins me in meditation. We remember our friends and family together. When we have company, they often join in our meditations, and it is a holy time shared by all.

Prayer should be the key of the day
and the lock of the night.

—OLD MAXIM

GIRL TALK #280: Today I will start a grocery list to save time, money and energy. No more impulse buying.

Once a week I go grocery shopping. I buy fresh vegetables and fruit. We snack on them all week. Whatever is left goes either into the soup pot or a fruit salad. Whenever I make soup, I freeze some in small containers.

I try to buy in bulk and spend one day a week cooking and freezing. That way, when I don't have time to make dinner from scratch, I can pull a serving from the refrigerator and add salad and a loaf of bread.

Once a month I visit the discount store and stock up on paper products, canned goods, boxed items and laundry goods. I save time by making only one trip a month, and I never run out of supplies.

If you are making numerous trips to the store for one or two items, you are wasting valuable energy. And I'll wager that you are spending far more than you should. If you have children, you may have to get an extra gallon of milk, but everything else should be able to wait until shopping day.

It's never too late in fiction
or in life to revise.

—NANCY THAYER

GIRL TALK #281: There have been times I have lived alone. Today I will remember that it can be an experience of pleasure and comfort.

Living alone is one of those paradoxes where it can be the best or the worst of times. Learning to make the most of living alone is good training for living with someone. This is true for women and for men.

When I met my husband, I was very impressed that he knew how to clean a house, prepare a meal and throw a party. He didn't expect me to be the homemaker. He was quite adept from living on his own.

Likewise, I have met many women in my practice who are totally dependent on their mates. They do not know how to drive, balance a checkbook or make travel plans. These women will find themselves like fish out of water if they become widows or divorcées and have to fend for themselves.

There are advantages to living alone. You are free to come and go as you please, without guilt or apologies. You can take a bath in the middle of the day or walk around naked. You can get up at all hours of the night and putter around. You can turn the lights on and read a good book at three in the morning. Nobody will object. With the right attitude, living alone can be a pleasure.

What life means to us is determined not so much by
what life brings as by the attitude we bring to
life; not so much by what happens to us
as by our reaction to what happens.

—LEWIS DUNNING

GIRL TALK #282: Today I will look for ways to enhance positive feelings I have about myself. I will celebrate my unique talents and virtues.

Self-worth is what life is all about. The more we have, the more we can enjoy our day-to-day experiences and our relationships. But too often we appoint ourselves the judge and jury and pass judgment on our actions, thus undermining our own good feelings. We chastise ourselves for missed opportunities and disappointments, which are often not our fault. We feel that others are better, and we are unforgiving of our own shortcomings.

Since we are all here on earth to write our own script, now is the time to stop putting yourself down. Instead, put yourself on a pedestal. If you don't, nobody else will.

Take out a clean sheet of paper and vow to be proactive about your destiny and your feelings about yourself. Look back only long enough to decide what needs improvement. Then let go of anything that is dragging you down. You, and you alone, can make your dreams come true. If only half of your plans and efforts are realized, you have come a long way, baby. Your self-esteem will be sky-high.

So find the goodness inside you and recognize your own excellence. As you feel closer to your spiritual self, your connection to God or your Higher Power becomes easier, and you will see the beauty of your own soul.

Self-esteem is so delicate a flower that praise tends to make it bloom, while discouragement often nips it in the bud.

—Alex Osborn

GIRL TALK #283: Today I will get my junk mail stopped.

Junk mail and telephone solicitations can be STOPPED! If you are swamped with advertisements you don't want, there is something you can do about it:

1. Do not sign up for free giveaways at the stores. Those lists are sold to thousands of vendors.
2. Do not give your address to anyone who calls you. Those names are sold to thousands of vendors.
3. Write to Mail Preference Service, P.O. Box 9008, Farmingdale, New York 11735, and tell them you want to be taken off all junk mail lists.
4. Clip your name and address from any catalogs or unwanted material and attach to a postcard. Return to the sender with a note to take your name off the mailing list.

Why do telemarketers always call when you are cooking or eating? Because they know you are home at dinnertime. But you can fight back:

1. Don't just hang up when they call. Tell them to take your name off the list.
2. Get Caller ID and don't answer the phone.
3. Write to Telephone Preference Service, P.O. Box 9014, Farmingdale, New York 11735, and ask to have your name removed from all telephone solicitation lists.

If you can't fight and you can't flee—flow.

—ROBERT ELIOT

GIRL TALK #284: Today I will make a diet plan for myself and stick to it.

Whether you are trying to lose a lot of weight or you can't seem to shed those last few pounds, you are in good company.

For years I wanted to lose ten to fifteen pounds. With traveling and eating out so much, it was impossible. Temptation was everywhere. Then one day I decided the "then" was now, and I set my goal and stuck to it. One year later I had shed fifteen pounds and I have never gained them back. These tips worked for me:

1. Set a realistic goal.
2. Exercise regularly, not just when you feel like it.
3. Give up five trouble foods (for me they were cheese, burgers, ice cream, fried foods and pizza).
4. Add three healthy, low-fat foods (for me they were bananas, popcorn and potatoes).
5. Drink plenty of water—eight to ten glasses per day.
6. Take the stairs instead of the elevator.
7. Change to non-fat products.
8. Stop snacking between meals.
9. Save dessert for special occasions.
10. Park at the edge of the parking lot and walk those extra steps to the store.

Insanity is repeating the same actions over and over and expecting a different outcome.

—Anonymous

GIRL TALK #285: Today I will think about the little people in my life and take every opportunity to bond with them.

There is nothing sweeter than holding a baby and nuzzling the little body in your arms. Babies have that new-baby smell that is delightful. And as much as adults need that bonding time with babies, infants need it even more.

There are many ways to bond with little ones. You can:

- Hold and rock them.
- Sing or hum to them.
- Change their diapers.
- Feed them.
- Keep a journal to share later.
- Give them a bath.
- Play music or dance with them in your arms.
- Make a tape of you singing to play when you're not there.

By bonding with a baby from the beginning, you will be rewarded by the toddler who comes right to you and smiles to show his or her love. As the child grows to a preteen and a teenager, continue the bonding with shopping trips, movies and nature walks. There is never a shortage of things to do. Even just being together and looking at old family photos can bring the two of you closer together.

So begin at the beginning if you can.

Life begets life. Energy creates energy.
It is by spending oneself that
one becomes rich.

—SARAH BERNHARDT

GIRL TALK #286: Today I am willing to make any changes necessary to further my position in life.

During the 1970s, I was working for a national training and research company. The position took me from Canada, through the U.S.A., to Mexico and to Europe. After so much traveling, I decided to leave the company to be closer to home. It was a difficult and bittersweet decision. But it was the right choice, especially since the president of the company and I were in constant conflict.

From that I learned that even when things are going just fine, sometimes it is better to quit. There may be a better opportunity lying just ahead.

I experienced this again when I retired from my programs in the Black Hills. I was at the peak of my career; however, the company had grown so large that the responsibility was overwhelming. It required more hours than I could give and still remain healthy and happy.

So I left the field I loved so much, and now I write. And I love that almost as much. It allows me to spread the word to a wider audience, without the traveling and at my own pace. So you see, there is always a pot of gold at the end of the rainbow. You simply have to follow your dreams to find it.

To wait for someone else, or to expect someone else
to make my life richer or fuller or more mystifying, puts
me in a constant state of suspension and I miss all
the moments that pass. They will never come
back to me to be experienced again.

—KATHLEEN TIERNEY CRILLY

GIRL TALK #287: I will make a commitment to make my inside match my outside today. I will also find new ways to love and nurture myself.

Virginia Satir was instrumental in making family therapy an accepted form of counseling. She was dynamic when she lectured. Instead of reading or talking, she made it an experience. She invited people to come on stage with her to demonstrate whatever family dynamic she was speaking about. They stood on chairs to illustrate power and they lay on floors to show how people walked all over them. She brought out the best in people with her loving, nurturing nature. Virginia was possibly one of the most affirming and affectionate persons I have ever met.

She had the ability to be brutally honest in a way that made me thank her for criticizing me. She had no patience for wishy-washy people. Her clarity and straightforward communication made me become more direct with others. And she always said, "Your health depends on making your inside match your outside."

Virginia was a tall woman with a large body. Her eyes were piercing, almost hypnotic. But it was her books, seminars and workshops that changed lives. Mine was one of them.

From Virginia I learned how to nurture and love myself.

A woman's life can really be a succession
of lives, each revolving around some emotionally
compelling situation or challenge and each
marked off by some intense experience.

—WALLIS SIMPSON
DUCHESS OF WINDSOR

GIRL TALK #288: Today I will commit to being financially responsible to and for myself.

Financial security can free you up to follow a dream. It allows you to reach your potential and gives you the opportunity to help others reach their maximum capability. It is a value to be respected and achieved.

Every day, every woman should repeat this mantra: *I have the right to the wealth and security that God has provided for me.*

Those of us who grew up in poverty, or as the poor relative, tend to have more difficulty in achieving financial success and a sense of insecurity in our ability to earn a decent living. But I have come to learn that we all deserve the good things in life.

If you are struggling with your financial situation, if you feel responsible for others, or if you have not found your comfort level in terms of money, you need to sit down and make a list of goals. Then formulate a plan to make those goals become a reality. *I Exist, I Need and I Am Entitled* is the title of a wonderful book by Jacqueline Lair and Walther Lechler. This book supports personal responsibility.

Even if it is not fully attained, we become better
by striving for the higher goal.

—MARCIA WALTON

GIRL TALK #289: It's never too late to start a new activity. Today I will choose one so I can reap all the benefits it has to offer.

At the peak of my career, if someone had said that my next major undertaking would be tap dancing, I would have laughed myself silly. Yet being part of a dance troupe has become a major part of my life.

Some people may say it's a frivolous or inappropriate thing to do at my age. I disagree. Tap dancing is wonderful exercise and a terrific way to socialize. I've established bonds with other women that are as deep as the ones I had in high school and college. Our shared experience offers support and encouragement when we cannot learn the steps or routines as quickly as some of the younger gals. There is a feeling of accomplishment and solidarity as we work toward a goal. Above all, it's fun and it doesn't feel like exercise at all.

Once we have the routines down pat, we perform at civic functions, casinos and festivals. The money that we make is donated to the needy, which means that we are not only having fun and instilling confidence in ourselves; we are also making the world a better place to live. That's a worthy combination.

I'm proud to be a member of the dance company and I plan to do this as long as I can—at least to eighty or beyond. When in Las Vegas, come out and see this showgirl tap to her heart's delight.

We do not stop playing because we grow old.
We grow old because we stop playing.

—ANONYMOUS

GIRL TALK #290: Today I will see if being adaptable is a skill I have developed. If not, I'll see if there are ways I can be more flexible.

T he only constant in life is change. Things change: People get married, separated, divorced; they get hired and fired; they make money and lose it. People are born and they die. Natural disasters and illness take us by surprise with their swiftness and devastation.

Learning to adapt and remain flexible are the only ways to adjust. When we are rigid, the stress is enormous. Just look at a tree in a hurricane to understand. The supple willow bends, while the tall and stately, yet rigid, elm will snap in half. Being flexible lessens stress and allows us to survive forced change with our physical and mental health intact.

When I became ill a few years ago, the doctors told me to stop vigorous hiking. It was a devastating limitation, giving up one of my favorite activities. Then I discovered the joys of tap dancing. And you already know how I feel about that.

I was flexible enough to accept the change in activity with grace and good humor. That's what it takes to turn a bad situation into a golden opportunity.

All our resolves and decisions are made in
a mood or frame of mind which
is certain to change.

—MARCEL PROUST

GIRL TALK #291: Today I will evaluate my intuition. Do I second-guess myself?

Intuition is simply our inner vision sending messages to our brain. It can be a blessing or a curse; it can be a help or a hindrance.

Insight may give us messages that are loud and clear, like when to leave a job, when to commit to a relationship, when to persist in a difficult task. But it can also be confusing and stressful, with messages like when to leave a relationship, when to give up something we like doing, or when it's time to move on if we want to stay put.

Messages are received daily—gut feelings that are trying to tell us something. Instead of filtering out the ones we don't want to hear, we must train ourselves to accept ALL messages—even those that challenge us. We should have the courage to trust these messages, honor them, and make decisions based on how we FEEL, not on what we THINK.

Intuition is rarely wrong. It's only inaccurate when we fail to recognize it and have the courage to follow our convictions.

It is only with the heart that one can see rightly;
what is essential is invisible to the eye.

—ANTOINE DE SAINT-EXUPÉRY

GIRL TALK #292: A meditation room would be nice to have in my home. Then, when I need comfort or inner peace, I'll have a place so seek solace.

When we moved into our log home in Rapid City, South Dakota, we wanted to make a meditation room—a place to say thank you. We collected angels, spiritual artifacts from the Lakota Sioux, religious art books, music and candles. Every morning we would meet whatever guests were staying with us in that room and share music and scriptures together.

The miracles that came out of that space were abundant, but none so clear as the wild forest fire that threatened to destroy our home.

Four thousand acres were burning, and we had been evacuated. I begged the firemen to let me return to gather our valuables. Amazingly, they let me. But once inside, I didn't know where to begin; we had so many personal treasures. When I got to the meditation room I looked around and was reminded of all the wondrous things that had happened because of the prayers said there.

I dropped to my knees and said, "Dear God, please protect this home and keep it from fire. If we lose it, please give me the strength to bear the loss." Then I left the house with nothing but hope in my heart.

For two days we stayed in a motel in town while the fire raged and heard nothing about the fate of our beloved home. When the roads were passable again, we hiked four miles from town to assess the damage. Incredibly, the fire had burned across our yard and had stopped within ten feet of our house!

My prayers had been answered. We didn't even have smoke damage. If that doesn't prove that our meditation room was a place of miracle-making, I don't know what does.

All miseries derive from not being able
to sit quietly in a room alone.

—BLAISE PASCAL

GIRL TALK #293: Today I will reflect on the lack of relationship with my grandfathers.

G randfathers come in every shape, size and temperament. Those who are most revered are the ones that play an important role in the lives of their grandchildren.

Both my grandfathers died when I was young, so there was an empty place in my life where they should have been. From my friends, however, I have learned a great deal about grandfathers. Grandfathers can be many things:

- Historians, who collect photographs and news clippings to make a record of the family for future generations
- Teachers, who share their skills with computers, cars, wood-working, finances, photography, cooking, music
- Role models, who impart important values about not smoking, drinking or taking drugs
- Caretakers, who help out when the parents have to work or who offer money when young families have financial difficulties

Sadly, grandfathers can also be negative role models. Sometimes a family must explain about an alcoholic or drug-addicted grandpa, or one that is violent or abusive. Youngsters need to be protected from these adverse role models. Every relationship presents an opportunity and a handicap. Grandfathers are no exception. And everything that can be said about grandpas goes for grandmas, too.

Gentleness is not a quality exclusive to women.
—HELEN REDDY

My daughter, Deborah, has four children, each of them a treasure. She is an excellent mother who nurtures, loves and cares for her offspring. She also home-schools her children.

When she first told me she was planning to do this, I was quite reserved about the effectiveness of the situation. All the children I had known had always gone to a traditional school. Since Deborah has an advanced degree in education, I was certain that she would see the value of regular schools. But she persisted in her endeavor.

When I visited her home I always noticed that it was very child-oriented. There were clocks, charts and words everywhere. She and her husband showed endless patience answering questions, and the children showed remarkable curiosity and ability to think for themselves.

The results of their homeschooling are beginning to show. Math has been taught in a practical way and the kids can use it in everyday life; their reading skills are truly amazing. I was worried about their social skills, but they have learned to interact and they show confidence and maturity.

Perhaps the greatest value is that the children love each other and feel respected. The qualities of trust, sharing, affection and creativity are all in place. My daughter tells me they may always be home-schooled or they may use public schools later. Now and then my son-in-law takes his son to school to see where Daddy teaches.

So I have learned to be more tolerant, to not pass judgment so quickly, to assess a situation and to evaluate it before condemning it. Whether or not these children ever choose to attend public or private school, they will have the best foundation a child can have. They love to learn. What lesson could be more valuable? And I'm grateful that my daughter has a mind of her own that was not discouraged by my concerns.

The mother's heart is the child's schoolroom.

—Henry Ward Beecher

GIRL TALK #295: If I need to ask for help from others I will see it as progress, not as interference or weakness.

As a public speaker and consultant, I found I could not keep up with the requests for my services. At the same time, in my city, there was a man who was trying to set up a series of programs to treat alcoholism in middle- and upper-class families. He asked if I would help him develop these programs. In return he would make me president of the company.

Until that point in my life, I had only myself to answer to. Now I would have to report to a board of directors. Did I want to give up my autonomy and enter the corporate world? It took a while to decide, but I finally told him yes.

Onsite Training and Consulting was incorporated in 1978, and I was the first president. With the help of a dozen business-people, we made training films and designed training events sponsored by corporations. Six years after forming the business, I bought it and moved it to the Black Hills of South Dakota.

There, we expanded again to include many treatment programs for eating disorders, addiction, nicotine dependence, and family and relationship issues. When I retired I sold the company. It is still flourishing, and the integrity and quality of the programs are first-class. There is a steady flow of people finding healing in their lives.

A rock pile ceases to be a rock pile the moment
a single man contemplates it, bearing within
him the image of a cathedral.

—ANTOINE DE SAINT-EXUPÉRY

GIRL TALK #296: Today I will enjoy miracles that come to me and also commit to making miracles for others.

One of my greatest pleasures is being able to share money. I love to buy cards and gifts to let people know how much I appreciate them. I love to make things possible for others in ways that they could not, or would not, do for themselves.

I believe that money is a gift that allows opportunities to happen. I also feel that the more we give, the more there is to give. As I help another, he or she can help someone else in turn.

When we all share financially, spiritually, intellectually and emotionally, we feel as though we are part of the universe. We are all connected by the energy that binds us together.

If you have ever been touched by a gift from someone else, perhaps now is the time to pass it on. It does not have to be a large sum or an expensive gift; anything that brings a bit of happiness to someone else will do the trick.

You can make miracles happen. Even five dollars given to a child can make a dream come true. A little deal can change a life.

There are only two ways to live your life.
One is as though nothing is a miracle. The other
is as though everything is a miracle.

—Albert Einstein

GIRL TALK #297: Today I will meditate on honesty in relationships.

In all relationships, there are times of misunderstandings, hurt feelings and disagreements. This is especially true in families. If these feelings are kept inside or ignored, they can fester and hurt until the people concerned become estranged.

I am blessed to have a daughter, Sandy, who refused to let hurt feelings and misunderstandings get in the way of our friendship. Sandy is an adult now and our relationship is open and honest. She has taught me the value of being honest, sharing what's on our minds, and facing disagreements with mutual respect. She confronts when necessary and loves unconditionally. She has my respect.

Every woman reading this page has these powers. Whether you utilize them and how effectively they work for you are very personal matters that only you can decide.

The greatest gifts are not got by analysis.
—Ralph Waldo Emerson

GIRL TALK #298: This will be the day I ask for grace. Then I will see what happens. It might be a good idea to ask regularly until I have inner peace all the time.

Grace is spiritual energy that is sent by our Higher Power when we need it. Sometimes we pray for it, at other times it surprises us with its arrival. It is a clear sign that we are not alone—that God is with us.

I am a shy person who has spent twenty years lecturing in front of large audiences all over the world. Grace was the reason I could do it, and do it well. The messages I had to deliver were important. I guess you might say it was my spiritual calling.

Whenever I walked onto the stage, knees trembling, palms sweating, I said a silent prayer that I would be able to get through the session. I was never disappointed. The power of grace is unlimited and available for the asking, any time of the day or night, like a twenty-four-hour spiritual convenience store.

When you experience a smooth day during which everything goes off without a hitch, you are having a grace-filled day. Is it any wonder that people sing the song "Amazing Grace" with such zeal and passion?

Ask, and it will be given to you;
seek, and you will find; knock, and it
will be opened to you.

—MATT. 7:7 NKJV

GIRL TALK #299: I will make a list today of sizes, colors and things I think my friends and family might appreciate. Then I'll begin searching for holiday gifts.

Whatever the reason, season or occasion, gift giving is always a pleasure—for both receiver and giver. At my house I have a gift resource center, a place where I've stored odds and ends that can be given on the spur of the moment to someone who needs a lift or a gift. I never worry when holiday time comes around, since I'm well stocked with presents. Last-minute shopping is not my style, and prices are better when they're not jacked up for the holidays.

Under my bed is a large, flat, plastic case that holds ribbon, paper and tags. When an occasion arises, I simply reach under and get whatever I want, with no pain, strain or credit card charges!

When we pay attention to our family and friends, we remember who likes books, who prefers tapes and CDs. We know the colors that each of our friends likes most. When we really know the people in our life, we can always be shopping and be ready. We will be able to avoid last-minute, impersonal gifts.

There is only one real deprivation, and that
is not to be able to give one's gifts to
those one loves the most.

—May Sarton

GIRL TALK #300: I am willing to be exactly who I am. When people come into my space, they recognize my personality by the choices I have made for myself.

B ette Midler is outrageous. When I first saw this tremendously talented woman, she struck me as a complete individualist. I loved her immediately for being what she is, and being proud of it. She marches and dances to her own beat, and she inspired me to become more independent and eschew expected conventions. I purchased black and white sunglasses, brightly colored clothes and fun costume jewelry. My taste in home decorations reflected my need to "nest," not impress. I felt increased freedom as I made carefree choices.

Whenever I put on an outlandish outfit, I think of Bette. When I see an artifact or brightly woven rug, I think of the lady with the golden voice and buy it. I'm sure decorators would get an instant headache looking at my decor. But it's ME. My clothes and my surroundings say who I am.

So, Bette Midler, here's to you: a debt of gratitude for taking this shy, introverted, wishy-washy Midwesterner and making her stand out in a crowd.

> *One reason I don't drink is I want to know*
> *when I'm having a good time.*
>
> —Lady Nancy Astor

GIRL TALK #301: Today I will contemplate what remarriage would mean in my life and what effect it would have on the people I know.

Marriage is a strong and powerful commitment between two people. Each must leave his or her own life behind so the two lives can be blended into a cohesive whole.

When one or both parties marry for a second, third or fourth time, this is not the case. Emotional baggage, and often children, come along for the ride. The enormous challenge of making a new marriage work requires maturity, compromise, acceptance, and a great deal of love and patience.

If either party has been divorced, there will be feelings of anger, hurt, betrayal, guilt and loneliness. Money certainly will be an issue, as will housing. Where to live can become a major stumbling block if one party must move into a home vacated by a prior spouse. New adjustments will take time, and it is unfair to expect a new relationship to have a fair start if old business is still unfinished.

If remarriage comes on the heels of one spouse's death, there will be a necessary grieving time that cannot be rushed. There will be guilt and comparisons, which is not fair to either party or to the memory of the deceased. Photographs of the departed should not be expected to disappear overnight, nor should the new spouse feel jealous of someone who no longer exists, except in spirit.

But all of this is easy to say and difficult to put into practice. Since I can speak from experience, I can tell you that when two people are successful in joining together in holy matrimony, with love and compassion and a willingness to work through the difficult times, remarriage can be one of life's greatest joys and achievements.

When one door of happiness closes, another opens.
Often we look so long at the closed door that we do not
see the one which has been opened for us.
—HELEN KELLER

GIRL TALK #302: I believe in my own capacity for goodness, and today I will look for the goodness in others. I will put myself in a few places where I can have my faith renewed.

Faith is believing in the moment. The past has been important and taught us many lessons. The future holds some wonderful rewards, but we are not yet there. So those who live in the present have the most trust that all will turn out for the best.

If we read the newspaper and watch the horrendous things portrayed on television, we may begin to doubt that life holds any worthwhile promise. But as humans, we have an inherent need to find faith in our culture, our legal system, our nation, our fellow men and women, and ourselves.

Faith is a healthy affirmation that people are worthy and good. There are many fine causes that are supported by selfless citizens who want to do the right thing. Instead of focusing on the negative, accent the positive and have faith that everything works out the way it was intended.

> *When we stop looking at whatever troubles us*
> *and turn to faith in God, the source of*
> *good, the difficulty disappears and*
> *a new condition takes its place.*
> —WILLIAM A. CLOUGH

GIRL TALK #303: Today I will consider my commitments and do what I can so people can count on me.

When George Bush was running for president, the chairman of my company told me that I was expected to attend a fund-raising prayer breakfast. It did not matter to him that I had already booked an 8 A.M. seminar. When I tried to get out of it, he simply said, "Figure it out and be there."

Naively, I thought that a 6:30 A.M. breakfast would be over within an hour, leaving me plenty of time to make my eight o'clock commitment. I was wrong.

When I arrived at the breakfast, I found to my dismay that my table was right in front of the podium—a prime location where I was effectively trapped if I didn't want to make a spectacle of myself leaving. So I stayed.

Finally, at 7:45, the emcee announced we were free to leave as soon as Mr. Bush was out of the room. The Secret Service quickly surrounded him, and as they started to move, I jumped up and joined them. Nobody said a thing. I simply became part of the moving mass of people that was getting a head start out of the building.

I thought nobody had spotted me—until the ten o'clock news came on. There I was, leaving the breakfast with the presidential party! My chairman was not amused, although I did catch him grinning. My children thought it was a great way to solve a problem.

> *Life is a series of problems. Some want to moan*
> *about them and some want to solve them.*
> —M. Scott Peck, M.D.

GIRL TALK #304: If I have not decorated for Halloween, I will do it today.

My favorite season is fall—with the harvest and the beautiful, earthy colors that warm my heart. Fall says we must give up the outdoor life of warm, lazy summer days and find our way back indoors, to get ready for another winter.

Halloween is the holiday that marks this change for me. A few weeks before, I decorate the house with pumpkins, which I have carved into jack-o-lanterns with funny faces. The original idea of All Saint's Eve has been forgotten, and Halloween has taken on a meaning of its own. It has become a night of fantasy, when children and grown-ups alike dress in outlandish costumes and pretend to be whatever they desire. It's a big costume party and everyone is invited. The prize is all the candy you can eat.

Nowadays the mall merchants offer goodies. It provides a safe, nurturing environment where the little ones can do their trick-or-treating without fear or embarrassment. It's a good example that rituals can change to fit the needs of modern times.

So if you are in the Halloween spirit, go out and have a great time. Enjoy a night of wild imagination, with ghosts, goblins, costumes and treats.

We have our brush and colors; paint
paradise and in we go.

—Nikos Kazantzakis

GIRL TALK #305: What are true riches? Today I will think about money and how I can be happy even if I don't have wealth.

While I was growing up, I didn't realize how poor my family really was. Looking back now, I see that it was the love and comfort that made me feel rich, although my clothes were made from feed sacks from my father's chicken hatchery. Our vegetables came from my mother's garden, and my dad's hatchery provided fresh eggs. Meals were always delicious and plentiful. On Sundays we had large family dinners with a bounty of food and merriment.

Since my grandmother worked for the Great Northern Railway, we received free train passes. I often went with her. We'd go to the dining car and, instead of ordering food, she would open her picnic hamper, which was stuffed with cold meats, cheese, bread and her famous doughnuts. It never occurred to me that we couldn't afford to buy the food served aboard the train. In fact, I felt sorry for anyone who couldn't enjoy my grandma's homecooked meals. In the corner of the cupboard, my mother kept a small metal box filled with coins, mostly quarters. Whenever a special occasion arose she would unlock it and provide me with whatever funds I needed.

Perhaps being penniless is a state of mind rather than a reality. We may have been cash-poor, but we were rich in resources and love.

> *Some things are very important and some are*
> *very unimportant. To know the difference*
> *is what we are given life to find out.*
>
> —ANNA F. TREVISAN

GIRL TALK #306: Today I will choose one behavior to reduce daily stress.

We live in a stress-filled world. Tension can be brought on by family, friends and work, as well as by cars and appliances breaking down. It is also brought on most commonly by lack of money. Since stress adversely affects our health, and money can help relieve some of our worries, something must be done.

The best way to remedy this situation is to use the funds we have available to reduce our overhead. In other words, maximize your cash flow by simplifying your life. That means giving up the extras, at least until money is no longer a worry.

Here are just a few ways that come to mind:

- Trade in an expensive car for an affordable one.
- Lower your car insurance premiums.
- Shop for less expensive clothing.
- Take care of your shoes; make them last longer.
- Avoid the mall and impulse shopping.
- Don't carry a lot of cash.
- Leave the credit cards at home.
- Browse, don't buy.
- Conserve on water, heat and air conditioning.
- Go to matinee movies, which are less expensive.
- Bring your own snack to the movies.

There is more to life than
increasing its speed.

—MAHATMA GANDHI

GIRL TALK #307: I will look at my creative urges today and let them flow. Hopefully, they will bring me hours of productive pleasure.

Creativity can take a myriad of different forms—writing, cooking, designing stained glass, orchestrating parties, playing music, taking photographs, gardening, plus a zillion more. Whatever activity brings you joy, takes you out of the humdrum of ordinary life and nourishes you, do it. When we like what we do, and feel a sense of accomplishment and productivity, it boosts our self-esteem. As our activities grow and expand, so do we.

As we create on the outside, our creativity creates us from the inside. New ideas and fresh awareness come to us as we become involved. Inspiration comes in waves, and life appears to rush by in a whirlwind of activity. Living creatively is going with the flow, trusting it and not limiting ourselves. Many of our greatest ideas come when we're not even looking for them, and they balance our lives by adding a new dimension that is play, not work. So if you have a talent, express yourself in whatever way gives you pleasure. Find a way to make it part of your daily routine. Some of the most creative artists started out with only a spark of an idea. By developing that artistic notion, they let their imagination take them to new and unlimited heights.

If you are seeking creativity, go out for a walk.
Angels whisper to us while we are walking.

—ALICE T.

GIRL TALK #308: I may walk only a mile a day or exercise for fifteen minutes, but today I will make it a regular part of my schedule.

Even with so much emphasis on physical fitness, the majority of Americans remain inactive. Those who exercise want to do it more, while those who avoid it do so with a passion. Yet there is no question that regular, moderate workouts keep us healthy, stave off depression and make the soul feel good. By following this three-point guideline, you can create a regular habit that will keep YOU in tip-top shape.

1. Choose activities that you enjoy. Decide whether you want to be indoors or out, with friends or alone.
2. If you are out of shape, get your doctor's approval before you start an exercise regimen. He or she may discover that you have a problem that you don't even know about (for me it was my heart). That way a suitable program can be devised to keep you healthy without aggravating any existing condition.
3. Set simple goals. If they are too difficult or too strenuous, you won't stick to them. Once you're in the exercise mode, you can always increase your mileage or the time you devote to whatever activity you've selected.

Whatever you do, it adds up. The average of three miles I walk each day tallies up to 1,000 miles a year! In three years I will have walked the distance of New York to California. It works for me. What works for you?

Getting started and being regular are what it takes to establish a healthy habit.

—Estelle Moran

GIRL TALK #309: Different cultures have unique places that they hold sacred. Today I'll reflect on which one I can visit.

The first time I went to the holy mountain at Bear Butte, South Dakota, I felt privileged to be accepted by the Native Americans who worship at that site. I began climbing the path upward, dwelling on the many generations of people who had used this same road as part of their spiritual journey. To my right were small sweat lodges. In the silent, still air, smoke curled toward the sky. Inside, people purified themselves in the hot darkness—ridding their bodies of toxins to prepare themselves for sacred truths.

There is a spiritual trail where ribbons representing people's concerns hang in the trees. Some have been there for many years. I added mine with my own prayers. The many colors of the many ribbons are comforting. The higher I went, the more I was surrounded by the beauty of trees, rocks and vistas. Nature's glory is breathtaking. Upon arriving at the top, I could see in every direction. I felt as though I were on another planet, one that was quiet and serene, with no problems, stress or hassles. I prayed on the summit, expressing gratitude to my Higher Power for allowing me to have such an awesome experience. I return as often as I can.

Never measure the height of a mountain
until you have reached the top.
Then you'll see how low it is.

—DAG HAMMARSKJÖLD

GIRL TALK #310: Today I will see what is healthy for me. I will nurture and protect what is, and I will get rid of anything that is not.

You would think that everyone would choose to be healthy. After all, who wants to be sick? Yet simply eating right and exercising are not always enough. When I became ill, I had to look beyond my own boundaries and into the environment. I began choosing restaurants that had non-smoking sections. If I was invited to a party where smokers would be present, I declined. I learned more about nutrition and exercise than I ever thought I would need to know. And I had to look at the people in my life. Just as there are toxic foods in the store and carcinogens in the air, there are people who are bad for our health. They drag us down and destroy our immune systems. I had to separate myself from anyone who was negative, highly opinionated or morbidly depressed.

My health is a high priority item, and I am the only one who is responsible for it. So it makes good sense to me to do whatever is necessary to protect it. How about you? What do you do to promote your state of health?

To gain that which is worth having,
it may be necessary to lose
everything else.

—BERNADETTE DEVLIN

GIRL TALK #311: Today I will be honest about what I need in my primary relationship. I am worthy of sensitive care and affection.

Little things mean a lot, especially in an intimate relationship. It's often not the big things that strain a union, but the small ones. Here are a few problems that I've heard over the years from my women friends:

- He never compliments me.
- He doesn't pay his way.
- He is jealous of anything that requires my attention.
- He doesn't want to meet my family.
- He doesn't remember my likes and dislikes.
- He ignores me in mixed company.
- He is not affectionate.
- He does not attempt to participate in the things I like.
- He is selfish with the remote control and his choice of TV shows.
- He expects me to accommodate his schedule.
- He forgets birthdays and anniversaries.
- He contradicts or corrects me in front of others.

Take a look at your mate, or the men you date. If they are guilty of more than two of the above, it's time to think about your choice of men.

> *To be told we are loved is not enough.*
> *We must feel loved.*
> —MERIAN JACOBER

GIRL TALK #312: Today I will accept the responsibility to be true to myself and know that my reality will be a product of my choices.

To overcome the pain of my parents' alcoholism, I became an overachiever. I overcompensated in all areas of my life. Instead of leading a balanced existence, I became a workaholic. Everything I did was in excess. It was no wonder that I burned out. In therapy, the more I learned about my need to be the family hero, the more I began to change. I learned to give myself a break now and then, to find an equilibrium that allowed me to get my work done without making me a nervous wreck. There were many changes I needed to make.

Later in life, when doctors discovered I had a serious illness, their diagnosis forced me to change again. New choices were necessary a second time, and I had to give up unnecessary obligations. It was time to simplify once again and adjust the scales so they tipped in my favor.

Today I live a healthy and relatively quiet life. I am also armed with the knowledge that my life is an accumulation of sound choices that have made me what I am today. My challenge is to keep making healthy choices.

> *The great victories of life are oftenest won*
> *in a quiet way, and not with*
> *alarms and trumpets.*
>
> —BENJAMIN N. CARDOZO

GIRL TALK #313: It is important to keep relationships positive so they bring joy, not pain. Today I'll see what I can do to improve the ones I have.

It can sound distasteful to talk about people as clutter, but at times they can bring disorder to our lives. When we let people sap our energy and intrude on our privacy and time, when we try to take care of everyone else's needs to the exclusion of our own, it's time for a drastic change.

To prevent this from happening, write down your top five friendships. This can be quite an eye-opener. Next, commit yourself to spending leisure time only with people who make you happy or bring you joy. Do not feel obligated to maintain friendships that don't make you feel good.

Learn to say "no thanks."

At work or at home, with friends, relatives or coworkers, if there is a situation that is bothering you, deal with it. Address the problem and move on. Who needs more stress in the form of a chink in a relationship? There's too much tension in the world already without adding more. Air the problem and resolve it. If you can't work it out, cross that person off the list. There's no time or room for toxic, negative people. Lighten your load and brighten your day.

It's only when we truly know and understand that we have
a limited time on Earth, and that we have no way
of knowing when our time is up, that we begin
to live each day to the fullest—as if it
was the only one we had.

—ELISABETH KUBLER-ROSS

GIRL TALK #314: Today I will listen to my own conscience. And when I hear the message I will act upon it.

We all have an inner guide. It is called intuition, conscience, a sixth sense or a gut feeling. Whatever the name, it nudges us into action. Therefore, it is important to listen to the clues it sends and the messages it gives our heart. Too often the point is lost or ignored, or worked into a logical solution that we don't put into practice. I recall a time when a friend called and wanted to take a walk. At first I said no, but a nagging feeling made me call her back and say yes. During our stroll she spoke about her mother, and our conversation led me to a revelation about my own mother, which led to a further healing for me. If I had not gone, I would probably still be struggling with that problem.

So take it from one who knows. When the inner guide calls, do not ignore the sound. We all have a purpose and a connection. And we can only find that by listening to the voices from the heart.

*There is guidance for each of us,
and by slowly listening, we shall
hear the right word.*

—RALPH WALDO EMERSON

GIRL TALK #315: The memories of people I have lost will be in my thoughts today. And I will turn to those I love and make the most of the time we have together.

When Beth and I met, we were both looking at our roles as wives and mothers, but what really bonded us together were our sense of humor and search for spirituality. Inevitably, no matter what was going on in our frazzled lives, we managed to have a good belly laugh and a good talk.

One night I was entertaining guests when the phone rang. I thought I'd let the answering machine pick up, and yet something told me I'd better answer it. Beth was on the other end.

"Sharon," she said, holding her voice steady, "the police are here. They've just told me our son has committed suicide."

I was speechless. Her son was twenty-two, in the prime of his life. Her only son was dead. How does one console a mother with such a grievous loss? My heart hurt and my soul wept and I wondered how she could survive.

As quickly as I could manage it, I went to see her. We fell into each other's arms and cried. She shared the details of his death, as well as her thoughts, feelings and fears. Her questions were only for God to answer, not I. Over time she began to heal; slowly she learned to smile again. Several months later, I heard her laugh.

Beth goes forward, not back. She has a loving husband and a daughter, and she had been blessed with grandchildren. Her son will never be forgotten, but Beth will recover and laugh again.

> *My grief was too deeply rooted*
> *to be cured with words.*

—ORINDA

GIRL TALK #316: Today I will listen to see if God speaks to me. I will trust my senses about authentic spirituality.

As a Catholic, I had always dreamed of visiting Rome. To me it seemed as though it would be the holiest place on earth.

When I finally arrived a few years ago, I felt an incredible elation as I approached Vatican City and St. Peter's Basilica. Yet when I left, I felt like a deflated balloon. Instead of being connected spiritually, I felt only sadness. The church that I had so long esteemed appeared to revolve around power and wealth, not love and faith. That visit started a renewed thinking about my feelings regarding the Catholic Church—a process that continues to this day.

However, there were other places in Rome that touched my heart and stirred my soul. At the Colosseum I could still hear the screams of the gladiators. At the Sistine Chapel—a magnificent and quiet place where Michelangelo worked miracles with a paintbrush—I had a truly spiritual experience.

The trip taught me to trust my feelings when it comes to God and spiritual matters. We can find holiness in a rock and find it missing from a cathedral.

> *Let nothing disturb you.*
> *Let nothing frighten you.*
> *Everything passes away except God.*
>
> —Saint Theresa

GIRL TALK #317: Retirement is a new beginning. So today I will reflect on what it will be like for me.

Retirement means different things to each of us. Some fear losing their identity when they leave active employment. Some picture living on a fixed income, playing shuffleboard and scrambling for early-bird dinners. These people feel that the productive time of their lives is over, and they wait for the clock to tick to the end. They avoid the word "retirement" like the plague, and they don't even allow their grandchildren to call them Grandma or Grandpa. Instead, they want nicknames because they're so terrified of being a nonproductive old person. How sad.

These days, retirement means redirection. It is a time to travel, volunteer, develop new skills and hobbies, connect with family and friends. The retirees I know are more active now than when they worked full-time! They have to squeeze their activities around an exercise schedule that is designed to keep them alive as long as possible.

When retirement is a positive state of mind, the possibilities for contributions to society are endless. To be a successful and happy retiree is one of life's greatest challenges. Are you up to it?

Positive thinking is the glue that binds
loose ends of our lives and keeps
us from falling apart.

—DARRELL SIFFORD

GIRL TALK #318: Today I will meditate on the chaos in my life and I will try to make some order of it. Perhaps I can stop juggling so many balls at one time.

There are times when I realize I am on overload. I am simply doing too many things at once. I am trying to please too many people and not taking the time to find a quiet place for myself.

When that happens, I must look at all my activities and begin sorting through them, finding a few things to let go of. It will make me lonely for a while, for these are all activities I like doing. But, as they say, something's got to give.

What is important is that I understand what is happening. Taking a good hard look at myself will help me put these changes into effect. Excess in any form does not serve me well. So I give myself permission to regulate my activities in a way that gives my life balance and harmony.

With the extra time, I will meditate an extra fifteen minutes a day. This will bring me closer to my Higher Power, and it will also bring me closer to myself.

> *Nowhere can a man find a quieter or*
> *more untroubled retreat than*
> *in his own soul.*

> —MARCUS AURELIUS

GIRL TALK #319: If I take a look at the larger picture of life, maybe I will see that everything is relative.

There are ways of feeling rich and ways of feeling poor. It has nothing to do with money. It's a matter of perspective.

My father owned a chicken hatchery. He was the only resource for chicken feed in our small town. The distributor brought huge sacks of grain to my father. Once the grain had been sold, he would distribute the sacks to the farmers so their wives could wash and iron them, and use them for clothes and household items.

The sacks could be seen as fabric for poor people. Or they could be seen as unique pieces of free cloth. Since it was my dad's business, my mother and I had first choice. Therefore, I grew up feeling lucky and special—in my own way, rich.

For years, all my clothes were made from feed sacks; however, they were the first choice of feed sacks. So it really doesn't matter what you have or don't have. Feeling rich is a state of mind.

> *No life is so hard that you can't make*
> *it easier by the way you take it.*
>
> —Ellen Glasgow

GIRL TALK #320: Today I will forgive myself for the mistakes I have made. Making errors does not make me a bad person, only an inexperienced one.

As a young wife and mother, I was grateful to live in a beautiful split-level home in a suburb of Minneapolis. The house had off-white carpeting, ivory drapes and elegant furnishings. The lower level had a playroom and a fireplace. It was quite a sophisticated dwelling for such a young homemaker. One winter day I decided to clean house. I lit the fireplace, put on a music tape and got to work. Just as I was finishing downstairs, I noticed smoke in the living room. There was trouble. I dialed the fire department and they arrived within a few minutes. By the time they found the source of the fire, there was a gaping twelve-foot hole in the living room wall. It seems that the twenty-six-degree-below weather had cracked the bricks, and the fire had moved into the insulation and then into the house. For three weeks we lived in a hotel until the repairs could be made.

Later that year it happened again. This time I had forgotten to close the fireplace screen tightly, and a few embers had touched the brand-new carpet, setting it ablaze. To avoid calling the fire department a second time, I grabbed the vacuum and sucked up the embers. I thought the problem was solved until I smelled smoke from the closet. Not only was the vacuum melted down, the clothes hanging in the closet were burned to a crisp.

I guess some lessons are hard for me to learn the first time around.

I think most of us become self-critical as
soon as we become self-conscious.

—ELLEN GOODMAN

GIRL TALK #321: A crisis can happen at any time, so today I will be available in case there is one. I will also not be shy if I have a crisis and need to ask for help.

Families in crisis are quite common. Take a number of people who are related to each other, add illness, money problems, loss, stress, hurt feelings and lack of communication, and you can see that problems will arise with regularity. Pulling together in a crisis requires a basic assortment of tools. Here are a few:

- Deal with the crisis one step at a time; don't try to solve all parts of the problem at once, or it will seem an overwhelming task.
- Accept the fact that transitions—weddings, births, deaths, moves and job loss—will be difficult. Support is needed during these times, not attitudes or bruised egos.
- Let go of the past. It's over and done. Move in the present and look to the future.
- Seek help outside the family circle for those problems that cannot be resolved.

Some families share a formal religious service and can find comfort that way. But no matter what, each person should respect and support the desires, opinions and wishes of each other family member in order to get through times of trouble.

We could never learn to be brave and patient
if there were only joy in the world.
—HELEN KELLER

GIRL TALK #322: Today I'll think about pets—those I have and those I have lost.

I grew up in a family that loved dogs. Skeeter and Pudgy were two of our pets, but I didn't really bond with either of them. They really belonged to my parents and siblings. So when they died, it was not a serious loss for me. However, when my own children wanted pets, it was a different story. Pepper was a brown terrier that became my bosom buddy after my divorce. She sensed a change had taken place in our household, and at night she would pad into my bedroom and settle down across my feet. The weight and presence of Pepper helped me heal in those early days of sleeping alone.

When she became ill with old age, it was a painful sight. Nobody could bear to have her put to sleep, even though she had to be carried outside to go to the bathroom. Then one snowy morning, after I had taken her out and settled her back on the rug, she looked at me, pleading with those big brown eyes to put her out of her misery. I took her to the vet for the last time that afternoon. It was so painful for me that I cried for two full days.

Since then there have been Snoopy, Tashia, Toby, Trixie, Jake, Mindy, BJ, Kaila and Nicky—all dogs owned by my children. I have come to see the value of the love shared between pet and master. Pets can bring out love, care and compassion the way no human can.

Love comes unseen, we only see it go.

—AUSTIN DOBSON

GIRL TALK #323: Today I will explore the child within me. Somewhere is a photo that will bring me back to that magical time.

Today, as a grown-up, there are many ways to experience and express my spirituality—through books, meditations and talks with God. Yet one of my favorite motivators is a photograph of me when I was five years old. I see a vulnerable little girl who was cared for by her Higher Power when nobody else could or would. I see her creativity, spontaneity and compassion. Her loving nature shines through, and I am proud to be intimately acquainted with her.

I know personally there were many times in her life when no one met her needs. Now, as an adult, I can care for the little girl within me. I can take care of her today, nurture her and commit myself to protecting her feelings.

It is important that we not forget the little girl that resides in each of us. It is a wonderful way of giving a deeper and more expansive love to your own children and grandchildren—as I have done with mine.

Look for the eternal child within you and promise to be good to her.

This above all: to thine own self be true.
—William Shakespeare

GIRL TALK #324: Good sleep patterns are important to my well-being. If I have problems, I vow to
take action to resolve them. A good night's sleep will
be my goal.

Experts say there is a growing problem of sleep deprivation
in this culture. They point fingers at several conditions:

- Late-night TV programming, which can seduce viewers to
  stay up past their bedtime
- Night shifts, which put the body's rhythms out of sync
- Business travel, which puts people in different time zones
- Too much stress, which interferes with our rest

The seriousness of this problem is underestimated. Chronic
tiredness impairs judgment and timing. It contributes to acci-
dents in cars and on the job. It increases tension, hostility and
impatience. Job and scholastic performance are diminished. Our
health suffers.

To improve sleep patterns, go to bed at a regular time—
preferably an hour earlier than usual. Drink warm milk and take
warm herbal baths. Avoid alcohol, rich foods and exercise just
before bedtime. Sleeping pills should be used sparingly, not as a
crutch. They can be addicting and they will leave you in a fog.
What happens if there is a midnight emergency and you are
drugged into a stupor?

There are sleep-disorder clinics if the problem is serious. For
the rest of us, try the tricks above and see if they help.

When I hope for nothing
but peace and sleep, the chattering echoes
of recent concerns race through my mind and
the more rest I seek, the less I can find.

—JOANNA FIELD

GIRL TALK #325: Taking no for an answer too easily might cheat me out of some very special experiences. So today I will go the extra mile in asking for what I want.

After a conference in New Orleans, several presenters (including me) wanted to hear some authentic Dixieland and jazz. We strolled down the street, stopping in here and there to listen to music. Finally we came to a club where the famous jazz trumpet player, Al Hirt, was performing. The show was sold out, so we tried to get tickets for the following day. But we were told they were being sold on a first-come, first-served basis.

The next day we scooted out of the conference and headed for Bourbon Street, but we were too late. The show was sold out. Frustrated and disappointed, we vowed to try a third time. Even though we left the session as early as possible the following day, we were told, "Sorry, sold out."

One of the people in our group decided to tell someone how he felt. He went back inside and came out a few minutes later with a big grin on his face. "We're in," he said proudly.

Inside there was not a seat available, much less a table for four. To our amazement, two waiters set up a special table for us right on stage! Then they brought out four chairs, and the host ushered us onto the stage for the best seats in the house.

> *It was a once-in-a-lifetime experience*
> *to say the least. You can't cross*
> *a chasm in two steps.*

—RASHI FEIN

GIRL TALK #326: Today I will say thank you to my female friends, and I'll say thanks to myself for nourishing such excellent companions.

Female friends are treasures. We bond together in ways that women and men cannot—even the most intimate of lovers. Women share the same feelings and experiences, the same highs and lows, frustrations and exhilaration that only another woman can understand.

The awkward years of puberty, dating, body changes, marriage, sex, pregnancy and birth are changes only another female can relate to.

There was a time in my life that female friends took a back seat to my career and to my male friends. At that moment, guys seemed more vibrant and interesting. Then, slowly, I realized that women have a depth of soul and a spiritual courage that make a better connection for me. In retrospect, I see that I separated from myself. I let my career and responsibilities define who I was. In other words, I gave myself over to others instead of being true to myself.

Today, I am happy to say, my female friends are on the top of my list when it comes to priorities. I cherish the time we spend together and I value their company, their thoughts and their input when I have a problem or a crisis. So cheers, gals—thanks for being there for me when I need you. I will try to reciprocate whenever you call.

I have learned that to have a good friend is the
purest of all God's gifts, for it is a love
that has no exchange of payments.

—FRANCES FARMER

GIRL TALK #327: Today I will give myself a pat on the back for not smoking. My commitment to protect myself will include being free of second-hand smoke, too.

If you smoke, STOP! Make it a top priority to end your addiction. Research has shown that smoking negatively affects your whole body. It damages the heart and destroys the lungs. It decreases bone density and increases blood pressure. It dries the skin on your face, causes wrinkles around your mouth and turns your fingers yellow. Each pack of cigarettes cuts hours off your lifespan and adds stress to your body. It smells awful, it's bad for your children and unborn babies, and it's expensive.

Even though the tobacco industry targets women and makes them feel that smoking is "cool," it really isn't. If you smoke, decide you are worth quitting. If you don't indulge, be grateful. Spread the word to others that smoking kills. Be a noisy advocate for nonsmoking areas in restaurants, social events and even the mall. Insist upon it.

If you or someone you know wants to quit, the withdrawal is fairly simple these days. The nicotine patch does wonders; so do hypnosis and other aids. There is also a Nicotine Anonymous group that offers a 12-step program to help you detox from this toxic habit. Look in your local phone book for more information. Or try an eight-day program called Onsite Living-Centered Program at 800-341-7432. It has helped hundreds and can help you, too.

The preservation of health is a duty.
Few seem conscious that there is such a
thing as physical morality.

—HERBERT SPENCER

GIRL TALK #328: Today I will find a sacred place I can use for myself so I can more easily feel the spiritual energy that is available to me.

If spiritual energy is everywhere, why do we need sacred places, like churches, to connect with God?

The answer is that we need to trigger the emotional bonding with our Higher Power in order to receive comfort. Having a special place doesn't necessarily mean a cathedral or a revival tent. It can be a corner in your home, a shrine, or even a table, like I have. It can be out in nature, near a mountain or an ocean. You can find it in the change of seasons or the quiet of a forest. When a crisis or problem arises in your life, it is much more comforting to retreat to this special place and meditate or pray for assistance or answers. Lighting candles or reading from scriptures, counting rosaries, ticking off prayer beads or even spinning a Tibetan prayer wheel all have the same effect—serenity and attachment to an energy higher than oneself.

Sacred places remind us of our connection to our Higher Power and offer comfort when we most need it.

If one advances confidently in the direction
of his dreams and endeavors to live the life which he
has imagined, he will meet with a success
unexpected in common hours.

—HENRY DAVID THOREAU

GIRL TALK #329: Independence is a wonderful thing. I pride myself on my ability to care for myself, and today I will reflect on what mastery means to me.

To master something means to know all there is about the subject. It is a measure of accomplishment.

Now is the age of mastery for women. Until the present day, women were expected to be homemakers and little more. But since the mid-1970s, women have been pouring out of the universities and into the work force in such large numbers, and with such quick and capable minds, they cannot be discounted or ignored.

Women are learning to take control of their lives and become independent of their male partners. The result is that they are enjoying autonomy, freedom and economic security for the first time in history.

Having mastered that stage, women have begun to look around for a life mate. The difference this time is that they are not financially or emotionally dependent on a man. Instead, they meet as equals—each bringing into the union a part of themselves they want to share. The neediness is gone and men should be glad to be wanted for themselves, not for what they can provide.

I can vouch for the fact that having a loving relationship with a partner on an equal footing makes the bond doubly satisfying. It's like having it all.

Each woman reading this book is on her own road to self-mastery. Some will be farther along than others. No matter where you are, you can have it all, too. It takes perseverance and time, it takes energy and an open heart, spiritual bonding and a positive attitude. Any woman should be able to put herself in a position of independence so she can take or leave a relationship on her own terms, instead of giving up her sense of self, her freedom and sometimes her life.

Where are you on the road? How far do you have to go, or are you already there? No matter where you are, move forward.

Do not stay frozen in time or space. Go ahead, get going. The rewards are many and well worth the effort.

No one can really pull you up very high, you lose
your grip on the rope. But on your own
two feet you can climb mountains.

—LOUIS BRANDEIS

GIRL TALK #330: Today I will find at least two ways to simplify my relationship with the telephone. Then I will appreciate the peace and quiet.

At the height of my career, the telephone rang incessantly, both at home and at the office. Even though I had an unlisted number, so many people had it that the ringing was a constant intrusion. So I decided to have one telephone, only for emergencies. I made special arrangements with a service that would only ring me if it was a dire predicament. All other calls were forwarded to a professional answering service that operated twenty-four hours a day.

While my friends and family didn't see why I needed to exclude myself from the telephone, it did save me from those annoying telemarketing and solicitation calls. It was truly amazing how much extra time I had without the constant interference.

I learned to treasure the quiet times during meals and conversations with my husband. I learned that I could live quite nicely without a telephone and that there was never an emergency that went unheeded, even though I did not pick up the line directly.

Today I have a telephone, but I screen most calls with the answering machine. My number, which is still unlisted, is changed from time to time to protect my privacy.

If you find your life overwhelmed with calls, you can get Caller ID to identify who is calling you. An answering machine is a must so you can screen calls, and most private lines have a call-back feature.

While telephones are a definite advantage, they can also be a drawback. But you don't have to be a victim. Take control of your time and life. Disconnect if necessary!

The ordinary arts we practice every day at home
are of more importance to the soul than
their simplicity might suggest.

—THOMAS MOORE

GIRL TALK #331: I am woman! Today I will challenge myself to be true to my convictions and take a stand on issues that are important to me.

In 1963 I read the book *The Feminine Mystique* by Betty Friedan, and my world began expanding.

During high school I had been active in finding increased medical care in rural communities, as well as in unraveling the dynamics of family systems, including addiction. I became a district, regional, and finally, a state speaker on these topics. Then I became a young mother, and my days consisted of changing diapers, sterilizing bottles and cleaning house. After reading Betty's book, I woke up from my "social coma." She inspired me to explore my values again; she challenged me to be the woman I always knew I could be. She did not let me hide my thoughts and opinions.

My sudden burst of energy and my expressed opinions were a shock in our social circle, where men talked and women listened. While it alienated some friends, I gained far more in return. And one important lesson was learned: There was always someone with the same opinion as mine. If it meant changing allegiances, that was a small enough price to pay. The reward was that I enrolled in college, standing behind my convictions with renewed self-confidence.

From Betty Friedan I have learned volumes about my role as a woman and the power I hold. She has inspired me to remain active and excited about every stage of my life.

Mankind has advanced in the
footsteps of men and women of unshakable faith.
Many of these great ones have but stairs in the heavens
to light others through the night.

—Olga Rasmainath

GIRL TALK #332: I am thankful for my friends and family and for the traditions and rituals that bring all of us together. On this day of Thanksgiving, I will say a prayer that we may all remain together.

Giving gifts is a tradition I cherish. So is giving thanks. Once a year we all get together to share time and food, stories and love. It is a treasured day for me, and I expect my sentiments are shared across the nation in the homes of all Americans. At least for one day, all differences can be set aside and compassion and respect prevail.

As the aromas of turkey, ham, baked potatoes, squash, and pumpkin and apple pies waft through the home, all the good memories of my youth and my married life are revived. And as I look around at my daughters and their husbands, their children, my son, my spouse and whichever friends have joined us for this special day, I am overwhelmed with gratitude for the life I have had. What more can one person ask than to have loving family and acquaintances nearby to share the bounty of this great land?

Whatever you do on Thanksgiving, know that I will be saying a silent prayer for each and every one of you—that your day is filled with love and peace and gifts of nourishment, both spiritual and emotional.

It is not what you give your friend but
what you are willing to give that determines
the quality of friendship.

—MARY DIXON THAYER

GIRL TALK #333: Today I'll reflect on a lesson I learned one dark night: If you're going to play in the sandbox, know the rules before you get in.

While I was living in South Dakota, I had the privilege of learning about a small subculture in America called the Harley-Davidson biker society. Every August, nearly 250,000 bikers and their spouses, mates and significant others gather in Sturgis, South Dakota, for a week of togetherness.

The town is small and every hotel, motel and campground is filled for miles around. Some brave townsfolk rent rooms for $150 a night, and downtown merchants watch with glee as their supplies dwindle and their cash drawers swell. During "Bike Fever," celebrities like Peter Fonda, Jay Leno, Malcolm Forbes and Elizabeth Taylor show up where least expected. Food and fun flow, and everyone seems happy.

After work one evening, I decided to see what all the hoopla was about. Six therapists and my husband and I dressed in traditional black Harley garb, pasted tattoos on our arms, slipped into our boots and silver jewelry and headed to Sturgis.

All went well until one of the guys went to the men's room and came back to our table white as a sheet. Seems he was spinning a tall tale about getting there on his "hog" when a huge biker, with arms that looked like they could lift a car overhead, began to challenge the facts. That, effectively, put an end to our charade, and we left in a hurry in our getaway car. We've had many great laughs about that night.

People are more fun than anybody.
—DOROTHY PARKER

GIRL TALK #334: Sometimes the choices we make may cause pain, but in the long run they are usually best for everyone. Today I'll think about some of the choices I have made.

Although my first marriage was a source of great pain and was emotionally devastating for me, my religion forbade divorce. In addition, my children were young and I had no viable source of income. But the distress was so severe, it was making me physically ill. Despite the credo from the Church, the only alternative was to seek a divorce. It was a choice not lightly made; in fact it was one of the most difficult decisions I have ever made.

My husband was furious when I filed the papers; my family disowned me. With no support system, I had to care for my three young children and work full-time to support them. During those difficult years, it seemed that when everything was too much, an angel would appear to rescue me or an event would unfold to get us through the crisis.

Divorce is never easy, yet there are times when it is the only alternative. When I wrote *Life After Divorce*, it helped me reframe the circumstances and see them as a necessity instead of seeing myself as a failure. I also realized that although I had filed the papers, I had not left the marriage first. Partners can abandon their mates emotionally long before a physical separation takes place.

As I look back at that difficult time, I give myself a message of appreciation that I worked through a terrible hardship. The result was that my children and I have thrived. It was a painful but correct choice.

I have now joined the fellowship of
those who live in pain.

—Dr. Thomas Dooley

GIRL TALK #335: I have creative desires and abilities. Today I will see what possibilities there are for developing my talents.

Outside many small towns is a place called the dump. That's where people take things they no longer need. It's not a place for garbage. Instead, you'll find broken toys, boxes without lids, dishes with chips and old furniture that has no place in the home any longer. Periodically a bulldozer rolls them under the earth and another pile starts.

When I was a child, the dump grounds were only a mile out of town. My friends and I would make regular trips there. For us it was a treasure trove. We'd bring large bags and go through the items carefully, selecting only those precious things we wanted. There were always pieces of costume jewelry, books, boxes, dishes for tea time, and odds and ends that we would take just for fun.

To this day, I love to create something new from something old. In thrift shops and antique stores I can spot a treasure instantly. The dump grounds enabled me to develop a creative eye and attitude; they helped me see beyond the obvious and ordinary. The supplies were throwaways, but the new products that came from them were gems that sprang from our fertile imagination and enterprising effort.

Imagination is the highest kite
one can fly.

—LAUREN BACALL

GIRL TALK #336: I am a woman who has gone through many stages. Today I will review some of them.

Our bodies go through many stages during the years, from birth to death. It's almost mind-boggling how much we change, grow, develop and shrink.

We started all soft and cuddly but unable to do anything for ourselves. Getting teeth and learning to walk were the first two stages toward our independence, for we were now mobile and we could chew food. The developments that took place during puberty were the next major passages toward womanhood—breasts and menstruation, which meant we could bear children. During the child-bearing years, although our bodies did not change much, they went through tremendous transformations—first with swelling bellies and breasts, then trying to return to our pre-pregnancy shape.

In the late forties and early fifties, the body began to change again. The skin and hair became drier, periods slowed down and then stopped, hot flashes and night sweats began, and insomnia often became a new kind of curse. We needed more time to rest and vitamins to boost our energy levels.

Moving toward the sixties, the blood vessels lose their natural protection provided by estrogen. Heart problems increase and osteoporosis creeps in, making bones brittle. We don't lubricate the way we once did, and intercourse can be painful as well as pleasurable.

As long as you know what's coming down the road, you can arm yourself with an exercise routine, a healthy diet, vitamin and mineral supplements, and hormone creams. These changes will eventually come to pass, just as all of our heads will turn white. But you can stave off the ill effects of growing older by being good to yourself.

May you live all the days of your life.
—JONATHAN SWIFT

GIRL TALK #337: Today is a good day to reflect on my inner wisdom. I will learn from my victories and my mistakes, knowing both outcomes leave me better than before.

Wisdom is the ability to judge soundly and deal sagaciously with facts. Simply put, wisdom is good sense. There is no way to develop wisdom except by living, learning and experiencing. We profit from our mistakes and our achievements. Nobody is born with it, we learn through trial and error.

Insight guides us through the dark corners of our spirit, where myths and problems try to bring us down. Prudence shows us the way out of conflict and dangerous situations. Discretion helps us find those who can guide and teach us, and who can help us improve our self-esteem and increase our knowledge.

We can pray for wisdom and it will come to us in the form of hunches that, if we listen, will give us a new perspective on an old situation. We all long for happiness, an easier life and the ability to reap the benefits that come with advancing age.

While nobody can give you insight or perception or the ability to be wise, the more experience you have, the more wisdom you will find right inside yourself.

The price of wisdom is above rubies.

—JOB 28:18 NKJV

GIRL TALK #338: There have been teachers in my life that were special. Today I'll reflect on some that helped me learn worthwhile lessons.

As a young child I was terribly shy. It was such a problem that it was considered a handicap. Although I would know the answers to the questions the teachers asked, I was unable to raise my hand, nor was I able to speak in front of the class.

In ninth grade, my English teacher noticed my struggle and offered to help me practice speaking. We stayed after school working on my problem. Through her affirmation and positive feedback, I was eventually able to break through my difficulty. Ironically, and probably because of her help, I found my calling as a public speaker.

The choir director was another teacher who directly impacted on my life. She was a single woman who lived in a rented house. Music was her main interest, and when she conducted our choir she drifted into a world of her own. The sophisticated clothes she wore and the beautiful rings on her fingers made me want to emulate her style.

These teachers and others invited me into places foreign and intriguing. They helped me find my way in this difficult world and encouraged me to find my own sense of self-worth.

Life is like a library owned by an author.
In it are a few books which he wrote himself, but
most of them were written for him.

—HARRY EMERSON FOSDICK

GIRL TALK #339: The teenage years are the most difficult. Today I will think about not criticizing the teenagers in my life. Instead, I will be more understanding and supportive.

Adolescence is a time of tremendous change, not only with bodily transformations, but with the need to find independence. Separating from family, whether physically or emotionally, involves challenging authority, testing limits and sharing daily life with peers instead of parents and siblings. Understanding and accepting the natural flow of growing up do not help solve the problems that arise from day to day. But they should make it easier to roll with the punches and not get caught up in power struggles and hurt feelings.

To help you cope, choose your battles. If you don't, you will be fighting all the time, over insignificant things along with the major ones. Battling over cars, safety, and drinking and driving is important, but quarreling over who's doing the dishes isn't. Since it is vital that teens develop a sense of self-worth, it is essential that they win a fight or two. Let them have their way with clothes, food and the music they want to play, even if it's not your choice. Get ear plugs. And beware of ultimatums—they can backfire with dire consequences.

Most important are keeping the lines of communication open, showing unconditional love and maintaining respect as a two-way street.

One of the oldest human needs is having someone
to wonder where you are when you
don't come home at night.

—MARGARET MEAD

GIRL TALK #340: This is the day to focus on my office to see if I can be more centered.

T he focal point of my office is a large calendar. When I put it up on January first, I write down all the important dates and activities so I know what's coming up and when.

On my desk are three writing pads. One is TO DO, another is TO BUY and a third is CALLS TO MAKE. Items are added and subtracted with regularity. By writing down these tasks I can keep my mind uncluttered with trivial thoughts about what to do and when.

My best ideas come at night while I'm watching TV or in a dream that wakes me up. I keep a pen and paper at my bedside to capture those moments. I know from experience that I won't recall the idea when I wake up in the morning. So I jot down enough key words so I'll remember when the sun comes up.

All of the telephone numbers I use on a daily or weekly basis are on speed dial. They are also on a large sheet under the glass top on my desk. I don't have to go hunting for my address book when I need to make a call in a hurry. A quick glance and the number is right there.

Hanging folders keep all my papers in order, so the top of my desk is always empty. This makes it easy for me to give whatever project I'm involved with my complete attention.

If you have an office at your place of employment or at home, maybe these tips can help you get organized.

Strive and thrive.

—ROBERT BROWNING

GIRL TALK #341: Today I will concentrate on healthy choicemaking until it becomes a natural and easy part of my life.

In my book *Choicemaking*, I wrote a poem that I taped to my bathroom mirror. It made making choices easier for me. I hope it can help you, too.

Choicemaking

Every day I have before me many choices
It's not easy to choose
For often the choice means letting go
Of the past
Of the present
I know what the past was
I know what the present is
But the choice propels me into the future
Whether or not I make the right one.

It's not easy to let go
It's not easy to fly into the future
It's like the space between trapezes
It's not knowing whether you'll be caught
It's not knowing whether you'll fall
It's not easy to trust.

That space between trapezes requires faith
I must admit that my faith is often shaky
I hope and pray that I'll make good decisions
That I'll be caught and will not fall.

God creates. People rearrange.

—JOSEPH CASEY

GIRL TALK #342: Being safe is a top priority for me. So today I will look around my home, my office and my car to be sure I have taken precautions.

Every few seconds a crime is committed against a woman. Rape, robbery, assault, purse snatching, kidnapping, carjacking, domestic abuse, murder. We need to take strong personal steps to lower our exposure to these dangers. So look at this list and see if you are guilty of placing yourself in jeopardy.

- Don't flash expensive jewelry or handbags.
- Don't withdraw cash from ATMs late at night.
- Watch where you exercise; avoid deserted places day and night.
- Avoid being intoxicated; you're easy prey.
- Do not be the only woman in a group of men.
- Don't fumble in your bag for your keys; approach your car and front door with keys in hand.

If your partner is abusing you, report it and make plans to leave. Keep away from anyone who is threatening or stalking you. Make sure the police and your family know the circumstances in case anything happens. In your home, protect yourself with adequate lighting outside, locks on the doors and windows. Start a Neighborhood Crime Watch.

Most important, pay attention to those you know. Rape and murder are usually committed by friends, spouses or acquaintances. In an argument, take any threat seriously. Keep yourself safe at all times.

Let us not look back in anger, or forward
in fear, but around in awareness.

—James Thurber

GIRL TALK #343: Today I will do my best to avoid situations that may be harmful in any way.

My first trip to Mexico was quite an experience. I went with a training group that had rented an entire motel outside Mexico City. I felt at a disadvantage not knowing any Spanish, but I tried my best to make my desires known. When I needed two pillows, I held up two fingers, then folded my hands and put my head down as though I were sleeping. That did the trick—sort of.

The bellboy brought two pillows along with my luggage. But when he opened the door to my room, he stepped inside and started to drop his pants. I was shocked to realize he thought I wanted company for the second pillow. I shook my head (the universal sign of NO WAY, JOSÉ) and he left looking quite disappointed.

There are some things that don't need words to be understood.

One cannot have wisdom
without living life.

—DOROTHY McCALL

GIRL TALK #344: Today I will honor the special place in my heart I hold for my aunts.

Although I had several aunts, four stand out as being exceptional. Elaine, Lorrie, Gertie and Harriet always made me feel special and important. Even as a youngster, they spoke to me as an adult; they asked questions that needed long answers. When I talked, they listened. Each in her own way gave me a gift.

Elaine, the sophisticated one, showed me how to dress and wear makeup. Lorrie, the essence of motherhood, taught me how to be a mom as I watched her lovingly tend her own nine offspring. She knew how to hold a family together, and I tried my best to absorb all she had to offer. Harriet, the schoolteacher, loved to learn. She inspired me to further my education. And Gertie was a domestic whiz; she made my favorite foods when I visited and I always felt welcome in her house.

Being an aunt does not have the responsibilities of a parent. Aunts can be more lenient and a bit more outrageous. My aunts would tell me family secrets and laugh at the funny things my relatives did. They let me stay up late and filled my ears with gossip.

My aunts now live quite a distance away, but I try to visit whenever possible. Walking in the front door is like returning to history, knowing there is a loving place waiting for me.

The reasonable thing is to learn
from those who can teach.

—SOPHOCLES

GIRL TALK #345: Today I will remember that everything has a purpose, and some things are more important than others.

The beauty of New Zealand is renowned. I have traveled through this amazing country by car, van, boat, jeep and air. One of my favorite experiences was to visit a sheep farm where nineteen different breeds of sheep were raised. They were everywhere, as far as the eye could see. To keep them from running wild, and to bring them in when necessary, sheepdogs were used. These brilliant pups can control huge numbers of animals, rounding them up and even sorting them out into different pens. Watching them made me realize each creature on Earth has its own purpose.

This lesson was driven home at the Waitomo Caves in Rotorua. A young Maori guide explained that the boat we were on was going to be pulled quietly and gently inside a cave. "You'll see something wondrous," he said. As we glided into the cool dark interior, the walls and ceiling of the cave were lined with glowworms shining eerily in blue. Millions of them cast an azure glow—until someone on the boat sneezed. Suddenly it was pitch black. These glowworms are extremely sensitive to noise, and the sound of the sneeze caused them to "turn off" their glow.

It was later explained that the only purpose of these glowworms is to produce light until they die.

So we each have our special purpose in life. The sheepdogs, the glowworms, you and I. Don't forget that. I won't.

Be not afraid of life. Believe that life is worth living and your belief will help create the fact.

—WILLIAM JAMES

GIRL TALK #346: Traditions give me comfort. Today I'll commit to nurturing them no matter what.

The first Christmas after my divorce was particularly painful. There was a nagging emptiness to remind us that we had changed as a family.

As the holiday approached and the radio stations began playing carols, I was flooded with memories. My tears flowed freely. I remembered my grandma coming to visit with cookies and other goodies. And I recalled my father dying on Christmas Eve. So I decided to have a different holiday—one that wouldn't fill me with sadness.

"Instead of a tree and lots of presents, I'm going to take you to Disney World in Orlando," I told my kids. Their faces brightened at the prospect and I felt reassured that my decision was the right one.

The first night in our motel room, my son astounded me by bringing in a small, artificial silver tree. He set it up and proceeded to decorate it with bulbs he had lugged along from home. He'd also brought presents. It touched my heart and added a homey warmth. At the tender age of twelve, he was already attached to the tradition and did not want to lose it. He told me it was important to keep what we valued and held in high regard. From my son I learned that rituals and traditions bring comfort and solidarity to hard times.

Great thoughts always come from the heart.
—Marquis de Vauvenargues

GIRL TALK #347: Self-care is important. So today I will pick at least two ways to take care of myself.

Time for oneself is very important. When we have many roles to play each day, the temptation is to go from the demands of one role to another without taking a moment for ourselves. Then life becomes hectic, chaotic and overwhelming. If we keep going at a frantic pace, we risk breaking down completely—or at least getting sick.

Time out does not have to be a major production. A few simple routines should do the trick.

1. Set the alarm early and use the extra time to enjoy the morning paper with a cup of coffee.
2. Get a massage or a manicure.
3. Try a facial.
4. Take a hot bath.
5. Set aside half an hour to read a good book.
6. Call a friend and chat.
7. Listen to your favorite CD or take a nap.
8. Go see a movie.
9. Have a glass of wine.
10. Order dinner out.

Habits are easily made. As you focus time, money and energy on yourself, your self-worth will increase. The result will be a happier, healthier, more well-adjusted you.

Life is there for the taking . . .
or the refusing.

—Anonymous

GIRL TALK #348: Today I will accept my own death. This should increase my commitment to having the fullest life I can possibly live.

When your first parent dies, it reminds you of your own mortality. With that realization comes a whole new set of feelings. Healing eventually comes, since there is still a surviving parent. However, the passing of the second parent brings a loss of security and identity as a child, or even as an adult.

When my mother was ill, I was in a state of denial about her death. My father had already passed on, and my belief was that she would always be there. The night she died, I told her how much I loved her and I told her of my gratitude. When I hung up the phone I did not believe she would really die. In spite of her poor health, I was still surprised to hear that she expired later that night. My grief and pain were deep; I knew there would never be a chance to connect with her again.

As the oldest child, I moved up a notch in the family hierarchy. It meant that I was in charge of family get-togethers; it was my responsibility to hold the siblings and their children together. I was no longer the middle generation; I was the older one, and my children had taken over the place once held by me.

My mother's death was also a red alert, reminding me to make the most of my life. The clock was ticking. That was a major factor in my retirement and my choosing to spend as much time as possible with my primary and extended families.

Once we acknowledge that we are mortal and that we will all die, then we can accept our demise with dignity and bravery. It will help us maximize the time we have left. It has helped me learn to walk fearlessly forward toward the end, enjoying the time I have left and making the most of every minute.

Do not seek death. Death will find you.
—DAG HAMMARSKJÖLD

GIRL TALK #349: It takes courage to open a family secret. Today I will reflect on anything that needs to be discussed to make our family closer in spirit.

In 1969, Margaret Cork wrote an important book entitled *The Forgotten Children*. Although it was not a bestseller, it remains an important book. In it she dealt with children from alcoholic homes. She wrote about their difficulties in school, their struggles in relationships, their feelings of shame, and their lack of self-confidence and self-worth.

In the aftermath of the book's publication, a woman named Joan Kroc brought together several professional people: psychiatrists, social workers, teachers and therapists. The only thing they had in common was the alcoholism in their homes.

The result of this meeting was the formation of a nonprofit group called The National Association of Children of Alcoholics (NACoA). Its purpose is to develop programs and distribute literature that will reach as many children in alcoholic homes as possible. I was honored to be the founding chairperson of this organization, and I found the intimacy and cooperation of this group a rare and precious thing. These virtual strangers met and shared deep and dark secrets on a basic level.

From Margaret Cork I learned to have the courage to go where others are afraid to tread. She has become a pioneer in helping children find a safe haven away from dysfunctional homes.

Children awaken your own sense of self
when you see them hurting, struggling, testing—
when you watch their eyes and listen to their hearts.
Children are gifts, if we accept them.

—KATHLEEN TIERNEY CRILLY

GIRL TALK #350: Today I will plan an annual exam for myself and find a way to remember it each year. I will commit myself to making healthy decisions regarding my sexual life.

To maintain ourselves sexually, there are many things to think about.

1. We need annual breast exams and PAP smears. After the age of forty, or earlier if breast cancer runs in your family, mammograms are essential. If you make the appointment at birthday time, you will remember it each year.
2. Make wise choices about birth control. A frank discussion with your gynecologist should help. Don't play around without taking precautions. It only takes one egg and one sperm to make a baby. One minute of fun can lead to a lifetime of responsibility.
3. Be aware of changes in your body—warts, lumps, discharges. Seek help immediately if something is not right.
4. Be aware of the symptoms of sexually transmitted diseases. It is imperative that you be tested. Early detection and treatment are important. You should also ask your partner to be honest, and you, in turn, should be forthright.
5. Practice safe sex. Before starting a new relationship, both of you should have an AIDS test. As many health professionals recommend, abstain until you know you are both healthy and in a committed relationship. Don't play Russian roulette with sex. It could mean your life.

It was a revelation to me, taking complete responsibility for my own actions.

—ANONYMOUS

GIRL TALK #351: There are many mysteries and cultural ways that are unfamiliar to me. It's good to be exposed to ways that are different from mine.

While in Hawaii, I happened upon a volcano that was usually dormant but that had erupted not long ago. From the top of a wooden walkway, I could peer down into the crater.

As I approached the rim, I could see a barrier had been constructed. Although it was singed, I could read the words *Do Not Go Beyond This Rope*. I got as close as possible but could not see the bottom of the crater. Just then a group of local Hawaiians approached, dressed in native garb and carrying large sacks.

To my surprise they lifted the ropes and proceeded to the very edge of the rim. Then they sat down in a row and opened their bags. First they put sticks of incense in the ground and lit them. As the fragrance filled the misty air, the scene became mystical and magical. They brought out chickens, lobsters, fresh fruit, vegetables and a variety of desserts. One by one they threw the food into the crater. I couldn't believe my eyes. Then they began throwing in money—nickels, dimes and quarters. And finally they opened a bottle of vodka and poured it over the rim.

Suddenly I realized I was watching a religious ritual. It was fascinating . . . until a young girl took off her shoes and began walking barefoot around the edge of the crater. It was so frightening I had to leave.

Later I found out that it was indeed a ceremony. Legend says that Madam Pele, the goddess of volcanoes, must be kept happy at all times so she doesn't blow her stack, causing an eruption. She loves to eat and she adores vodka. So the natives keep her supplied and she stays quiet. To test Madam Pele's mood, a young girl walks around the rim. If Madam is happy, the girl can walk without harm; but if Madam is miserable, the girl will fall in.

At the bottom of the hill I was quite relieved to see the youngster coming down the walkway. However, when I asked if any girls had fallen in, nobody would give me an answer.

*Without heroes we are all plain people and
don't know how far we can go.*

—BERNARD HAHAMAD

GIRL TALK #352: I have certain skills and talents that need nurturing. Today I will take a look at what I am about.

While I may have retired from my professional life as a therapist and speaker, I am far from having nothing to do. These days my joy and satisfaction don't come from sitting in an office and helping others find solutions to their problems. Instead, they come from writing—from taking my many experiences and insights and making them come alive through words.

I would like to think I have left a legacy of highly trained therapists to carry on my work. I would like to believe that the thousands of people who heard me lecture, or who attended my seminars, were helped in a positive way.

Now, through the books I have in print, I would like to imagine that my gift has helped others find the inspiration and help they need to work through their difficult times, or to be motivated into action by one of the pages in *Girl Talk*. If I have helped even one woman get her life together, the effort will have been worthwhile.

So as this book winds down, I hope that you have enjoyed what you have read and that some of the stories and ideas have touched you in some way. We have thirteen yet to go, then Happy New Year and start all over again.

You were there when I needed you.
You stood above all the others with your strength
and guided me. To each of you I offer my
being, my love and all that I am.

—Deidra Sarault

GIRL TALK #353: Today I will reflect on my first major encounter with death. On that day I lost both an important person in my life, and my innocence as well.

As the holidays begin to roll around, I always reflect on the shock and horror of my first major meeting with death. I was a new mother with a two-year-old son and an infant daughter. On that Christmas, my parents were to meet their granddaughter for the first time.

We had gathered excitedly around the Christmas tree, waiting to hear their car tires crunching into the snow that blanketed the driveway. They were late and I said a prayer that they were driving safely. Then the phone rang, intruding loudly on our joyous evening. When my husband returned to the living room, I knew from his ashen face that something was wrong. But nothing could have prepared me for the words he uttered.

"Your father has died," he said as he held me in his arms. "We need to leave now and see your mother."

My head spun. Nothing made sense. They were supposed to be at my home for a celebration. This was not happening. Through the fog in my brain I called for a baby-sitter and we began the hundred-mile ride through a blinding snowstorm, trying to comprehend the situation. Perhaps it was a car accident or a heart attack. After all, he was only forty-six.

Dozens of friends and relatives were at my parents' home when we arrived. My uncle took me aside and told me that my dad had been found a few hours after committing suicide. I tried to console my mother, brother and sister even while I was reeling inside, grappling with my own grief. As the oldest child, the funeral arrangements fell on my shoulders. I made the necessary decisions, then drove back home to be with my babies.

The trauma sent me into a tailspin. A deep depression followed. Part of me died with my dad. Nothing in my life would ever be the same again. I tucked away all the special memories of growing up, and an older, more solemn woman left her childhood home that night.

Eventually, with the love and help of many people in my life, healing took place and I was able to function once again. It took a long while until I was able to participate in life more fully and appreciate the family I had created.

Death can be the natural order of things, or it can be an unexpected tragedy. It is never easy, but suicide can be the worst. The suddenness, the finality, the reasons unknown make the survivors wonder what they might have done to prevent it. Suicide leaves many questions and no satisfactory answers. It only causes pain and confusion. And while the survivors' wounds will heal, they will always wonder, *why?*

It isn't for the moment you are stuck that you need courage, but for the long uphill climb back to sanity and faith and security.

—ANNE MORROW LINDBERGH

GIRL TALK #354: If I make a mistake it's best to own up to it and fix it. Today I will realize that nothing can be gained by compounding one mistake with two, just to save face.

One Christmas we decided to give our son a new bike. It had several gear shifts and was just the one he wanted. To save money, we bought it unassembled; my husband said he'd have no trouble putting it together. When I suggested that he assemble it a few days before Christmas, he scoffed at me. Waiting until the last minute was his way of doing things.

Needless to say, on Christmas Eve he was out in the cold, dark garage trying his best to get the bike together. He didn't have a clue. The stores were closed and he had two choices: to tell our son he didn't have the bike he had wished for, or to find a quick fix for his problem. I left the garage angry and frustrated; only Santa could be of service that night.

A few hours later I returned to the garage and was horrified to find two piles of parts. Apparently my husband had borrowed a similar bicycle from a neighbor and had taken it apart to see how it was assembled. Now the problem was compounded, and two boys would be without bikes.

Christmas Day meant a whole lot of explaining, and the following morning my husband found, to his dismay, that hiring someone to put two bikes together was twice as expensive as assembling one! That's certainly learning the hard (and costly) way.

> *Someone has said that the greatest cause of ulcers*
> *is mountain climbing over molehills.*
>
> —MAXWELL MALTZ

GIRL TALK #355: Today I will remember the women who came before me in my family and say a thank-you prayer.

Nine months of swelling and extra unwanted pounds, painful labor, 10,000 diapers changed, 5,000 baths given, 1,000 books read, countless loads of laundry done and meals prepared, numerous hours of help with homework, and millions of miles chauffeured. And that's not counting sleepless nights, groceries bought, dishes washed and floors swept.

These are the tasks that become second nature to mothers. It's a good thing we don't keep score. A mother's love goes far beyond the call of duty because it's not about duty. It's about keeping a lineage alive—a heritage of love. And with raising the next generation comes learning parenting skills, instilling family values and passing on traditions. Stories are passed down, and legacies remain alive through the spoken word.

A mother's love can be stored in many places. For me it's a blue metal box that my mother once kept quarters in for special occasions. My best treasured recipes are in this box. We all have ways of creating traditions. My hobby of taking photographs will help keep memories alive for my children and all the children that are born in the years to come. May they always know a mother's love is forever.

A mother is not a person to lean on but a
person to make leaning unnecessary.
—DOROTHY CANFIELD FISHER

GIRL TALK #356: Connections to our past can come from the most unusual places. There is a great comfort in knowing we are tied to many people all over the world.

As a girl, I remember my father playing a lawn game with his friends. He called it Roly-Boly. It may be better known as bocci ball. Back then it was played by a group of men who stood around drinking beer from brown bottles and wagering bets.

With the unexpected loss of my father, I had many unanswered questions. He had been orphaned as a child, but he never told me anything about his growing up. I always felt I had time for him to fill in the blanks. But when he died, I felt disconnected from his history completely. My only way of connecting was to look at telephone books when I traveled abroad to see if I could find anyone with the name of Roelandt. I never did.

Then imagine my surprise when I went to Brussels, Belgium, and found three pages of Roelandts. I envisioned some of them as my distant relatives. The concierge where I was staying was kind enough to photocopy the pages, and I made plans to revisit and explore my roots. That resolve was confirmed when I passed a little park not far from where I was staying and saw men drinking beer out of brown bottles and wagering bets on a game of Roly-Boly!

It seemed God was giving me a message that my dad was doing well, maybe doing a little betting of his own—wherever he is.

From harmony, from heavenly harmony,
this universal frame began.

—JOHN DRYDEN

371

GIRL TALK #357: Today I will clean out all my catalogs. It's too late for this season and next year will bring a whole new bunch of them.

Ordering from catalogs by mail saves me a tremendous amount of time and energy. They are filled with creative choices from thousands of sources—far more than I could find in a mall or even several malls. Throughout the year I curl up with my catalogs and mark all the gifts I want to buy. Then I highlight them or mark sticky notes on the pages.

I leave myself plenty of time for the gifts to arrive. I know it can take up to two months, or even more if they are out of stock. When they begin to roll in, I mark them off on my gift list, wrap them in pretty paper, put a note tag on so I'll remember who it's for, and wait for the next shipment to arrive.

In my house I have a closet specifically for gifts. That way nobody can spot his or her present beforehand and start asking questions. I even have a lovely quilted basket that my daughter gave me to hold the catalogs. Yes, you might say I am highly organized when it comes to gift-giving.

By having all my presents in order I can really enjoy the coming holidays without having to rush here and there with everyone else, sweating in hot stores and being jostled by rude shoppers and ignored by overworked, underpaid clerks. I can sit back with a glass of wine and watch the logs crackle in the fireplace. You can do it, too. All it takes is planning.

*A place for everything and
everything in its place.*

—ANONYMOUS

GIRL TALK #358: Today I will explore what qualities make a person special. Then I will nurture those qualities within myself.

My life has been graced by wonderful family and friends. While family comes with the territory, so to speak, friends are made by choice. Of course, we cannot possibly be friends with everyone we've met, so there is a selection process that takes place. In looking carefully at this I can see that while the people I have bonded with are of different backgrounds and have different interests, we share certain qualities. My friends all have a sense of adventure and the desire to make the world a better place. They have the courage to stand up for their convictions, and we are all here to support one another in times of crisis and times of joy.

My friends are like a patchwork quilt—different colors and textures—and nice to be with on a cold winter night. I treasure these relationships, the special bonds that we share. When we cannot see or speak to each other for long periods of time, we manage to reunite and pick up exactly where we left off months, or even years, ago. The glue that holds us together is caring, sharing and giving lots of space while being joined together.

All you need is deep within you waiting to unfold and reveal itself. All you have to do is be still and take time to seek for whatever is within.
—EILEEN EADDY

GIRL TALK #359: Today I will realize that rituals and traditions are meant to bring people together.

Who says Christmas has to be on December 25? In my family, not everyone can get together on that exact day. So for the past ten years I have been celebrating whenever it is convenient. Some years it's the first week in December. Last year it was the third week in January.

The idea of choosing a date agreed upon by all members occurred when my children got married. Their spouses had commitments to their own families and it became a tug of war, timewise and emotionally. There were too many obligations, too much stress and too much unhappiness to make it a joyous occasion.

When I first suggested this to my children, they were relieved and intrigued. The shift in time allowed them to fulfill social obligations with coworkers and friends as well as their in-laws. Now everyone looks forward to a relaxed getaway and more presents. There are other side benefits also: airline tickets are less expensive, planes and airports are less crowded, and we have plenty of time to spend with one another instead of scrambling to make other plans.

So if your family is torn helter-skelter with obligations, think about having Christmas (or any other national holiday) on a different day. It works!

Oh, come all ye faithful.

—JOHN READING
ADESTE FIDELES

GIRL TALK #360: Today will be filled with pleasure and excitement for me, as well as being a spiritual experience.

Perhaps no holiday has the power to tug at the heartstrings the way Christmas does. The shopping, the cards, the food, the presents, the decorations and the get-togethers filled with rituals and traditions. It seems every year the season gets longer and the calendar gets fuller. Some believe that it is too commercialized. Maybe so. Or it may be that the feeling of love and the need to celebrate has become so strong that we need to stretch it to the limit.

Despite the commercial side, we should not forget that Christmas is the promise of a better world. We want to believe that a savior has come during our times of tribulations and that he or she will lead us through the desert of our lives to the oasis of spiritual nourishment. When we accept Christmas, we believe in the goodness of humankind and expect the best from humanity.

To make this holiday enjoyable, and to be relaxed and free from stress, stay within your budget and do not overextend yourself. Keep food preparations simple and easy. Allow yourself time to meditate on what you want for the coming year and what you are thankful for. Be kind to yourself and to others. Enjoy the day.

At Christmas play and make good cheer,
for Christmas comes but once a year.
—THOMAS TUSSLER

GIRL TALK #361: Today I will get my finances in order so I can start the new year right.

There was a time in my life when I was very poor. Then I began making money, but I didn't know what to do with it. I had no idea about investments, stocks, bonds or mutual funds. So there I was, with cash for the first time in my life, and it was doing nothing at all for me.

Even if you don't have a lot of money, it's a wise idea to learn about how your resources can work for you. Become knowledgeable about retirement accounts, IRAs, mutual funds and CDs. Learn how much you need to save in order to have a sizable nest egg. It's an old notion that women can't grasp these things. We can understand them perfectly well. And once you gain some knowledge, it is very rewarding.

Make sure you never sign anything you haven't read completely. Ask questions. Did you know that if you sign a joint income tax return, you can be held liable for half of anything that may be due? So know what you are doing. If it means hiring an accountant or C.P.A., the money will be well spent.

There is no reason every woman cannot be successful. Make an effort. Promise that this coming year you will do at least one thing to make yourself better acquainted with your money matters.

It takes money to make money.

—KEN MARTIN

GIRL TALK #362: Today I will think about what I will leave behind that may be of value. It could be something large or small. What is important is that it will show that I passed through.

Few houses in America more accurately reflect the personality of their owners than Thomas Jefferson's Monticello in Virginia. The house took over forty years to construct and it tells the story of the man—a dreamer, a creator, a visionary, an inventor. Jefferson believed in respect and freedom for all people, even though he housed 200 slaves on his property.

The house is spacious and filled with his inventions—from his clock/calendar on the wall to his early version of a copy machine. In the library are circular shelves that could be closed and shipped by carriage or ship. On the grounds are lush flower gardens, orchards and vineyards. Even the graveyard has a special feeling about it, as though God has touched it.

Of all the presidents, Jefferson left perhaps the greatest legacy. Since his death, generations of visitors have been transported back in time to understand that earlier era and appreciate what he contributed to our society and to the world.

> *Look not mournfully into the past.*
> *It comes not back again.*
> *Wisely improve the present. It is time.*
>
> —HENRY WADSWORTH LONGFELLOW

GIRL TALK #363: I am an ordinary woman who has led an extraordinary life. Today I will reflect on what I am passing on to my children and to others.

My greatest accomplishment during this lifetime was raising my three children. In return, they have given me their friendship and love, and six lovely grandchildren. I treasure my relationship with my husband and nurture my professional and social connections. I have traveled worldwide, designed addiction programs, trained therapists, authored fifteen books, made two films and several videotapes, spoken at hundreds of conferences and listened to thousands of problems. I garden, entertain, travel, walk and tap dance. You might say my life is hectic. It was. Until I learned to simplify.

On several occasions, at turning points in my life, I have had to make choices. I eliminated the negative so I could accentuate the positive. It's difficult each time, but the reward is that I feel lighter and less stressed. I have more time for me, which means I can be more creative and less crabby. Over time I have learned that it is part of life's journey, and in the end, when some things have been let go, I feel more fulfilled and less empty.

There will always be people and activities that I want to keep. So something else has to go. That's what life is all about— choices. It comes with the art of living and with the limited time we are here on earth to enjoy it.

Besides the noble art of getting things done,
there is the noble art of leaving things undone.
The wisdom of life consists in the
elmination of nonessentials.

—LIN YUTANG

GIRL TALK #364: Today I will visit a place of beauty and let my spirit and senses be renewed. The location I choose will touch my heart and soul.

For anyone who wants to feel close to God, try the Butchart Gardens in British Columbia, Canada. I felt as though I had arrived in heaven. Nature's colors and designs intoxicated my senses. Through the day I wandered this magical land visiting the rose garden, sunken garden, and Italian and Japanese gardens. There were snapdragons taller than any I had ever seen. Was it the soil that was blessed or was it the tender concern of the people who lovingly tended the plants, shrubs and flowers? I only knew there was something holy about the site. Upon leaving, I wrote this:

I believe that man will not merely endure. We will prevail. Man is immortal, not because he alone among creatures has an inexhaustible voice, but because he has a soul, a spirit capable of compassion, sacrifice and endurance. And most important, an ability to appreciate beauty and God's design.

*The real voyage of discovery consists
not in seeking new landscape but
in having new eyes.*

—MARCEL PROUST

GIRL TALK #365: Today I will think about New Year's Eve and what it means to me. All forms of celebration are possible. What matters is that I choose to celebrate in a way that reflects my values and interests.

As a young woman, one of my worst fears was not having something special to do on New Year's Eve. On that night of magic and romance, I was afraid I wouldn't be invited to a party and that I would be alone. Yet I really don't like drinking, or raucous dinners, or the frenzy of the revelers in Times Square. To be honest, noisemakers don't add much to my enjoyment of life.

Over the years, this holiday has become one of my least favorites. Perhaps it has to do with the year ending, as opposed to New Year's Day, which is a new beginning. Maybe I feel life is going by too quickly, and this night makes me reflect on how the years are speeding up. I want the clock to stop; I want more time.

It must be that the last day of December is the end of another year, and I don't want to be celebrating with noise and merriment. Instead, I prefer a quiet time and space to say thank you for all the events that have transpired during the previous 364 days. I want to pamper myself. So I now turn down invitations and instead make my favorite meal, share it with my husband by candlelight, fill my bathtub and slip in with a glass of champagne. It no longer matters if I stay up until midnight. I need a good night's sleep so I can be ready for the next day—the first day of the year, and the first day of the rest of my life.

Give to the world the best you have and
the best will come back to you.

—MADELINE BRIDGES

Cross-Reference Index

Numbers correspond to affirmation number, **not** page number.

A

Acceptance, 6, 26, 42, 47, 60, 69, 81, 103, 108, 123, 128, 142, 154, 174, 175, 181, 183, 186, 195, 196, 200, 209, 210, 225, 232, 235, 241, 245, 252, 258, 275, 281, 282, 286, 290, 291, 294, 301, 317, 321, 339, 348

Accomplishment, 1, 5, 11, 15, 17, 23, 34, 46, 48, 54, 60, 64, 68, 76, 85, 92, 96, 101, 110, 123, 129, 133, 136, 139, 144, 148, 151, 152, 158, 164, 171, 172, 180, 182, 184, 187, 192, 194, 204, 208, 213, 214, 227, 239, 241, 243, 244, 249, 267, 283, 284, 289, 294, 295, 300, 301, 307, 308, 329, 335, 338, 352, 357, 362

Addiction, 50, 56, 91, 113, 116, 117, 123, 130, 138, 174, 177, 200, 203, 223, 244, 257, 266, 293, 295, 327, 349

Affection, 39, 41, 47, 94, 112, 118, 128, 132, 143, 150, 151, 167, 197, 205, 212, 251, 273, 285, 322, 332, 344, 355

Aloneness, 16, 30, 58, 96, 120, 138, 147, 153, 198, 201, 217, 225, 257, 281, 348, 356

Anger, 28, 30, 94, 135, 167, 170, 215, 218, 245, 262, 278, 354

Appreciation, 18, 36, 45, 55, 69, 81, 88, 93, 120, 125, 127, 128, 132, 143, 150, 159, 168, 182, 200, 205, 212, 220, 226, 227, 228, 231, 235, 244, 263, 269, 274, 296, 305, 319, 326, 331, 332, 338, 362

Assertiveness, 6, 15, 20, 28, 31, 46, 54, 80, 92, 136, 157, 159, 160, 169, 170, 175, 179, 184, 204, 214, 215, 219, 230, 255, 259, 270, 277, 283, 303, 313, 318, 325, 330, 334, 361

Awareness, 1, 22, 40, 63, 81, 138, 142, 146, 161, 167, 195, 198, 206, 243, 257, 291, 310, 314, 323, 337, 342, 361

B

Balance, 4, 16, 26, 34, 37, 51, 72, 112, 113, 124, 143, 161, 213, 235, 245, 264, 272, 290, 307, 312, 318, 339

Beauty, 76, 93, 108, 125, 139, 151, 155, 163, 178, 220, 226, 231, 309, 364

Beliefs, 13, 15, 60, 91, 142, 154, 160, 198, 217, 219, 282, 291, 302, 316, 328, 346, 360

Body Image, 6, 42, 57, 68, 85, 98, 108, 111, 119, 135, 157, 170, 179, 189, 203, 219, 226, 255, 258, 261, 266, 275, 284, 298, 308, 327, 336, 342, 347, 350

C

Choices, 4, 12, 20, 28, 31, 32, 34, 40, 44, 56, 60, 61, 64, 72, 78, 83, 90, 95, 97, 103, 110, 113, 115, 118, 124, 128, 136, 142, 145, 146, 149, 157, 160, 162, 169, 171, 183, 184, 185, 192, 204, 210, 214, 218, 219, 224, 227, 228, 233, 241, 242, 243, 244, 254, 261, 264, 266, 270, 271, 276, 284, 286, 289, 294, 295, 297, 306, 310, 312, 318, 327, 330, 334, 341, 352, 358, 363

Communication, 18, 52, 59, 62, 84, 100, 102, 122, 139, 150, 153, 168, 175, 188, 193, 194, 197, 200, 211, 215, 225, 240, 245, 246, 249, 250, 251, 255, 257, 272, 273, 278, 285, 297, 314, 321, 339

Confidence, 17, 48, 80, 117, 127, 133, 152, 157, 159, 192, 204, 230, 232, 243, 255, 282, 289, 298, 300, 329

Courage, 6, 15, 25, 30, 63, 117, 123, 157, 158, 160, 169, 178, 180, 198, 204, 214, 217, 219, 237, 241, 247, 268, 286, 295, 303, 331, 334

D

Decisions, 4, 6, 31, 56, 61, 73, 78, 83, 99, 103, 105, 118, 119, 122, 134, 136, 137, 146, 148, 157, 160, 162, 171, 181, 183, 184, 187, 192, 198, 199, 204, 210, 213, 214, 221, 227, 232, 241, 244, 257, 266, 271, 276, 284, 286, 288, 291, 295, 310, 312, 318, 327, 330, 334, 356, 359

Destiny, 21, 26, 142, 146, 152, 169, 174, 179, 184, 195, 204, 209, 210, 212, 217, 224, 227, 228, 233, 237, 238, 239, 249, 252, 257, 272, 286, 290, 302, 314, 317, 329, 331, 348, 349

Dreams, 2, 57, 60, 152, 214, 277, 286, 296, 329, 356

E

Emotions, 2, 7, 20, 41, 77, 94, 118, 132, 133, 135, 142, 176, 179, 199, 207, 218, 225, 245, 246, 272, 278, 282, 297, 315, 321, 346, 356

Excellence, 64, 68, 85, 92, 110, 113, 123, 139, 144, 151, 159, 169, 176, 196, 202, 206, 217, 231, 240, 242, 243, 247, 269, 281, 294, 307, 337, 362

Experiences, 6, 9, 39, 48, 58, 61, 65, 71, 81, 86, 98, 99, 103, 105, 109, 112, 114, 117, 118, 125, 126, 131, 135, 143, 153, 155, 157, 158, 166, 173, 174, 180, 181, 184, 186, 191, 192, 200, 204, 207, 212, 214, 220, 225, 227, 228, 231, 233, 234, 237, 238, 240, 244, 250, 253, 257, 260, 271, 276, 286, 292, 295, 301, 303, 309, 314, 316, 320, 322, 325, 331, 333, 338, 343, 345, 346, 349, 351, 353, 364

F

Faith, 2, 9, 13, 21, 26, 35, 44, 100, 119, 138, 142, 155, 169, 188, 209, 217, 237, 252, 274, 277, 279, 282, 291, 292, 298, 302, 316, 328, 360

Fear, 25, 31, 58, 61, 154, 157, 174, 177, 342, 351

Food, 3, 59, 109, 140, 143, 151, 168, 201, 202, 203, 205, 208, 261, 263, 280, 284, 305, 310, 332, 351

Forgiveness, 40, 128, 198, 268, 278

Friendship, 41, 59, 114, 115, 123, 127, 139, 153, 194, 201, 205, 208, 239, 244, 268, 278, 297, 313, 315, 326, 358

G

Gifts, 18, 23, 36, 39, 52, 85, 93, 112, 121, 123, 128, 165, 205, 216, 228, 249, 252, 256, 296, 299, 305, 354, 357, 360

Goals, 4, 33, 54, 60, 63, 79, 91, 113, 136, 142, 144, 145, 152, 162, 164, 190, 200, 213, 220, 230, 277, 284, 288, 289, 308, 329, 361

Grief, 30, 132, 139, 154, 170, 174, 177, 218, 234, 245, 251, 268, 301, 315, 348, 353

Growth, 29, 40, 44, 66, 68, 72, 78, 90, 94, 98, 103, 110, 118, 122, 131, 136, 142, 146, 149, 151, 152, 155, 158, 164, 169, 174, 176, 179, 183, 184, 192, 195, 196, 198, 202, 212, 219, 224, 230, 231, 232, 233, 235, 237, 239, 241, 243, 252, 257, 258, 272, 282, 289, 295, 307, 323, 329, 331, 336, 338

H

Happiness, 2, 77, 97, 112, 118, 127, 137, 140, 143, 156, 163, 168, 179, 199, 207, 210, 218, 220, 242, 248, 264, 281, 301, 305, 313, 322, 332, 344, 347, 367

Harmony, 18, 26, 47, 82, 96, 109, 120, 124, 125, 139, 143, 151, 155, 163, 165, 168, 188, 193, 199, 209, 213, 215, 225, 235, 245, 264, 269, 276, 285, 301, 309, 321, 339, 360

Healing, 6, 7, 20, 30, 44, 50, 80, 85, 91, 111, 116, 119, 135, 138, 153, 157, 170, 179, 180, 187, 193, 198, 205, 218, 223, 231, 240, 244, 257, 268, 275, 278, 312, 349, 353

Health, 6, 9, 42, 51, 85, 113, 124, 127, 134, 135, 139, 149, 157, 163, 164, 170, 180, 189, 196, 199, 203, 218, 231, 238, 240, 261, 275, 284, 290, 306, 308, 310, 327, 336, 350

Higher Power, 2, 9, 13, 21, 26, 35, 40, 63, 71, 88, 96, 97, 100, 104, 109, 110, 117, 120, 142, 149, 155, 188, 202, 207, 209, 217, 223, 228, 237, 252, 279, 282, 297, 298, 309, 315, 316, 318, 323, 328

Holidays, 1, 45, 100, 121, 130, 140, 153, 167, 185, 216, 304, 332, 346, 353, 354, 357, 359, 360, 365

Home, 5, 12, 59, 74, 82, 96, 130, 141, 156, 168, 183, 208, 213, 247, 276, 292, 294, 304, 305, 320, 330, 332, 340, 342, 353, 357, 359, 360

Hope, 9, 56, 97, 123, 135, 138, 157, 180, 199, 210, 217, 258, 302, 360

Humor, 7, 12, 19, 25, 38, 48, 61, 70, 86, 99, 106, 116, 126, 153, 159, 166, 173, 181, 186, 191, 200, 215, 218, 238, 253, 264, 274, 303, 320, 325, 333, 343, 354

I

Identity, 14, 17, 28, 50, 74, 118, 132, 149, 169, 181, 186, 203, 206, 226, 241, 300, 317, 331, 338

Imagination, 57, 63, 111, 120, 152, 181, 201, 216, 307, 335

Independence, 66, 83, 90, 158, 184, 192, 197, 204, 214, 224, 230, 262, 286, 329, 339

Intimacy, 55, 102, 122, 127, 155, 197, 211, 301, 326, 350

J

Joy, 2, 37, 41, 49, 70, 71, 93, 112, 125, 139, 143, 163, 207, 285, 313

L

Laughter, 7, 12, 38, 126, 159, 170, 215, 218, 289, 344

Limitations, 46, 60, 110, 142, 161, 175, 227, 241, 259, 272, 277, 290, 312, 363

Loneliness, 41, 58, 120, 147, 153, 165, 177, 198, 217, 318

Love, 3, 39, 41, 45, 112, 118, 198, 210, 251, 332, 355, 360

M

Meditation, 26, 35, 40, 57, 67, 75, 82, 96, 120, 124, 163, 188, 279, 292, 328

Miracles, 6, 9, 71, 98, 104, 117, 118, 138, 209, 212, 223, 228, 237, 292, 296, 316

Money, 10, 33, 46, 54, 60, 73, 77, 79, 89, 95, 105, 137, 145, 158, 162, 171, 185, 190, 192, 201, 216, 221, 230, 245, 248, 259, 265, 270, 277, 280, 288, 296, 305, 306, 354, 361

Motivation, 1, 46, 54, 80, 91, 96, 116, 133, 136, 138, 142, 144, 148, 157, 169, 184, 192, 208, 214, 219, 249, 277, 284, 296, 300, 307, 310, 327, 331

N

Nature, 76, 97, 125, 143, 151, 155, 163, 178, 185, 220, 231, 237, 254, 309, 364

O

Opportunity, 31, 62, 64, 78, 83, 136, 147, 152, 171, 192, 200, 204, 209, 210, 215, 227, 228, 233, 238, 244, 271, 276, 285, 286, 290, 295, 303, 317, 357

Optimism, 88, 97, 104, 127, 131, 133, 135, 139, 150, 153, 157, 164, 170, 180, 182, 186, 189, 193, 196, 199, 218, 232, 247, 258, 264, 269, 277, 282, 319

P

Parenting, 2, 8, 9, 11, 28, 29, 38, 65, 71, 80, 86, 94, 98, 102, 112, 118, 128, 132, 158, 167, 175, 177, 192, 207, 245, 246, 250, 262, 273, 274, 285, 294, 305, 339, 346, 348, 354, 355, 359

Passages, 29, 50, 66, 67, 78, 90, 98, 103, 112, 118, 122, 131, 146, 164, 175, 177, 183, 195, 196, 198, 210, 224, 232, 234, 241, 251, 258, 281, 286, 290, 305, 317, 322, 329, 331, 334, 336, 337, 348, 353

Peacefulness, 75, 93, 109, 120, 155, 163, 165, 176, 217, 235, 365

Play, 32, 37, 70, 140, 201, 209, 304

Pleasure, 49, 70, 74, 97, 111, 125, 130, 139, 140, 143, 147, 151, 156, 163, 185, 194, 199, 201, 208, 216, 220, 263, 269, 281, 289, 296, 307, 313, 332, 347, 360

Priorities, 4, 16, 34, 40, 51, 53, 79, 105, 129, 137, 148, 157, 179, 189, 196, 214, 221, 230, 270, 288, 306, 310, 312, 318, 326, 327, 342, 347, 363

Purpose, 15, 17, 24, 31, 33, 46, 60, 78, 91, 99, 108, 138, 142, 144, 146, 152, 160, 164, 169, 171, 176, 180, 184, 200, 204, 213, 216, 224, 229, 243, 249, 265, 273, 279, 283, 288, 294, 297, 314, 317, 345, 361

R

Relationships, 2, 8, 9, 16, 22, 28, 41, 44, 47, 50, 56, 69, 71, 80, 87, 94, 101,

102, 103, 112, 114, 118, 122, 127,
128, 132, 139, 141, 146, 147, 149,
150, 159, 167, 175, 177, 191, 197,
198, 205, 210, 211, 225, 232, 234,
239, 242, 244, 245, 246, 250, 251,
262, 267, 268, 278, 285, 293, 297,
301, 311, 313, 321, 326, 329, 334,
339, 344, 348, 353, 355

Relaxation, 7, 16, 57, 59, 75, 82, 96, 109,
120, 127, 140, 147, 163, 165, 168,
185, 189, 201, 240, 263, 347, 357

Renewal, 1, 20, 30, 35, 40, 52, 56, 68, 70,
80, 88, 97, 98, 100, 113, 119, 136,
138, 142, 149, 151, 153, 155, 163,
165, 170, 178, 187, 188, 193, 198,
210, 217, 231, 235, 237, 241, 272,
275, 282, 302, 312, 318, 331, 367

Resourcefulness, 5, 15, 45, 46, 64, 72,
90, 107, 126, 137, 144, 148, 156,
158, 164, 166, 169, 171, 181, 187,
192, 201, 204, 205, 213, 214, 216,
219, 221, 227, 228, 229, 238,
243, 247, 259, 265, 277, 286, 290,
294, 295, 303, 319, 325, 330, 342,
357, 361

Responsibility, 34, 44, 78, 80, 134, 144,
157, 158, 179, 184, 195, 259, 266,
310, 312, 350

Rituals/Traditions, 1, 2, 3, 23, 36, 45, 51,
59, 75, 76, 100, 121, 130, 156, 163,
165, 172, 180, 185, 188, 191, 194,
208, 215, 216, 234, 263, 273, 304,
328, 332, 346, 355, 359, 360, 365

Role Models, 12, 28, 30, 43, 55, 62, 71,
84, 92, 94, 101, 114, 123, 127, 132,
135, 140, 151, 154, 159, 171, 179,
184, 198, 212, 225, 239, 247, 257,
268, 293, 294, 300, 315, 331, 338,
344, 349

S

Security, 41, 69, 73, 95, 134, 164, 305,
323

Self-Worth, 14, 17, 42, 45, 60, 73, 80,
85, 89, 103, 105, 108, 123, 136, 138,
158, 169, 196, 198, 203, 206, 221,
225, 226, 230, 243, 246, 255, 270,
282, 289, 307, 327, 329, 331, 337,
338, 339, 347, 349

Serenity, 26, 40, 75, 93, 96, 120, 124,
143, 147, 154, 155, 163, 176, 178,
217, 231, 235, 237, 281, 309, 330

Sexuality, 55, 122, 162, 167, 197, 253,
336

Sharing, 1, 2, 8, 18, 36, 39, 41, 47, 52,
59, 62, 71, 84, 87, 102, 117, 121,
127, 131, 135, 139, 140, 147, 150,
153, 154, 155, 159, 168, 172, 179,
180, 188, 193, 194, 197, 201, 202,
207, 210, 211, 212, 216, 231, 239,
244, 245, 247, 251, 263, 272, 273,
292, 296, 305, 315, 326, 332, 346,
352, 355, 359

Solitude, 21, 35, 67, 82, 96, 155, 163,
177, 217, 237, 281, 318, 365

Solutions, 4, 41, 48, 53, 54, 70, 72, 79,
83, 91, 96, 99, 105, 119, 124, 137,
138, 149, 153, 159, 161, 162, 165,
166, 170, 174, 175, 184, 187, 189,
190, 192, 198, 199, 201, 205, 210,
214, 215, 225, 227, 228, 229, 232,
235, 238, 245, 246, 271, 272, 277,
278, 284, 286, 291, 303, 306, 310,
313, 318, 321, 327, 334, 342, 347,
350, 359

Special Places, 9, 49, 67, 87, 109, 125,
131, 139, 143, 155, 168, 178, 193,
207, 220, 231, 237, 240, 250, 260,
276, 292, 309, 316, 328, 335, 345,
351, 356, 362, 364

Spirituality, 2, 9, 26, 35, 39, 52, 65, 81, 88, 96, 104, 109, 110, 117, 138, 142, 155, 169, 174, 188, 202, 209, 217, 223, 237, 252, 257, 269, 279, 282, 292, 298, 314, 316, 323, 328, 360

Stress, 7, 17, 26, 40, 51, 58, 61, 85, 113, 115, 120, 124, 144, 158, 161, 170, 182, 189, 211, 213, 215, 216, 235, 240, 245, 264, 290, 306, 313, 359

Success, 24, 48, 144, 152, 157, 159, 164, 169, 171, 190, 200, 204, 214, 219, 241, 259, 284, 286, 294, 295, 317

T

Talent, 49, 74, 139, 204, 209, 239, 243, 249, 289, 297, 307, 335, 352

Thankfulness, 9, 28, 55, 65, 81, 88, 103, 114, 118, 125, 127, 132, 135, 143, 155, 158, 159, 168, 198, 204, 205, 207, 212, 225, 227, 228, 231, 235, 240, 251, 274, 292, 300, 309, 331, 360, 367

Time, 16, 51, 53, 74, 82, 91, 96, 107, 115, 123, 129, 131, 134, 140, 145, 148, 150, 151, 161, 172, 185, 187, 190, 192, 194, 196, 208, 211, 213, 216, 229, 249, 252, 256, 265, 270, 280, 283, 299, 313, 317, 318, 326, 330, 332, 340, 347, 357, 359, 362, 363, 367

Trauma, 6, 20, 30, 61, 135, 157, 170, 174, 177, 218, 232, 240, 246, 268, 290, 301, 315, 321, 342, 353

Trust, 13, 28, 47, 141, 197, 210, 217, 292, 314

U

Understanding, 22, 50, 81, 102, 110, 115, 128, 149, 153, 154, 161, 169, 174, 194, 195, 198, 209, 215, 224, 225, 235, 245, 250, 278, 291, 321, 337, 339, 344, 348, 361

V

Validation, 14, 73, 89, 92, 138, 150, 159, 198, 204, 219, 225, 230, 259, 275, 282, 289, 314, 323, 329

Values, 24, 97, 101, 122, 125, 136, 155, 160, 182, 199, 202, 206, 217, 219, 246, 247, 269, 270, 294, 319, 331, 346, 355, 360

Vision, 15, 57, 123, 133, 142, 144, 146, 152, 164, 171, 184, 192, 204, 227, 233, 237, 252, 271, 276, 285, 291, 294, 295, 307, 314, 317, 322, 329, 337, 349

W

Wealth, 10, 33, 54, 60, 73, 79, 95, 162, 171, 190, 221, 230, 247, 248, 277, 288, 305, 319, 361

Wholeness, 6, 9, 20, 41, 80, 97, 108, 113, 118, 125, 128, 138, 142, 150, 154, 155, 157, 164, 169, 170, 177, 179, 189, 193, 196, 197, 198, 210, 217, 225, 226, 232, 237, 245, 257, 268, 272, 278, 282, 289, 310, 312, 314, 319, 329, 347

Y

Youth, 8, 22, 29, 38, 39, 41, 50, 55, 58, 60, 69, 72, 78, 86, 87, 94, 99, 111, 121, 128, 131, 140, 143, 167, 175, 227, 239, 245, 262, 285, 293, 294, 304, 319, 322, 323, 338, 339, 344, 346, 351, 355, 356

About the Author

Sharon Wegscheider-Cruse is the founder and former president of Onsite Training and Consulting, currently located in Tennessee. She is the author of *Another Chance—Hope and Help for the Alcoholic Family, Coupleship, The Family Trap, Choicemaking, Learning to Love Yourself, Experiential Therapy, Family Reconstruction, Grandparenting, Life After Divorce* and *Dancing with Destiny*.

Sharon and her husband, Dr. Joseph Cruse, divide their time between Las Vegas, Nevada, and Marine on St. Croix, Minnesota.

Also from
Sharon Wegscheider-Cruse

Dancing with Destiny
Turning Points on the Journey of Life
This inspiring book encourages readers to look for and pay attention to moments in their lives charged with intense personal meaning. It explores these events and the life-transforming effects they have on people's lives. Wegscheider-Cruse examines these occurrences from the perspective of a therapist, providing examples that clarify their essence. She shares with readers several moments she danced with destiny, and relates stories of others who have had similar experiences.
Code 4576.............$10.95

Code 2824 ....$8.95

Code 4397............$7.95

Code 4265 ....$9.95

Code 4648 ....$8.95